Aurea Vidyā Collection[1]

——— 15 ———

[1] For a Complete List of Titles see page 175.

The Regal Way to Realization

(Yogadarśana)

This book was originally published in Italian in 1982 as Patañjali, *La Via Regale della Realizzazione*, (*Yogadarśana*), by Associazione Ecoculturale Parmenides (formerly Edizioni Āśram Vidyā) – Third Revised Edition 2010.

First Published in English in 2012 by
Aurea Vidyā
39 West 88th Street
New York, NY 10024

Printed and bound by Lightning Source Inc. at locations in the U.S.A. and in the U.K., as shown on the last page.

ISBN 978-1-931406-15-4
Library of Congress Control Number 2012952170

On the cover: Manuscript commentary of Patanjali's *Yogasūtra*.

Patañjali

The Regal Way to Realization

(Yogadarśana)

By

Raphael

(Āśram Vidyā Order)

AUREA VIDYĀ

"Hear then, O son of Samkṛti, I will expound for you the doctrine of *Yoga* with its eight means. First the prohibitions and the observances, then the positions, and finally the control over the vital breath. Next comes abstraction, the supreme patrimony of knowledge. Then concentration, meditation and contemplation crown, O sage, the discipline."

Śrījābāladarśanopaniṣad I.4.5

"Without *Yoga* how could ever knowledge grant liberation? Without knowledge then, how could *Yoga* afford liberation? Therefore who ardently aspires to liberation, more than anything else, should strive to pursue both Knowledge and *Yoga*."

Yogaśikhopaniṣad I.13-14

TABLE OF CONTENTS

INTRODUCTION

The term *yoga* stems from the root *yuj*, which denotes the "act of subjugating" and, in our specific case, resolving both mental and physical turbulences in order to obtain perfect *unity of consciousness* that goes beyond the boundaries of thought, hence beyond the categories of time and space. There are many types of *yoga*, from the *Haṭha* to the metaphysical *Asparśa*.[1] The *yoga* we address here is the *Rājayoga* codified by Patañjali, the regal (*rāja*) *yoga* which leads to reintegration. *Yoga* is not a religion, as this term is commonly understood, rather it is a science, the science that studies the being in its totality. It is philosophy as well, because it offers a vision of life and of the nature of the being. Inasmuch as science it is of an experiential order, thus eminently practical, and is therefore constituted of both theory and praxis.

Yoga, like all traditional Doctrines, does not try to convince or impose on anybody its own philosophical convictions and its own praxis. It lives and expresses itself in the dignity of that which it is. If someone has an erroneous conception of it, this is because (especially in the West) at times it has been made into a simple profession, a commercial undertaking, and a parody, thus the degradation of that which is sacred, although there are exceptions to this.

---

[1] For the *yoga* paths refer to, Raphael, *Essence and Purpose of Yoga,* The Initiatory Pathways to the Transcendent, Element Books, Shaftesbury, U.K.

Individuals live at different stages of awakening, of intellect and consciousness development. Therefore, it is often difficult to create relationships, not because we are insensitive, but because we are on two different wave bands, living on opposite planes and in different vibratory states. And without doubt this can happen within the same family group, couples, or between companions and friends.

What then could the attitude of the student of *yoga* be toward the social world or the "collective unconscious"? We would say an attitude of utmost reserve, and possibly of silence; the collective unconscious is constrained by some exclusive and peculiar *necessities*: working in order to survive, involvement in family to avoid loneliness, acquisition of material things, amusement and dismissal of any type of study whose purpose is not peculiarly material. The collective unconscious does not live, but lets itself be lived; it does not create, but is dependent; it does not think, but lets itself be thought. It is an enormous sedimentation, incrustation, a rubble of beliefs, opinions, faiths, emotions and passions, of material and sensory interests and of convictions not supported by reason. All these have been perpetuating themselves for millennia and are superimposed on pure intelligence.[2]

It may seem truly strange and unusual that neither research, even when regarding philosophical, spiritual and psychological truth, living according to certain principles not based on common opinion (*doxa*), or self-refining, are not appreciated by the majority. This is self-evident and, unfortunately, one cannot but to accept it the way it is. Human beings always put their hopes in a distant object

---

[2] For the various forms of learning according to Plato, see, Raphael, *Initiation into the Philosophy of Plato*. Aurea Vidyā. New York.

(appearance), rather than finding the real truth close by, i.e. within themselves. In his *Pithian III*, Pindar says: "The most inconclusive category of people is of those who denigrate what is close and turn their attention toward what is far away, letting their unrealizable hopes pursue ghosts."[3]

On the other hand the sincere researcher who feels a precise "vocation" and an authentic instruction from his consciousness cannot but pursue his path. To betray others is not allowed, but to betray oneself is suicide.

Who essentially is *Yoga* addressed to? To those who, due to direct experience, supra-conscious intuition, faith in the principle of transcendence, maturity of consciousness or thirst for seeking truth, can hear the "call" for the *comprehension of oneself.* And *Yoga* is the science of knowing oneself in order *to be*.

> "In fact I would say that temperance [σωφροσύνη = mastery of the polarities, desires, etc.] is knowing of oneself, in accordance, with such definition, with the author of the votive inscription at Delphi. In truth, the sentence seems to be inscribed there as a welcome from the god to the visitors." (Plato, *Charmides*, 164d)

While generally the individual is multiplicity, dichotomy and conflict, *Yoga* leads the being to find himself again as *unity*. In an individual's life we always find contradiction, and often opposition, between thought and action; consciousness is torn by restless psycho-physical energies which even cause paranoid states and neuroses of various kinds. *Rājayoga* fills the separations, makes whole the world of duality and embrac-

---

[3] Pindar, *Pythian III*, "Odes and Fragments". Sansoni. Florence. (Italian Edition).

es, in a flight, both the sensible and the intelligible spheres. Pursued with loyalty and vocation, *Rājayoga* unveils Beatitude and Fullness, which are of pure consciousness, beyond any event-object of any order or degree. From the desire of appropriation, which is centered on the ego (love of oneself), the *Yoga* of Patañjali leads to the unveiling of Love that donates itself and offers itself; Love that is not weakness, passivity or passionateness, but a solar and all-knowing *comprehension*.[4]

There is another consideration which should be reflected upon. Some may think that only the Eastern Tradition is eminently practical, realizative and interested more in the ultimate Subject than the formal object, and is directed more toward consciousness than to mental erudition as an end in itself. This thought can be very reductive. In the West there has always been an initiatory Tradition, which, in order to be such, propounds the effective, practical and vital transformation of the entity.[5]

For example, the ancient philosophy was one of a realizative and transforming order. It did not have as its finality mere conceptual speculation, but the realization of a style of life and a state of consciousness. By propounding a vision of the true being, which is authentic Good, the philosophical dialectics was, as it should be, a precise process of liberation of the Soul from the mundane illusions, the dianoetic projections and the various sensory pleasures. Over time, though, with the

---

[4] Cp. Raphael, *The Science of Love*, "Conception of Love". Aurea Vidyā, New York.

[5] With regard to the Western Tradition, see the following works by Raphael: *Orphism and the Initiatory Tradition, Initiation into the Philosophy of Plato* and *The Threefold Pathway of Fire*. See also by Parmenides, *On the Order of Nature*. Aurea Vidyā. New York.

prevailing materialistic and positivistic outlook, this conception began to fade and even lose the very essence of philosophizing in order *to be*. In modern times, to state one's resolve to *live* and coherently express the philosophy of a Parmenides, Plato or Plotinus, could seem anachronistic. Thus, those few who want to perpetuate the "vision of life" of the Western philosophical Tradition (what the East would call: *jñānamārga* or way of Knowledge, that ὀδός which the goddess proposes to Parmenides) must be in a condition of reservedness.[6]

Therefore, although *Rājayoga* rests on a philosophical vision of life, it is eminently practical. Its operative context is developed in five sequences which embrace the expressiveness of the being in its entirety.

Individuality	1. Rules for the ethical conduct of life Purification of the powers	Preliminary (1st & 2nd means or *aṅgas*)
	2. Position (*āsana*) and *prāṇāyāma*. Purification of the vital body	Physical & prāṇic (3rd & 4th means)
	3. Abstraction from the senses Beginning of re-entry of Consciousness on itself	Emotional sphere (5th means)
	4. Re-education of the psyche and control of the mind	Mental sphere (6th and 7th means)
Immortal *puruṣa*	5. Isolated Unity *Samādhi*	*Puruṣa*-consciousness (Transcendence of the individualized state)

[6] Cp. Plotinus, *Enneads*, VI, 9-11, and Plato, *VII Letter*, 341.

We can also give a synthesis of the content of the four chapters (*pādas*).

PĀDA I

Sūtra	*Subject*
1-4	Definition of the *Yogadarśana*
5-11	The five types of modifications of the mind; possible effects (painful and non-painful.) Their classification.
12-14	Suppression of the modifications of the mind through *abyāsa*.
15-16	Efficacy of *vairāgya* (conscious detachment).
17-18	*Saṁprajñātasamādhi* and *asaṁprajñātasamādhi*.
19	The various possibilities to realize *samādhi*.
20	The basic elements of *samādhi*.
21-23	*Samādhi* gives itself to those who have a strong yearning, practice diligently the appropriate means and give themselves to Divinity.
24-28	The principle of the God person (*Īśvara*) is established.
29	By practicing these means the obstacles disappear and consciousness draws inwardly within itself.
30-31	Source of the distraction of the mind. *Vikṣepa* or externalizing of the mind. The qualities that allow the recognition of a distracted mind.
32-39	Means to eliminate the obstacles of *vikṣepa*.
40	Psychical powers (*siddhis*) and their limits.

Sūtra	*Subject*
41	Exposition of the unity of knower, knowing and known.
42	*Savitarkasamādhi.*
43	*Nirvitarkasamādhi.*
44	*Savicāra* and *Nirvicāra.*
45-46	The subtle objects extend to the *aliṅga* stage: therefore to all the *pratyayas* which can be meditated upon the plane of *prakṛti.* These gross and subtle objects are part of meditation with seed.
47-48	Only in the state of *nirvicāra* there is "light" (universal *buddhi.*)
49	Empirical knowledge is different from intuitive knowledge.
50	*Sabījasamādhi* (with seed.)
51	*Nirbījasāmadhi* (without seed.)

PĀDA II

Sūtra	*Subject*
1	The preliminaries of *Yoga* (*kriyā*): *tapas, svādhyāya, īśvarapraṇidhāna.*
2	The preliminaries of *Yoga* (*kriyā*) lead to the attenuation of the *kleśas.*
3-9	Theory of *kleśas* and their listing. Their causal source is *avidyā* (ignorance of one's own real nature.) Definition of *avidyā.*

Sūtra	*Subject*
10-11	Methods for the solution of the *kleśas*.
12-15	The *kleśas* lead to all sorts of conflictual experiences, they are generators of *karma* and rebirth. For the discerning Sage experience is tantamount to conflict and misery.
16	Future misery can be avoided.
17	It is necessary to avoid the identification of the viewer with the visible.
18	What is the visible.
19	The four stages of the *guṇas*.
20	The viewer is pure consciousness.
21 & 23	The visible is only a means and not an end.
22	For the Liberated in life the visible is as if it was no longer in existence.
24	Oblivion of the *puruṣa* is the cause of the identification with the forms-bodies of *prakṛti*.
25-28	Solution of the identification.
29-55	Explanation of the eight means or *aṅgas*, *yoga*.

PĀDA III

Sūtra	*Subject*
1-15	Continuation of the explanation of the eight means or *aṅgas* up to the eighth means of *samādhi*. What is *saṁyama*.

Sūtra	*Subject*
16-56	Listing of the *siddhis* obtained by doing *saṁyama* on specific *cakras*. Perceptive faculties and sense organs produced by *prāṇa*. Control of the *pañcabhūtas*. The non-attachment to the *siddhis* leads to *kaivalya* (III.51).

PĀDA IV

Sūtra	*Subject*
1	The *siddhis* are the result of birth, drugs, *mantra*, ascesis and *samādhi*.
2-3	Only that which is in potency can become manifest.
4-6	A sole mind, the real one, is the cause of the manifold minds.
7-11	Birth of the *saṁskāras*, *karma*, desires, and so on. Their operative workings. Solution of their cause (*avidyā*).
12-15	Thesis on mental perception and free will.
16	Surpassing of solipsism.
17-21	Mind is only a relative vehicle and *puruṣa* witnesses the movement of the mind.
22	Self-awareness of one's own nature.
23-25	Nature of *citta*, in its broad sense, and of the *vāsanās*. All that which is manifested must be transcended.

Sūtra	*Subject*
26	*Viveka* acquires its highest relevance when it discerns what is from what is not.
27-28	There can be *pratyayas* also in the intermediate state between Being and non-being. It is necessary to eliminate the *pratyayas* as was done with the *kleśas*.
29	One who is able to take *vairāgya* to its furthermost limit, even with regard to the sublime heavens, attains the *dharmameghasamādhi*.
30	Thus ensues the freedom from all *karmas* and *kleśas*.
31	Difference between sensory knowledge and illumination.
32	The *guṇas* can cease to trap the incarnate consciousness.
33	Time theory.
34	Definition of *kaivalya*.

Chapter I

SAMĀDHI PĀDA

1. Now [comes] the exposition of Yoga.*

2. Yoga is the suspension of the modifications of the mind (cittavṛtti).

3. [When this has been effected] then the seer rests in his essential nature.

4. In the other modalities [when the seer is not founded in himself] there is identification with the modifications [of the mind.]

These four *sūtras* sum up the whole essence and finality of *Rājayoga*. "*Yoga* is the suspension of the modifications of the mind;" which is to say, *yoga* consists in bringing the 'conformed movement' (*māyā*) to solution, sound into the without sound, to transcending the becoming of the psyche, and bringing consciousness to stabilize itself in itself, with

* Square brackets added.

itself and for itself. *Yoga* is to realize oneself as Being-*puruṣa* without conceptual superimpositions or mental projections. *Yoga* is to resolve oneself into Essence by tearing oneself away from *prakṛti* or substance. When consciousness is not resting on itself this means it is assimilated to the movement of the *guṇas*. An instinct, an emotion or a thought are qualified energy movements involving and compelling *puruṣa*-consciousness. This involvement, which veils and alters, leads to conflict and pain. Emancipation from the intra-individual and universal modifications leads to the Point at the center, to the *parapuruṣa*.

What is designated with the term *citta* is the causal characteristic of the *antaḥkaraṇa*, which is the totality of what we call content of the mind; it is the formal substance of the psyche; in it also reside the *saṁskāras* (impressions that are present in the mental substance.) *Citta* in *pāli* means "attitude" and is the sum total of the repetitive attitudes.

What is, on the other hand, designated with *vṛtti* are the modifications or the alterations of *citta*. What the mind projects as form (conceptual formal thought) is called *vṛtti*. *Citta* can be impelled by internal subconscious stimuli (*saṁskāras*) or by external ones. Under this pressure, consciousness not only turns out to be burdened by contents of varying nature, but also deeply upset, shaken or modified, thus losing its centrality and clarity. The process of solution of the *vṛttis* normally occurs in three stages: slowdown, control or mastery, solution or transcendence. Also, it is well to consider the fact that the mind is the subject and the world the object, but, behind the subject-mind is *puruṣa*, as incarnate reflection, which is beyond object-subject and world-ego, and which can integrate and transcend them. The entire relational sphere, like time-space, world-ego or universe-God, is constituted by those categories which are born of that subject, which can exist just if put in relation to something: gnosiological polarity.

The mind is not self-existent and self-illumined or self-conscious and in fact, *puruṣa* gives it consciousness and movement, and *puruṣa* is the witness (*sākṣātkāra*) of the movement of both mind and body. Mind and "matter" have in common *puruṣa* as their sole *substratum*, therefore the mind is just the means through which the object is perceived, but the *true Human being* can do as well without both the means and the object because he is *causa sui*.

The non-realized knows himself through his instrument which acts as a reflector, while realization consists precisely in being conscious of one's own essential nature without any intermediary. Under the former perspective it would seem that the mind is the ultimate subject witness, but that is not the case, the mind only reflects the witness, as a mirror reflects the *image* of the entity.

Through discernment (*viveka*), the incarnate *puruṣa* begins to comprehend the workings of the mind and its nature, up to the point of no longer regarding it as first cause, but as simple operational instrument.

It is well to clarify one fact for the benefit of the Western student: whoever follows *yoga*, or generally speaking an Eastern realizative school, has certainly come across the word "consciousness"; in fact, the majority of schools state that, in its most profound expression, the entity is nothing but Consciousness (*caitanya*). There might well be disciples, or initiatory schools, who, because of the particular cultural *forma mentis* they live in, are not able to conceive of themselves as consciousness, but simply as thought. Western literature, then, conceives a human being as an "ego" determining himself in a world of phenomena, but it never presents him as unaltered Consciousness. Leaving aside the greater part of that culture for which consciousness represents a simple epiphenomenon of the physical material structure, the Western initiatory Tradition has defined the entity primarily through its attributes, such as will, intelligence, activity, potency, and so on. Also in the latter domain you can discover the lack of a precise reference to consciousness. Consciousness still remains as a function of contents of different nature, in the absence of which there is no consciousness left either. What is not recognized is that the cause can also subsist independently of the effect or of an incidental attribute.

If we refer to the Eastern Tradition, and to the Indian one in particular, consciousness is held as an essential factor, rather it is the start and the end of the research. Let us also be precise and point out that Patñjali's *Yoga* is one of Hinduism's six *darśana*, in line with the *Veda-Upaniṣad* Tradition.

All those qualifications (will, intelligence, and so on) are nothing but superimpositions on consciousness, which is *ipseity*. The *Upaniṣads* state: the *ātman-brahman* is *caitanya-sākṣin*. The *ātman*, as pure Consciousness, is witness of the superimposed states or conditions, including the vehicles or bodies of manifestation themselves; it is also, *caitanya-svarūpa*, essence of pure Consciousness. The "ego" itself (*ahaṁkāra*) into which the positivist culture is woven, as also the esoteric one often is, is nothing but a superimposition (*adhyāsa*) on pure Consciousness.

Consciousness, which normally we affirm in the waking state and beyond, is nevertheless a mere reflection of the principial Consciousness, therefore, when we talk of *puruṣa* "identifying itself", we are in fact referring to this reflection, the ray of light which appropriates certain vehicles.

Gauḍapāda and Śaṅkara developed this theme in the *Māṇḍūkya Upaniṣad* and concluded that each and every thing appears and disappears from the horizon of our consciousness, or Presence, but not the latter.[2] If we take the three states of waking, dream, and deep sleep without dreams, we observe that in the waking state we are aware of the physical object world; in the dream state that world disappears, but consciousness does not, because it is aware of the objects of dream, and this is self-evident; and in the state of sleep without dream, the object of dream disappears, but not consciousness; we can in fact say to be aware that we had no dreams nor experiences of any kind.[3] As it can be noticed, the object, in its various configurations and levels of reality, may be there but may also not be there, and yet it does not disappear from consciousness, which is precisely aware of the presence or absence of a concept, idea, or emotion, or of the empirical ego itself.

If we study the psychological mechanisms of perception we observe, generally, that we come to know ourselves by way of attributes of *prakṛti*, and not as pure awareness. The attributes function as a mirror and in it we reflect and know ourselves; it is under this perspective that we maintain: "I am strong-willed", "I am emotional", "I am mental", "I am self-assertive", "I am weak", and so on. According to *Yoga* we

---

[2] Gauḍapāda, *Māṇḍukyakarika*, The Metaphysical Path of Vedānta. Translation from the Sankrit and Commentary by Raphael. Aurea Vidyā. N.Y.

[3] According to the *Māṇḍukya* and other *Upaniṣads*, beyond the threefold world there is the Fourth which is beyond knowledge and consciousness itself.

come to know ourselves through the *guṇas* (energetic qualities of the mental substance *prakṛti*.) The entity's tendency is to define itself as: "I am *this* or *that*", where the "this" or "that" are expressive forms of thought. These ideations come after the "that which one is", but unfortunately, with identification, we arrive at considering ourselves no longer as "I am that which I am", but as mere ideation, hence become alienated (II.6).

When the incarnate reflection of consciousness – that ray of consciousness which makes us recognize ourselves as entities with a name and a form and positioned in a well-defined space and time – reunites with its source, it realizes itself in what *Vedānta* calls *ātman*, whose nature is fullness (*pūrṇatā*), and which *Yoga* calls *puruṣa*.

Because this state, as it is outside of the qualitative frame of reference, cannot be described in words, it must be realized directly; let us say that it is a matter of actualization of consciousness. We can consider that the realizative process of *yoga* consits in putting oneself in the state of *puruṣa*, transcending the world of name and form or world of *māyā* or, better, *integrating* the duality or dichotomy of *saṁsāra* into pure consciousness.

5. The modifications [of the mind] have a fivefold aspect and are painful and non-painful.

Having defined the character and finality of *Yoga*, Patañjali now considers the nature of the *vṛttis* both in relation to our response to them, and to their mental-emotional content (*pratyaya*) which is presented to the subject.

The following *sūtras* give the indications and the means to dominate and transcend these *vṛttis*.

6. [They are] right knowledge, non-discernment, imagination, sleep and memory.

7. The bases for right knowledge are: direct perception, inference and testimony.

8. Non-discernment represents a false notion [because] not founded on the real nature [of the object.]

9. Imagination, evoked by words or notions and without foundation, is fantasy.

10. Sleep is the modification which includes the sense of emptiness.

The modifications of the mind examined are: *pramāṇa* (right knowledge) and *viparyaya* (wrong knowledge or non-discernment.) Those are the two kinds of knowledge that derive from the contact of the senses with the external world. Instead, *vikalpa* (imagination) and *smṛti* (memory) derive from the contact with subconsciousness, and are subjective. *Nidrā* (sleep) is the state in which there are neither objective nor subjective representations, but, as there is in it a potential condition of activity, this state is not to be confused with *nirbījasamādhi*. The distinction is very important because if not comprehended it is source of delusion. We will explain this with an example: many *sādaka*, having meditated for a long time with *mantras* or *yantras*, think they have resolved the modifications of the mind, also because they see themselves as more peaceful and more detached from the external world. But, at a certain moment and for various and undetermined causes, they see many modifications of the mind or subconscious contents resurface with more strength and create even a crisis in them. This means that they have simply inhibited, pushed back their "modifications" into the unconscious, without having resolved the very roots of the movement of the *kāma-manas*. It could even be said that their non-correct and therefore non-resolving meditations constituted a "drug". It also happens that, when falling asleep, we enter a deep state of sleep (*nidrā*) in which the thought modifications are brought to the latent state, but as soon as we wake up they return full of life and vigor. True liberation does not occur when we "flee", or inhibit our *vāsanās*, but when we consciously resolve the *roots* of the very movement.

11. Memory consists in holding on to the experienced object.

12. Control [over the modifications enumerated before occurs] with constant exercise and non-attachment [detachment].

The control of the instinctual, emotional and mental movement happens by detaching consciousness from it; and it is necessary to "observe" the whole reactive psychic world in order to find oneself as observing *puruṣa*-witness. As was indicated earlier, we generally are conscious of the object (anxiety, hunger, pleasure, and so on) but not of the ultimate subject. Who is hungry, pleased, and so on? As long as we are identified with the pleasure-pain superimpositions we cannot comprehend the Witness subject. Our assertion is always like this: I am pleasure, I am pain, and so on, and we therefore recognize ourselves to be conscious as "living objects". *Yoga* though tells us that the individual is *puruṣa*, an entity which transcends the various attractive-repulsive movements. Pleasure-pain is a *qualitative* modification of the physical and mental vehicle, which modification we mistake for the very *puruṣa*. In other terms, to use an analogy that Śaṅkara used, we mistake the rope for the snake. The snake we see in place of a piece of rope is a projection or a simple mental movement. Behind the body-volume there is the quality and behind it there is the witness-*puruṣa*. In the measure in which there is identification of *puruṣa* with the body-quality, a limit is established, a prison is erected; hence the "fall". This error of perspective is fatal to the being who does not comprehend his essential nature. In *Vedānta*, as in *Yoga*, the error represents *avidyā*. It is necessary to consider that the empirical mind itself is a "modification" of *prakṛti*, and as such must be transcended.

13. Of these, the constant exercise is a commitment to be firmly founded [in the suspension of the modifications.]

14. But this [abhyāsa = exercise] becomes stable when it is practiced for a long time, incessantly and with zeal.

15. Non-attachment is conscious mastery on the part of he who has stopped thirsting for visible and audible [revealed] objects.

16. The supreme [detachment] is represented [also] by a complete freedom from the guṇas as the result of the awareness of the puruṣa.

The withdrawing or detachment (*paravairāgya*) of the consciousness from the sense objects, both visible and audible, is realized by degree: first through a withdrawing into oneself and a becoming conscious of the subject, then, by persevering in detachment, one masters the reactive world, although still existent; in the end, you have *puruṣa* living in a condition of total freedom from the movement of *prakṛti* and therefore from the *guṇas*.

> "For the incarnate soul practicing restraint, the sense objects vanish, but their taste (*rasa*) persists; however, this vanishes too when the Supreme has been seen."[4]

Rājayoga is based on the *Sāmkhya darśana*[5] which rests on the following vision of Reality: there are two factors, one called *puruṣa* and the other one *prakṛti*, they correspond to essence and substance, to the universal father and mother; the first is masculine and positive, the second is feminine and receptive; one responds to the stimulator and the other to the mother nature generatrix of the world of names and forms. *Prakṛti* is fecundated by *puruṣa* by induction, like a seed by a ray of sun. Thus fecundated, it produces *Mahat*, the great universal mind, and then the *buddhi*, the *ahaṁkāra* (the sense of ego), the *manas* (the analytical distinctive mind) and finally the various subtle and gross elements: *tanmātras* and *bhūtas*. All the substantive forms express three types of qualities (*guṇas*): *sattva*, corresponding to balance, harmony, light, and purity which also represents rhythm in conformity

---

[4] *Bhagavadgītā*, The Celestial Song, Translated from Sanskrit and Edited by Raphael, II.59, Aurea Vidyā. New York.

[5] For this *darśana* see, Īśvarakṛṣṇa, *Sāṁkyakārikā*, with Gauḍapāda's Commentary.

with pure existence and "intellective light", and is the condition of neutrality which transcends and integrates *rajas* and *tamas*. *Rajas*, corresponds to activity and impelling energy, to heat, desire and expansion, to movement, development and passionate drive. And *tamas*, corresponds to darkness, inertia, to passiveness and condensation, it represents the inertial tendencies turned downward, and is equivalent to ignorance (*avidyā*).

The *prakṛti*, therefore, expresses particular qualities which are the combination of the three *guṇas*.[6]

Puruṣa is free in its condition of absoluteness and, if it so wishes, can determine itself along indefinite lines of life expressions. One of which is that of being with a name and a form produced by *prakṛti*. Hence, as earlier mentioned, the "fall"; *puruṣa* although free from any conditioning, can also become relatively entangled in the net of what *prakṛti* produces, to the point of *forgetting oneself*.[7]

Yoga, in the end, is taking oneself back into one's own Essence of consciousness, namely returning into one's own primordial nature, unconditioned and devoid of formal superimpositions, that is, into the unconditioned *mahāpuruṣa*. Wherever there is conflict and suffering, in every type of existence, there you will find identification with what one is not. Beatitude, the one that responds to total *fullness*, can only be found in the state of Being; leaving it, means believing to be that which one is not. Sense pleasure, which the "fallen"

---

[6] For further clarifications on the *guṇas*, one can refer to ch. XIV, and related commentary, of the *Bhagavadgītā*, The Celestial Song, Translated from Sanskrit and Edited by Raphael. Op. cit.

[7] For further study on this subject see Raphael, *Tat tvam asi*, ch. "The Origin of Subconsciousness". Aurea Vidyā. New York.

entity enjoys, is nothing but a diversion, a compensation, a surrogate, also because in the world of becoming everything is contingent and aleatory. The most trustful and resolving message which the *Yoga darśana* transmits to us is a stimulus to resume our true nature, indicating the way by which to reconquer it and, therefore, how to leave the sphere of projections and identifications. The condition of freedom of *puruṣa*, is called *kaivalya* by Patañjali: that is, isolation of *puruṣa* from the formal movement of *prakṛti*. Thus, this treatise describes the means to leave the world of qualities (*guṇas*) and that of bodies-quantities (*dehas*). It expounds theory and practice of awakening and re-integration.

These *sūtras* are very clear; *abhyāsa*, the practice of *yoga*, becomes firmly stable when carried out with great zeal and for a long time. Detachment (*vairāgya*) is the conscious mastery over sense objects of any nature, while supreme detachment (*paravairāgya*) is the complete freedom from the *guṇas* so as to be pure *puruṣa*.

*17. The condition of knowledge is that accompanied by argumentation, by reflection (*vicāra*), by beatitude and by the sense of the pure "I am".*

18. One other [cognitive contemplation] occurs with the [sole] residue of the [subjective] impressions [when it is] preceded by constant exercises that suspend every activity of the mind.

These *sūtras* expound two types of *samādhi*: *saṁprajñāta* and *asaṁprajñāta*.

First of all, what is *samādhi*? It is not a "trance", the way we mean it in the West, nor a state of hypnosis or a paranormal phenomenon, and not either something pertaining in one way or another to the sense or psychic world in its extent. *Samādhi*, in its highest expression, can be defined as direct knowledge of the truth. Where the subject, the object and the very knowledge become one, there you have *samādhi*.

Saṁprajñāta means *samādhi* with *prajñā*, and *prajñā* means knowledge. *Asaṁprajñāta*, instead, means *samādhi* without *prajñā* (the *A-* being privative.) But the latter is not the opposite of the former; their difference is this: in *saṁprajñāta* you have *samādhi* with a particular mind content (*pratyaya*), while in *asaṁprajñāta* there is the absence of any content whatever. This is a purer *samādhi*, and higher, because it leaves out the object of thought, the *pratyaya*, or seed for contemplation. To better comprehend the two *samādhis* we can observe how the mind works. The mind proposes a *pratyaya*-seed which can be a philosophical, mathematical idea, or an image whatever; with this operation the *saṁprajñāta samādhi* is put into practice. Then the mind can do away with the seed, remaining, therefore, totally available and concentrated on itself: it is a condition of extreme self-vigilance and self-luminosity; consciousness can reflect itself in its pure state, thus it is no longer "consciousness of...". In this position, consciousness, devoid of any superimposition of *pratyaya*, is in *asaṁprajñātasamādhi*. Thus, in *saṁprajñāta* the mind and consciousness are extroverted, they give themselves to the thought, while in the *asaṁprajñāta* the mind is quiet and available. Thus between a *saṁprajñāta* and the next *saṁprajñāta*, you have *asaṁprajñātasamādhi*.

There are four kinds of *saṁprajñātasamādhi*: *vitarka* when the mind, and therefore the consciousness behind it, is concentrated on a particular thought or *formal* seed; *vicāra* when the mind operates through non-specific, intuitive discernment; *ānanda* when it operates through the archetypes or the Ideas, which, although possessing their own specific identity, are recognized to be part of the One-all; and finally, *asmitā* when the mind operates on the plane of total unity. And, therefore, we have four types of knowledge: empirical-specific, universal, that of the cause as principle, and that of the pure transcendent Being, i.e. first, or primordial Cause. Up to here, however, we are on the plane of *prakṛti* and of the *mūlaprakṛti*, which is nature containing the indefinite modalities of the manifest development of the undifferentiated unity. With the *asaṁprajñātasamādhi* we find ourselves on the plane or state of the non-manifest, that is, when consciousness rests definitively on itself (*nirbījasamādhi*).

19. It is brought about naturally by one who is disembodied and by one who is absorbed in the principial prakṛti.

Samādhi or contemplation can be brought about in a natural way by those that already are in the subtle states (supra-physical) and by those who are in the same causal body at the potential state. These ones seem to posses the *kaivalya*-isolation, but it is not so because if they have not resolved the unconscious impulses (*vāsanās*) they need to be born again in a new cycle of life.

20. Some other [yogis] attain it by faith, virile will, memory, concentration and intelligence.

Knowledge of *samādhi* can be attained through faith (*śraddhā*), will (*vīrya*), memory (*smṛti*), meditation-concentration (*dhyāna*) and, finally, discerning intelligence (*prajñā*).

In other words, *samādhi* is attained through an unwavering faith, a firm and persevering conviction of the Reality which is within us, a conscious will to transcend all the obstacles of whatever nature and degree, an assimilated experience enabling us to evaluate what is the next step to take, a profound and prolonged concentration and an intelligence that perceives things for what they are. These five qualities would have to be integrated.

As a consequence, the two preceding *sūtras* indicate two types of *yogis*: the former ones who acquired *samādhi* by birth and the latter ones by the practice of *yoga*.

21. It is very close for those with an extremely strong will.

22. [But with] one distinction, depending on whether [the will] is light, average or powerful.

23. Or [contemplation can be attained] with abandon to Īśvara.

Yogadarśana, contrary to *Sāṁkhya*, admits a God-person or *Īśvara*. We can recognize that, although Patañjali founded his *darśana* to a great extent on the *Sāṁkhya* metaphysics, here the sāṁkhyan dualism is surpassed. And anyway, *Yoga* is of a practical order, nowadays we would say scientific, and therefore does not enter into a doctrinaire disquisition on the nature of *Īśvara*. To go deeper into this Principle, Patañjali seems inclined to refer to the speculations of *Vedānta* or the *Upaniṣads*.

24. Īśvara, principial Puruṣa, is not contaminated by afflictions, by actions and [their] enjoyments and by [latent] seminal impressions.

25. It is the supreme principle of omniscience.

26. Due to the fact of not being conditioned by time, It is even master of those who came first.

27. Its designation is the prāṇava (the syllable Om.)

28. Its incessant repetition and the meditation on its meaning [are the means.]

29. Hence the disappearance of all obstacles and the attainment of introspection.

Īśvara is not contaminated by the afflictions (*kleśas*), by the actions (positive or negative *karma*), by the enjoyment of the actions and by the *saṁskāras* or potential seeds which gradually impel into becoming. *Īśvara*, as can be noticed, is beyond movement and non-movement, and beyond any dualism. It is the supreme principle of knowledge itself. As it is outside of time, and therefore of space itself, it is the "Elder", the "Ancient of Days", that who is the First of the first being. Its sound-name is *Om*, whose constant repetition leads to introspection and to the disappearance of the obstacles. *Īśvara*, as the supreme principle of life, expresses absolute

Intelligence and omniscience; due to its intrinsic nature, it transcends the very totality of manifestation; in this way it is both transcendent and immanent, in that, as *essence*, the totality of life prevails. It is the hub of the wheel: which, although still, makes the wheel of becoming turn. In *Vedānta* terms it represents the first *determination* of *nirguṇa Brahman* (non-qualified); that is to say, the God-person, the first *yogi* in his *kaivalya* aspect.

Every *jīva* (or Soul) manifests, in proportion to its awakening, the primordial Intelligence. It could be said that the time-space difference between *jīvas* consists in their greater or lesser expression of the Intelligence as principle. A *jīva* unveils this Intelligence, more or less, depending on whether it succeeds in making its own substance luminous, in purifying its vehicles of contact and clearing the intellect. Although the *jīvas* are sparks of the same "central Fire" (hence the unity of life, and thus of all *jīvas*), yet in time and space not all *jīvas* express it adequately. Many *jīvas* veil themselves on different existential planes, and they make themselves less luminous, because they project image-forms of various nature, which cover the primigenial Spark they are. *Vedānta* talks about projections superimposed on the *ātman*, which is the equivalent of *puruṣa*.

Therefore, according to the various combinations of the *guṇas*, the individual expresses himself along a line of greater or lesser Intelligence (*cit*). As a consequence there is a hierarchy of entities, and so we are unity, insofar as principle, but we have diversities insofar as expressions of that principle, and at times, even marked diversities between the various entities.

Therefore, we need to further differentiate the principial Intelligence from that of the individualized *jīva*. The former *comprehends* the universal life in its totality, while the latter, although reflection of the first one, works in order to organize and direct a particular, individual life, often to the disadvantage of other individuals and the universal. The stronger the individualization the more the being is in opposition, first of all with himself, as he does not express synthesis and harmony, and then with his fellow creatures. The consciousness of a *jīva* which has brought back the part to the whole, and which has thus overcome the sense of ego and the distinction typical of the ego, expresses itself with the universal-principial Intelligence. What we are saying is admirably expounded by Plotinus through these words: "I strive to bring the Divine which is in me back to the Divine which is in the universe."

A consciousness made universal unveils itself in terms of Being, Synthesis and Unity and no longer in terms of you and me; it does not see the individuals as such, but as a "field of energy" interrelated and unified by the Principle.

30. Indisposition, inertia, doubt, negligence, indolence, attachment to objects, wrong perception, inability to identify a point of support (concentration), and instability, represent the mind distractions and the obstacles.

31. Accompanying the causes of mind distraction are pain, desperation, body stimuli, [irregular] inhaling and exhaling.

32. [Necessary] to remove them is an intense application on a single principle [of truth.]

Patañjali enumerates nine obstacles which are elements of distraction of the mind:

Indisposition concerns the physical body and when the body is ill, the mind, not yet resolved, puts the attention there, obviously hindering the concentration on *abhyāsa* (*yoga* practice).

Inertia regards primarily the psyche. However healthy your physical body may be, the psychic body can be apathetic, abulic, and inertial. On emergence, such state could seem as lack of desire or absence of a reason to be active, these being the signs of an advanced consciousness, but in reality it is no so; inertia is a psychic "illness", a pathological state, and not a *yoga* position of consciousness. Unfortunately it is a great obstacle for the *sādhanā*, and who falls a victim of inertia, of mental inactivity, of lack of volition is unlikely to make big strides on the path.

The gnawing of *doubt* eats into and paralyzes every incentive, volition and decision. A doubting being has no alternative but that of always finding himself in a condition of paralysis and conflict. Doubt must be substituted by faith, by intuitive discernment or by experimentation guided by will.

Negligence is carelessness, and is the non-fulfilment of one's own duty or *dharma*, in our case the *dharma* inherent in the state of the *sādhaka* (disciple). It is a widespread "illness" among disciples. At the beginning of the *sādhanā* there is diligence and emphasis, also in carrying out the *yoga* techniques, then slowly the inertial force (the inertia the *sūtra* is talking about) gets the upper hand and the *abhyāsa* wearily drags along, precisely with negligence.

Indolence is the lack of reaction to the external stimuli, is abulia, certainly not due to having achieved the fifth *yoga* means or *pratyāhāra*. It is a psycho-physical attitude that unfortunately damages any kind of aspiration or quest.

Attachment to the mundane objects of the senses represents another source of stagnation and hindrance. There are many *sādhaka* who, even though they want to realize *Yoga*, and hence the union with their own Essence, yet, due to a subconscious inertial force, are attracted by the world of sense objects. You could say that a clear contradiction exists in them: on the one hand they want to "let go" of that which they are not, on the other hand, there is a tendency to hold on to that which is not. In time-space a crisis juncture may occur when consciousness is obliged to make precise choices.

Wrong Perception has great importance on the path of *Yoga*. Some disciples, for example, give wrong interpretations to experiences which may have occurred at the physical, psychic and even spiritual level. Experiences of sound, light, images, and so on, may be interpreted in the wrong way. Events at the profane level are source of wrong evaluations. An incorrect interpretation of the Doctrine is part of this picture as well. Discrimination-discernment (*viveka*) and humility are factors in an appropriate approach to events of a social as well as a spiritual life.

The *inability* to identify a point of concentration derives from a lack of continuos and diligent practice.

Instability is the inability to "fix oneself" on the experienced state. It often happens that the *sādhaka*, having touched a certain state of consciousness, can no longer stabilize it, fix it, and make it permanent. The subconscious gravitational force swallows him up again into the old rhythm; this is a condition common to many students of *yoga*; what is needed, of course, is a greater purification of the various *saṁskāras*.

Mind distraction is accompanied by pain, which may be related to the individual *karma*, or caused by other beings or by nature itself. It can also be caused by desperation, due to frustration of some not satisfied desire; by body stimuli or a disharmony in the nervous system deriving from causes of various nature, and finally, by irregular breathing also deriving from various factors.

To avoid the mind scattering, it is necessary to concentrate on a certain object. A mind still subordinated to psycho-physical movements is dispersing in a thousand directions and continues to be vulnerable to any kind of stimulus. Through concentration on a single object, the mind polarizes and no longer perceives the various physical and sense stimuli; also, in the long run, this attitude puts the mind under the control of the *buddhi*, the higher intuitive vehicle.

33. Purification (calm) of the mind substance is obtained by cultivating the attitude of friendship, compassion, contentedness, and equanimity with regard to happiness and pain, and to virtue and vice.

34. Or by the exhaling or the retention of the breath (prāṇa).

35. Or through a [supra-normal] sensory activity able to determine mind stability.

36. Or [with] the luminous and painless [state.]

37. Or [when] the mind has those who have transcended passions as an object.

38. Or having as support the knowledge of the states of dream or sleep without dreams.

39. Finally, through meditation (dhyāna) on an agreeable object.

Many methods are now enunciated to make the mind calm, purified and quiescent. By developing equanimity, non-opposition and the comprehension of the polarity of life, the mind is purified. By breathing rhythmically, emotions are restrained. By concentrating on a particular activity, the mind is quiescent; for example, by concentrating on the top of the head, or on the *ājña* center, while observing the breathing of *prāṇa*, the mind becomes calm and consciousness elevates itself beyond the physical; or, by concentrating on the lotus of the heart (*anāhatacakra*) the mind remains absorbed. Some types of concentration may produce luminous states or great peace, but these are only instrumental conditions fostering a quiet mind. Concentrating on Those who have "won the world" can be of great benefit; there are beings, and even living ones, who represent a symbol which is not only polarizing for the mind, but also cathartic; moreover, fixing the mind on some data seen in the state of *svapna* and *nidrā* (*taijasa* and *prājña*), which are states of consciousness beyond the gross physical. Finally, by concentrating on a simple pleasing object of meditation, the mind polarizes on the object of meditation.

40. His mastery [of the yogi] extends from the smallest atom to infinite greatness.

41. In that one whose modifications of the mind (vṛttis) have been halted, the fusion of the knower, the knowing and the known object, arises as in a clear crystal.

Through the mastery of the mind the *yogi* can firmly contemplate any datum at will, from the smallest to the largest.

A still mind, serene and available is saturated with *sattva* and therefore, like a crystal devoid of impurities, reflects reality for what it is, without any superimpositions. Having arrived at this condition one transcends the threefold factor that determines the impulse to "come out" of the state of Being.

42. That state of concentration called argumentative (savitarka) is mixed with speech, idea (meaning) and knowledge.

43. When memory is purified and the mind loses its form and only the real knowledge of the object [of concentration] shines, one has the state of concentration without argumentation (nirvitarka).

44. And thus are explained (referring to the two prior sūtras) also the argumentation and the without argumentation states in which subtle objects inhere.

The *savitarkasamādhi* of *sūtra* 42 represents a type of knowledge in which there is the representation of subject-object, resulting from the mixing of name and meaning-idea or concept which the name expresses. This meaning is still an effect of simple sense perception. With *savitarkasamādhi* you have the type of knowledge which is defined as empirical, imaginative and representational (perception, concept and name.) We are used to speculating on the *mind representation* more than on reality itself.

The *nirvitarka* of *sūtra* 43 represents a higher *samādhi*, i.e. that in which the mind reflects a datum of knowledge for what it is, and not for what the mind imagines. This entails having overcome the subconscious projections. Beyond "conventional knowledge" (*savitarka*) there is a knowledge which is supra-sensorial and meta-empirical (*nirvitarka*).

45. The subtle object terminates in aliṅga.

The different degrees of density of the substance terminate in the *aliṅga* state, the last state of the *guṇas*.

46. These concentrations (samādhis) are called with seed.

A seed (*pratyaya*) is any object on which one exercises *saṁyama*. This is constituted by the combination of *dhāraṇā*, *dhyāna* and *samādhi* (concentration, meditation and contemplation or ecstasy.) The seed can be of gross (*sūtra* 42) or subtle (*sūtra* 43) order.

47. When you have the maximum purity in concentration without argumentations inner calm is attained.

The *sūtra* highlights that when the maximum purity or *sattva* condition of the *nirvicārasamādhi* (without mind reflection) is attained, only then inner calm and pacified psyche are achieved. And more, only in this purified state of *sattva* the truth of things can be recognized.

48. Here [in this inner calm] knowledge is reached.

49. Knowledge acquired through testimony and inference, resting on objects of a particular order, differs from higher knowledge.

Knowledge of the supra-conscious *samādhi* is different from that obtained through the five senses with the analytical-descriptive mind acting as conceptual factor; in other terms, the senses furnish information and the mind draws the concept. So, the senses transmit certain items of information of a flower – color, porosity, form, and so on – and the representational mind draws the relevant concept. This, therefore, is the result of the information given by the senses (hence sense knowledge), and it is of an indirect order, or, in case the mind is considered as another sense, it can be said to be of a direct order; yet it is always of the sense type. In fact, *sūtra* 7 of this chapter enumerates direct perception, inference and testimony as useful means for right knowledge. But one must bear in mind that *Yoga* places this type of knowledge on the plane of "modifications of the mind", those which, in fact, must be transcended. On the other hand the individual himself, as he recognizes that this type of knowledge is not perfect and absolute, must resort to particular devices to validate it. Hence the repetition of the event at will, the general terms of the statement, or a testimony made by others, and so on. But, although these devices narrow the margin of imperfection, they are nevertheless not absolute, and therefore it can easily be said that our empirical knowledge is not absolute knowledge. Then, in what sense and for what reason is it often stated that empirical knowledge is the only valid one?

For *Rajayoga* things stand in a different manner. With empirical cognition we never have knowledge of a datum, but merely of our own conceptualization of it, and if the individual had no faculty of a different order, he would be deprived of the true reality of things.

This first chapter is very important because it defines *Yoga*. It enunciates the causes of pain-conflict, and puts the foundations for the correct position of consciousness to adequately follow the *sādhanā*. It also makes the distinction between empirical sense knowledge (movement of thought) and supra-sensorial or pure intellective knowledge, in order to free the consciousness of the neophyte from the perceptive sense world. Finally, it defines *samādhi* with seed and without seed, to which, the latter *samādhi*, the neophyte will have to turn his attention.[8]

50. The impression generated by it prevents any other impression.

51. When also this impression [which prevents any other impression] is transcended, all [impressions] being eliminated, samādhi without seed is attained.

The higher knowledge that we saw in the preceding *sūtras* still refers to knowledge of a seed, of an object operating on

---

[8] For the various types of *samādhi* refer to Śaṇkara, *Dṛgdṛśyaviveka*, Discernment between *ātman* and non-*ātman*. Translation from Sanskrit, and Commentary, by Raphael. Aurea Vidyā. New York.

the plane of *prakṛti*. When the mind works on a seed any other seed and any subconscious impression (*saṁskāra*) is removed or excluded; when that sole seed is transcended, then the reflection of consciousness resolves into *puruṣa*. In other terms, when the neophyte is able to operate in the last stage of *sabījasamādhi* (*sa-bīja* = with seed), that is the *asmitā* of *saṁprajñāta*, and therefore in the *aliṅga* state of the *guṇas*, he can enter with ease in *nirbījasamādhi* (*nir-bīja* = devoid of or without seed) and create in this way the identity with *puruṣa*.

Rajayoga, thus, constitutes that Teaching which favors the realization of one's own *universal Identity*, as opposed to the "individualized culture" which instead propounds the identity with one's own empirical or phenomenal ego.

For *Yoga* the latter represents nothing other than a mere superimposition on the ontological 'I'.

Chapter II

SĀDHANĀ PĀDA

1. Ascesis, self-knowledge and abandon to Īśvara constitute the preliminary (kriyā = practical) yoga.

2. It entails the attenuating of the afflictions (kleśa: affliction-misery) and the realization of samādhi.

The first *sūtra* serves as introduction to *sūtra* 32 of this chapter, where the eight *aṅga* or means (*aṣṭāṅgayoga*) are expounded in detail. *Tapas, svādhyāya, īśvarapraṇidhāna* are three of the components of *niyama* (second *aṅga*); they represent the active and preliminary part (*kriyā*) of the *abhyāsa* and, conducted with perseverance and diligence, they put the *sādhaka* in a condition of attenuating the maculations or impurities and of attaining *samādhi* in a balanced way and without any danger.

3. Ignorance (avidyā), egotism (asmitā), attraction (rāga), repulsion (dveṣa), attachment (abhiniveśa) [to life] are the causes of conflict-affliction.

These are the maculations that cause afflictions (*kleśas*), and their removal entails the solution of the *kleśas*. Often the maculations are assimilated to the same *kleśa* (see, for instance, the *Śvetāśvatara Upaniṣad*: I.11) and one can say that they belong to non-discernment, and therefore to *avidyā*, as per *sūtra* 8 of Chapter 1. *Kleśa* means pain, affliction, suffering or sorrow. A life supported by *avidyā* produces *kleśa*, pain, also when it apparently seems to offer physical or psychic pleasure. The *kleśas* (see *sūtra* 4) can be found at the latent, or potential state, attenuated, weak or intermittent, i.e. when they alternate with opposite qualifications and, finally, at the fully active state. The four states correspond to the evolutionary degree of the *sādhaka*.

This second chapter is of an extreme importance because it puts the accent on the cause of human pain-conflict and on the means through which to eliminate it. It can be said that here Patañjali expounds the whole psychology of the intra-individual movement, regarded as a complex of qualities-energies that condition existence in its daily course.

4. Ignorance (avidyā) is the source of the other [kleśas] whether they are dormant, attenuated, intermittent or fully active.

The source and the cause of the other four *kleśas* is *avidyā*; which is ignorance about the real nature of being.[1]

The *Vedānta darśana* also maintains that the cause of bondage is ignorance, that is *avidyā*. It is the task of *Yoga* and also of *Vedānta*, as epilogue and end of the *Vedas*, to resolve *avidyā* and cause pure Consciousness to shine forth. If

[1] For further aspects on *avidyā* see, Śaṅkara, *Aparokṣānubhūti*. Aurea Vidyā. New York.

one does not arrive at this first cause, that operates through the process of projection (*vikṣepa*) and of veiling (*āvaraṇa*) of the *puruṣa*, one ends up acting always and exclusively on the effects, which obviously cannot solve the problem of conflict and pain.

5. Avidyā consists in mistaking the impure, the impermanent, the pain and the non-ātman for the pure, permanent, happiness and the ātman.

As it was already pointed out, obviously *avidyā* does not regard erudition or lack of erudition, as erudition pertains to the descriptions of phenomena, the quantity of notions or opinions about things. *Avidyā*, on the other hand, is ignorance with regard to the nature of Reality, or the taking for real that which is not real. Thus, if we say that the being is the physical body, or vice versa, we mistake the relative for the absolute, and that which makes us fall into this error is precisely *avidyā*. When we mistake a simple piece of rope for a snake, we have fallen into *avidyā*, because we have mistaken the nature of one datum with that of another datum.

If, instead, we ignore the composition of nitrogen, this ignorance is about the *quantitative* and *descriptive* condition of the element nitrogen, is about phenomenology. From what was said it follows that there are two types of knowledge, but between the two there is no opposition because one is of metaphysical order (ultimate reality of a datum) and the other one is of empirical or physical order. On the traditional plane, *Sāṁkhya* and *Yoga* in this case, there is no opposition between religion, philosophy and science: there is a single knowledge susceptible to different applications on different planes of existence. According to rigorous logic, we should consider the metaphysical one to be knowledge par excellence, precisely because it regards the nature of Being. This, therefore, is knowledge by identity because the nature of Being cannot be considered *object* of knowledge, since it does not admit dual relationship, relation or distance. Being is one and one only, or without a second. The nature of Being is such that only by reinstating oneself into it it can be comprehended. There are some materialists who disavow metaphysical knowledge as they consider it "escape from reality" (material, of course), but a metaphysician recognizes that the most live in *avidyā* because they mistake the relative for the absolute, the phenomenon for the noumenon, and the empirical ego for the Being.

Patañjali covers the solution of *avidyā* in *sūtras* 26-27 of this *pāda*.

6. Egotism (asmitā) corresponds to the identification of the seer with the power of seeing [with the instruments of contact.]

Asmitā derives from *asmi* which means "I am". The *sūtra* maintains that when the "I am" fuses with the *quality* and with the form-object it becomes: "I am *this*". In this way, when we see a tree we can ascertain three elements:

a. "I am" (seer)

b. The eyes which observe (instrument of contact)

c. The tree (object)

The "I am" through the eyes sees the tree. When there is fusion of the "I am" with the tree (the seer and the seen) we have this proposition: "I am the tree". What have we obtained with this event? That the seer has fused with the "seen", or the subject is assimilated to the object; or, still, the subject dissolves into the object. The same thing occurs with the sense organs; in this instance the seer-subject fuses and dissolves in the eyes, which only are instruments of contact. We can say together with Śaṅkara that the object is superimposed (*adhyāsa*) on the subject. Hence also the various identifications: "I am the car, I am the father, I am the mother, the professor, and so on". But the object, such as father, mother, professor, and so on, is superimposed to that "I am" which is behind and beyond the object itself. This assimilation with what, in truth, we are not, causes us to lose the Identity with ourselves; we "fall" into *avidyā* or ignorance precisely because we *forget* our authentic nature. This is Narcissus who, by looking at his reflection in the water, fuses with his projected object-image (*vikṣepaśakti*)[2] and falls into delusion. This can also be an identification with a certain content of the psyche, but the process is the same, and hence we state: I am anxiety, pride, and so on. It can even happen that there is an identification with the very instrument of relation or contact: the gross physical, the hands, the eyes, and so on, as we have already seen.

From this perspective originate ideologies corresponding to materialism, idealism, spiritualism, etc. When there is an assimilation of the subject with the gross physical object, or with its five senses, obviously it follows that the interpretation of life is of a material character, and all we see we classify as matter-body. The idealist, instead, is assimilated to thought and is of the opinion that all reality is thought-idea. And thus, the universe is nothing but thought-idea and Deity itself is conceived as Idea, or Thought of thought. An inner distinction needs to be made between what is permanent, constant and identical to itself and what becomes, appears and disappears. We are *conscious* of the arising of an emotion, its develop-

---

[2] For *vikṣepaśakti*, cp. Śaṅkara, *Vivekacūḍāmaṇi*, The Crest Jewel of Discernment. Translation from Sanskrit and Commentary by Raphael, *sūtras* 113, 115, 140, 143, 144, 343. Aurea Vidyā, New York.

ment and its decline. We can therefore deduce that, of the two, consciousness is the constant.

If we have comprehended the mechanism through which the perceptive-cognitive process and the incarnate consciousness operate, we can understand the expressions of absolutism existing in humanity, we can recognize how ideologies are the outcome of the identification of the subject with the object – be it the physical body, the mind or other. When the Point at the center is realized or consciousness is free of superimpositions, there is a new way in which you see things. The "I am" does not become "this" any longer, but comprehends itself as "I am That I am", *'Ehjeh 'Ašer 'Ehjeh*, according to the doctrine of the traditional Qabbālāh.[3]

When we will realize the "I am", free of its attributes, superimpositions, or objects (no matter what name we may give to it), we will truly have taken a step forward on the Way of Return. This is the Way of dis-identification, detachment (*vairāgya*) from the qualities (*guṇas*) and from the forms (*rūpas*) through which those qualities express themselves. Only in this way the microcosmic "I am", free from its qualitative and quantitative prison, will spread its wings toward that Being which is and does not become, and which constitutes the metaphysical foundation of all appearances.

Puruṣa is surrounded by the *buddhi*, the *manas*, and by the *rūpa* (body), and these are vehicles, sheaths establishing contact and rapport; they are compounds expressing qualities-attributes. In this way, again by analogy, the nucleus of the atom, although *equidistant*, is surrounded by several layers of electrons, which constitute its expressive body. The "sense of ego" is born of the identification of the *puruṣa*-consciousness

---

[3] Raphael, *The Pathway of Fire according to the Qabbālāh*, 'Ehjeh 'Ašer 'Ehjeh (I am That I am), Aurea Vidyā, New York.

with the vehicles. The task of the neophyte is to come out of this identification, which does not correspond to truth, by relying on *vidyā*, i.e. on the recognition that *puruṣa* is a reality which rests on itself, for itself and in itself (I.3).

Why does the embodied *puruṣa* identify with its own vehicles of expression? Because this is one of the manifold possibilities available to *puruṣa*. We can say, because it is free to do so. *Puruṣa* is free to determine itself along the line of conflict-pain (*avidyā*), or of beatitude-fullness (*vidyā*) or still of the metaphysical *kaivalya*, that is, of total detachment from the world of appearances of *prakṛti*. *Avidyā* and *vidyā* represent the vital polarity – the first creates identification and the "sense of ego", with all the consequences that might be ensuing, and the other creates sattvic harmony and right relation – while *kaivalya* takes one beyond all polarity and thus beyond the three *guṇas* or the *nāma-rūpa*.

> "Two [things] are there in the Indestructible, in That which transcends *Brahmā*, in the infinite: deeply concealed there lie both knowledge and ignorance. Ignorance, in truth, is destructible, while knowledge, in truth, is immortal. But That who controls knowledge and ignorance is other [from them.]"[4]

For obvious reasons, we often resort to analogies; these pertain to a conceptual dimension, and because we are dealing with things which are in no way conceptual, by necessity we have to resort to analogies and precise and "substantial" points of reference, which can make us "intuit" the truth of things. Analogy is not identity, suffice it to remember this in order not to render material those things which are not of a

---

[4] *Śvetāśvatara Upaniṣad*, V.1, in, *Upaniṣad*, Edited by Raphael. Bompiani. Milano. (Italian Edition).

material order. What is "matter" for *Sāṁkhya* (*prakṛti*) does not find an equivalent in our Western context. For *Sāṁkhya* matter is not "material". The term that can possibly make us best comprehend the concept of matter in *Sāṁkhya-Yoga* is that of *substance*, according to the acceptation of Greek philosophy.

7. Attraction (rāga) is founded on pleasure.

8. Repulsion (dveṣa) is founded on pain.

9. Attachment (abhiniveśa) is strong desire for life, it self-perpetuates automatically and can dominate also an erudite person.

Attachment to form, to the life of the vehicle, and to the compound is tenacious, so strong as to create restlessness even in the erudite and the learned ones who span over the many fields of the Scriptures.

We can recognize that in this *sūtra* Patañjali enunciates three factors:

a. Attachment to life stems from the desire, the "thirst" for acquisition.
b. It perpetuates in an automatic fashion due to its peculiar and intrinsic operative dynamics.
c. It dominates even an erudite who is knowledgeable in the Scriptures.

Let us pause on these *sūtras* because their comprehension may make us turn in the right direction and clear the ground for our ascesis (*abhyāsa*).

Attachment, adhering to the world of formal life or to a particular existential plane is not cause, but effect; the effect of an impulse, a yearning or a parching thirst which we call *desire*.

"Desire is an intense feeling that drives a search for possession, gain or the accomplishment of what satisfies a physical or a psychical need."[5]

Others state that desiring also means "feeling the want of..." Also according to Plato, desire is a want or deprivation of our forgotten fullness; and this matches Eastern Tradition.[6]

Desire, therefore drives the being out of himself and into the appropriation of something he is lacking, so that *thirst* can be quenched. But we could ask ourselves: is this thirst or parching heat cause of itself, or is it itself an effect? If we carefully follow the psychological sequence of extroversion, we notice that desire is a link between a specific subject, who desires and wants, and an event-object not yet possessed. We, therefore, have three factors:

a. A subject

b. A desire, as impulse or driving force

c. An event-object which the subject wants to seize

In this way we have an efficient, an instrumental and a final cause. If things are so, then the accent, besides putting it on the event-object or on the drive-desire, should be put on the subject, which, in final analysis, represents the determining cause. To understand the process we can resort to an example. What takes place, when we are thirsty? The same movement that we examined earlier:

---

[5] From the Treccani Dictionary. (Italian edition). Also, "A strong feeling of wanting to have something or wishing for something to happen", Oxford Dictionary.

[6] Cp., *Bhagavadgītā*, The Celestial Song, Translated from Sanskrit and Edited by Raphael. Op. cit.

a. An external object we lack

b. A desire-thirst arising from...

c. A physiological need

Therefore, through the embodied instrumental cause of desire-thirst, a physiological need urges the fulfilling of a necessity of the being. It can also be added that, following our example, every physiological satisfaction affords a more or less psychological satisfaction; and consciousness adheres so well and so profoundly to pleasure (*rāga*) that it becomes progressively unable to comprehend if it is pure necessity or pleasure that drives the repetition of the event. What matters is to single out the motivating cause within us which, in its turn, creates the desire or the thirst.

What is driving one toward desiring formal and phenomenal living? Someone might answer: the nature of being itself, which is lacking. If this corresponds to truth, we have to resign ourselves and continue living pushed by *dveṣa-rāga*. We should not even complain because such is our nature, and the very idea of "want of..." should not arise, nor should any satisfaction arise either. If the nature of water is to be humid, it cannot have any idea of dryness or of solidity because these are not contemplated in its nature. The fact that we have an idea of emancipation, transcendence, completeness, immortality, or of absence of desire, and so on, means that all of these are contemplated in our nature. We are, therefore, forced to search for the motivating *cause* which drives us into the world of conflict (*rāga* and *dveṣa*.) Which one is then the cause? Someone may say: pleasure. But we have seen that pleasure is just an effect arising from the resultant of several factors. And the same is for pain.

Someone else, with a deeper introspective capability, could say: the motivating and originating cause is constituted by the *vāsanās*, and by the *saṁskāras*, i.e. by the subconscious tendencies that push for the expressing and ripening of events.

A psychic content is a solidified coagulum having its own:

a. Vitality-necessity
b. Quality-tendency
c. Purpose-finality

Now, this content-seed, or energy coagulate, can be cultivated and fed for entire incarnations, or rather, we can say that a *manvantara* itself is the manifestation of unresolved seeds (II.12 and following). The thirst for formal life arises, then, from a "necessity" stored in a *seed* so powerful as to involve even one who is knowledgeable in these matters and understands these dynamics; but, it has to be recognized, that this happens because mere erudite knowledge is not enough to resolve the imprisoning content.

The second factor to which we referred at the beginning, is the fact that this seed self-perpetuates automatically due to an intrinsic operative dynamics. Let us try to comprehend this point. When, with the power of our creative mind, we "form", i.e. we give a form (mass) to the undifferentiated energy, the form-seed thus obtained has a life of its own, and is at times even independent. We can say that we have created an "entity", a child of ours with its own quite autonomous existential position. In terms of Physics we would say that energy was converted into mass. This "entity" – and such it is, and Plotinus confirms it – is qualified by our tendency, vitalized by our energy (*prāṇa*), by the mind (*manas*) and directed by our purpose-aim (positive or negative.) Have we realized how difficult it is to resolve a seed-content? And why is this? Because it does not obey any longer to our will, because it escapes our decision; quite the opposite, it happens that this extremely vital "entity" takes over to the point of overturning the sense of reality. From being constructors we have turned into being constricted. This is duality: we are not alone any more, we have to live together with "children" which we have created and which possess their own vitality, dynamics, and vital demands. There are even moments when a nagging thought crosses our mind, that of giving up. We have no other choice, we would otherwise create severe frustrations in the field of our psychic space. But are we then bound to be vexed by our "creatures"? Are we made to be devoured by our very own dreams? Should we, free thinkers, submit to the impositions of our thoughts? Are *rāga* and *dveṣa* our executioners? We can be comforted by observing that all which is born, also must have an end.

At this point let us make a synthesis so as to make the comprehension of the *sūtras* easier:

a. Attachment to life is the fruit of desire or thirst
b. Thirst, in its turn, is the effect of unresolved *vāsanās*
c. A content, a *vāsanā*, is an "entity" with its own intrinsic, although relative, energy
d. It is qualified by our own movements-tendencies

Moreover, has the thirst, which is leading us to *not-being*, its own underlying motivation? The answer is: yes, the motivation, or cause, is *avidyā* (II.3-5 and 24-26). And, due to the fact that it gives us the illusion of being *this* particular nature, e.g. the physical body, *avidyā* drives us more and more to thirsting for a physical body, and so on. Due to our free will, we can think-project many things up to the point of believing to be these things and falling into disowning and forgetting what in reality we are. The entity is a creator and can also identify itself with its own creations, submitting to an inevitable alienation, and its entire conflict cannot be eliminated until its alienation is resolved.

With *sūtra* 9 the listing of the maculations ends. *Sūtra* 10 an 11 give the indications on how to destroy them.

10. These [kleśas,] becoming subtle (weakened), are brought to solution.

11. Their activities are suppressed with meditation.

The impure, disharmonious and tamasic qualifications must be gradually toned down, controlled and then brought to solution. What matters in this work of solution is the persistence in purpose, unity in goal, meditation and the unshakable certainty that sooner or later victory cannot but come. *Yoga* is eminently practical and whoever draws near to the *Rajayoga* of Patañjali must be moved by a strong aspiration for *kaivalya*, for liberation from the five above-mentioned fetters. If a profound need for *self-comprehension* in order to be is not there, the fruits will truly be poor. *Sūtra* 10 offers the solution of the potential seeds being taken back into their causal state, that is, into the undifferentiated *prakṛti*. This occurs by separating the incarnate consciousness (or incarnate ray of *puruṣa*) from the qualities-*guṇas* and then with the reabsorption or integration of the quality in the very consciousness. Therefore, it is not a question of inhibiting, but of integrating, dissolving (the alchemical *solve*) and transforming mass into energy that is no longer qualified. It would be like taking a piece of ice back to its original state of water. If the *puruṣa* is the "demiurge" in its own psycho-physical environment it can "solve" or "coagulate" according to intention. It is therefore good to keep this sequence in mind:

Puruṣa --> *guṇa*-quality --> *rūpa*-body-form

Puruṣa, in order to manipulate the *guṇas*, must be behind the body-*rūpa*. Hence the necessity to carry out a "separation" from the qualified energy movements (I.3-4).

Sūtra 11 proposes bringing back the active seed to its potential state, and practicing *dhyāna* as a valid means. And it cannot be in any other way, if one considers the fact that every action is nothing but the effect of a conscious or unconscious meditation.

12. The reserve of karma rooted in the kleśas is experienced in the visible (present) or invisible (future) life.

13. When the root [of karma] is subsisting, there will be the [consequent] maturation: birth, life span, with its [related] experiences.

14. They (birth, etc.) imply joy or pain depending on whether their cause is merit or demerit.

15. For he who discerns, there is only pain-conflict because of change, sorrow, karmic impulses, and the opposition created by the workings of the guṇas and the modifications of the mind (vṛttis).

The reserve of *karma* (*karmāśaya*), or causal body where all the *saṁskāras* are latent, obviously must be resolved, otherwise the *kleśas* mature and give rise to effects in the present or in a future life. Which kind of effects? First of all, birth, growth, illness and death, and already this is a conditioning; pleasure and pain, depending on whether the *karma* is of merit or demerit (you harvest what you sow, states the

Christian Gospel); but, as pleasure is of a contingent order it will manifest as anxiety and fear of losing that which has been conquered. We said elsewhere that pleasure and pain are the two faces of the same coin and, because they belong to the world of becoming and *avidyā-māyā*, they cannot but take one, in final analysis, to a single conclusion, which is agitation. Sense happiness is only emotional exaltation and not fullness of life or *pax profunda*.

Between *kleśa* and *karma* there is a vicious circle: the former produce the latter, and this one brings the *kleśas* into manifestation. But since *Yoga* is of a practical order, you need to experience directly, by way of the *observing consciousness*, birth, growth, and the expression of the *guṇa*-qualities. As an example, one can take whatever physical or psychical pleasure and follow it with the utmost attention, from its birth to its objective ripening. And thus not by way of a recall of what already happened (which is what we generally do), but in the immediacy of its own expressing. We will then become aware of the extent by which *we are determined by*, rather than we determining ourselves. But determine ourselves we can, and *Yoga* confirms it.

16. The future pain-conflict is to be avoided.

This *sūtra* is important in that it highlights one more characteristic of *Yoga*, i.e. the immediacy of realization. One who is willing to shake off the pain-pleasure pair of opposites and the bondage of *saṁsāra*, necessarily must stop their causes *now*, in this very life, so that the future unveils in the present. A spiritual purpose cannot be projected in the future, it must be actualized in the present as otherwise it has no existence whatsoever. In order to neutralize the present and future effects, we must eliminate the determining causes; and unless we take the causes into consideration, we will never have a change in the effects; and physical "death" itself does not solve the problem because those causes, *kleśas* or *saṁskāras*, since they are always present in our mind, throw us back into *saṁsāra*-pain. According to *Yoga*, and any initiatory Doctrine, it is necessary "to die while alive"; natural death is nothing but a passage from one state to another and does not alter our daily events, as sleep does not alter our daily vicissitudes.

You may ask yourself: does the curb imposed on the *kleśas* not represent inhibition? *Yoga*, we have seen, talks of solution and not of inhibition, of *integration* and transcendence of *saṁsāra* and not of psychological escape from the process-becoming. In any event, the work of an instructor can be of great benefit, although few are the available disciples.

It is well, though, to remember that psychological inhibition implies duality: i.e. an *agendi* (acting) subject that wants an object, separate from itself, on which to apply its will. The object may, in the majority of instances, very well resist, hence the conflict. There is inhibition when *two* are involved, but when the entire consciousness self-determines itself there is non-inhibition. When the entire consciousness deliberates to get up from a chair, in this act there is no inhibition; if duality is found in it, this is because complete consciousness is not there. And further, the "second" (*kleśa*, *saṁskāra*, and so on) is not something totally different from ourselves, but a projection of ours, something we have created, a thought of ours turned into mass. In this condition no one is to be fought, there just have to be comprehension and solution. From here stems the *thirst for liberation*, and one of the most fundamental requirements of the disciple, is a profound issue of transcendence always present in the consciousness of the *sādhaka*. If there is a unity of consciousness, purpose, and will any further element is integrated and resolved.

17. The cause of that which must be avoided is the identification of the perceiver with the perceived.

In ultimate analysis, what is the cause that must be avoided? It is the identification of the perceiver with the perceived, it is the merging of the subject with the object, the fusion with the *prakṛti* and its modifications (*guṇas*). The entity identifies with the physical body, with the senses, with the machine (we talk about the machine civilization) which he himself produces, with the ideologies of mind body, with the world of things, and from here conflict and pain arise. The whole of human sufferings, wars waged for the "noblest of ideals", and so on, are born of the identification of the individual with his passions and the things of the world. *Asmitā*, we have seen (II.6), is the merging of consciousness with the instruments of contact: sensory organs and vehicles of expression. This must be avoided in order not to "fall".

18. The visible (perceived) is made up of elements and sensory organs, has light, activity and inertia as its nature, and experimentation and liberation as its end.

And what is the visible, the perceivable and the objective? It is *dṛśyam* the spectacle, the *prakṛti*, the changeable *māyā*, it is all that which is not *puruṣa*, appearance-phenomenon, the sensory world, i.e. the world of names and forms.[7]

And what is the nature of this *dṛśya* made of? Of the three *guṇas*: *sattva*, *rajas*, and *tamas*. And what is its purpose? To offer experiences and in the end, since these lead into duality, the very liberation from the experiences. And

---

[7] For further investigation see, *Dṛgdṛśyaviveka*, Discernment between *ātman* and non-*ātman*. Translation from Sanskrit, and Commentary, by Raphael. Op. cit.

in what sense can we speak of liberation when the *puruṣa* is always equidistant from the spectacle? The question is an appropriate question. The *puruṣa* is free in its nature and in its state, and its nature is such that it cannot be any different from what it is. What needs to be changed is the distorted "attitude", the perspective toward things and toward *prakṛti*. If someone believes to be... Julius Caesar, he falls into an error of "identification"; in fact he is not Julius Caesar and never will be, but unfortunately he considers himself so. What must an individual, who considers himself what he is not, do? He must "recall into his memory" his precise identity, recognize himself for what he has always been and always will be, and *liberate himself* from the projected image. When this will happen he will no longer act as Julius Caesar. As long as the individual does not gain back his true nature, he is conditioned by his alienation, cause of conflict and bewilderment, because it is based on a false projection.

This represents the joyous message and the most profound truth *Yoga*, and the entire and real metaphysical Tradition, offers us (Plato's "remembrance-anamnesis" or meta-empirical memory can be mentioned here.)[8] This message wants to tell us: you are free and immortal entities, yet you believe to be slaves of your senses and mortal things; if you want to resolve your fundamental problem at its root, leave all the social cure-all, and so on, and recognize yourselves for what you really are. True completeness and peace can only dwell in one's own Essence, in one's own nature of Being, beyond any identification with the perceptible and the visible. All the socio-political ideals are enticements because already based on the illusion that we are *dṛśyam*, the spectacle. An event

[8] Raphael, *Initiation into the Philosophy of Plato*, ch. "Platonism and *Vedānta*", and *Orphism and the Initiatory Tradition*, ch. "The Soul's Ultimate End". Aurea Vidyā, New York.

based on an illusory datum cannot but be an illusion. Humanity's vital problems can be resolved only when revolutions are brought about inside, rather than on the outside, of the entity. When more than the institutions, albeit valuable, consciousnesses are transformed, the vision of life and the relationship of oneself with oneself is mutated, and consequently with the others; and furthermore the relationship with the world of nature and forms is also changed. To work on the effects only means putting off the conflictual problems of human kind; but attaining or pursuing a *yoga* vision of life and of being, implies knowing how to fight the internal "enemies" rather than the external ones, and for many this is extremely hard and arduous.

19. The constituent states of the guṇas are: the specific, the non-specific, the differentiated and the undifferentiated.

The three *guṇas* give rise to four stages of development that regard the specific (individual-material), the non-specific (subtle-substantial), the differentiated (the archetype of a specific datum) and the undifferentiated (principial-unity) where all data resolve into unity.

Seen under the aspect of the constituent bodies we have this chart:

Bhūtas	= elements of the gross vehicle	Individual-particular
Tanmātras	= subtle elements	
Buddhi	= universal-intuitive perception vehicle	
Prakṛti	= primordial substance	

In the primordial undifferentiated state the three *guṇas* are in perfect equilibrium; every modification, and therefore manifestation, of *prakṛti* represents a loss of that equilibrium or principial harmony; all the entities participate of the three *guṇas*, in accordance with their consciousness development.

With reference to consciousness it goes that, the specific (*viśeṣa*: distinction, peculiarity) regards the knowledge in reference to a particular object: selective empirical knowledge. The non-specific (*aviśeṣa*: non-distinction, non-characterization) regards the underlying idea we conceive about the *species* of the object. The differentiated (*liṅga*: subtle character) is the constituent element, the specific indication of an object in order to distinguish it from another of the same species. The undifferentiated (*aliṅga*) is devoid of elements, of sign and imprint because the concept-idea and the very distinctive sign of the object have been integrated into unity. Therefore we have: the generic, the specific, the particular indication of a specificity and finally, the integration of the whole into consciousness as the synthetic cognitive unity. Another example for illustration is the following: among many objects made of gold, silver, brass, lead, and so on, we select that of gold (*viśeṣa*) which belongs to the metals *classification*; of this object we then define the *species* (*aviśeṣa*), i.e. belonging to the gold species (and not silver or other); we then define it for what it is in respect of other objects of the same species, we attribute to it a sign, a mark, a name; finally these descriptive aspects are resolved into consciousness, which represents the synthetic cognitive unity by immediacy. The four stages mentioned by Patañjali are susceptible to further developments; in any case we can stop with what we have already described.

We can give a concise frame with the states of both consciousness and the *guṇas*, leaving everything to the intuition of the *sādhaka*.

States of consciousness	States of the *guṇas*
Vitarka	*Viśeṣa*
Vicāra	*Aviśeṣa*
Ānanda	*Liṅga*
Asmitā	*Aliṅga*

For the states of consciousness of the *saṁprajñātasamādhi* see I.17.

20. The seer (puruṣa) is pure consciousness alone; although pure, it appears as seeing through the contacts of the mind.

Patañjali having talked about *dṛśyam* (the spectacle), now addresses *draṣṭā* (seer-spectator-*puruṣa*, in the text.) What does the seer represent? Patañjali is very clear and explicit: *mātra*: only, and *dṛśi*: pure consciousness, which has knowledge in itself.

An how did the seer fall into *prakṛti* and in the forms?

Truly, the seer has not fallen, he is always pure consciousness, but appears maculated due to the modifications of the body-vehicles.

Let us read from the *Sāṁkhyakārikā*:

> "From contrast it follows that the soul (*puruṣa*) is witness, isolated, indifferent, perceiving and non-acting."

Gauḍapāda's comment is the following: "... But, how is it possible that the soul (*puruṣa*), if it is non-acting, reaches the determination to embrace what is right or, vice versa, reject it? To do this the soul must be acting. Yet it was said that it is non-acting..." Therefore, how is it all possible?

"The dissoluble, in itself insentient, becomes sentient thanks to the union with the soul (*puruṣa*); on the other hand the soul, although indifferent (non-acting), becomes active thanks to the own activity of the constituent elements."[9]

Prakṛti is not the cause of itself. The *puruṣa* is the only one determining *prakṛti*'s modifications and represents the catalyst which, even as equidistant from the substance, in fact, is determining its various productions.

In which way does the *puruṣa* seem to enjoy pain-pleasure, the right and the wrong? The *puruṣa* is not the one undergoing modifications, but, rather, the vehicles-bodies interrelated with the three *guṇas*. Let us use an example: the sun ray hits a vegetable seed making it productive, active and capable of birth, growth, and ripening, in other words, capable of *modification*. When coming in contact with the seed, the sun ray appears enjoying the modification, but in fact, not the sun ray, but the seed experiences the movement. The *puruṣa* is enveloped by various sheath which are the ones undergoing modifications; it sees and feels always through them; and the *puruṣa* is not produced, but cause of production; it is not the known, but cause of knowledge; it cannot be conquered as if it were any object, but unveiled, and realized. Its unveiling, or its revealing, will be imperfect if the means of contact is vitiated by some maculation-defect. Ignorance (*avidyā*) is the veil which is found between *puruṣa* and the vehicular reflection. So, when the sides of a lantern are made pure and transparent (sattvic) the light inside is visible in its natural splendor. When we observe a cold corpse we are still seeing a body, but its "inner" light has retreated and the appearance (like the lantern's) has become cold and dark. The "reflection

---

[9] Īśvarakṛṣṇa, *Sāṁkyakārikā*, with Gauḍapāda's Commentary, *sūtras* 19, 20.

of consciousness" of the transcendent *puruṣa*, the ray that illumines and determines the sheaths and the *guṇas*, identifies itself with the movement (*cittavṛtti* of *sūtra* 2, Chapter I) of *prakṛti* (pleasure-pain, action, non-action, emotional and manasic ideals, and so on) and this is due to a simple act of identification with it, to the extent of sharing the vicissitudes of the *guṇas*, which belong to substance. However, this falls within the possibility of the incarnate ray of consciousness itself. In this way, the individual may think, not think, think and identify with his thinking, or not identify. To embrace thinking totally means to lose and annul oneself in thinking, and this entails the belief of being effect, relativity, and duality with all the relevant consequences.

Also the atomic nucleus stays *unaltered* and *equidistant* from its sheaths, the electrons, which, on the other hand, perform movement and quality under the influence of the nucleus. If the nucleus (proton-neutron) were to consider itself electron it could be considered as "fallen" into *avidyā*, into ignorance with regards to its nature. This example, albeit of physical order, can nevertheless be illuminating.

One last consideration: The *sūtra* indicates that the *puruṣa* is pure awareness-consciousness alone. One must ponder over this definition because often consciousness is considered as epiphenomenon of the physical body. We do not need to go any further; the attentive disciple will know how to experiment with the statement of the *sūtra* beyond any preconception of the "collective unconscious". See again the comment to *sūtra* I.4.

21. The nature of the visible (that which is seen = prakṛti) is only as a function of It (puruṣa).

The visible, or perceivable, in that effect, is obviously as a function of the cause. When the cause draws back into itself, not only the effects disappear but also the cause as such (in that reflection of the incarnate consciousness.) We can say: the incarnate consciousness is the subject and *prakṛti* (together with its indefinite modifications) the object; beyond this polarity is the transcendent *puruṣa*.

22. For one who has reached the goal, it (the visible) becomes non-existent, yet it is not destroyed as it is [still] shared by the others.

23. The connection between the power of the holder (puruṣa) and the power of what is held is cause of experimentation of their respective and essential natures.

24. The cause [of the connection] is avidyā.

25. In the absence of it [avidyā] the connection disappears. [This] is the remedy and the Isolation [kaivalya].

In fact, for one who has attained *kaivalya* the visible is dissolved, while it still subsists for the non-realized entity. For the *kevalin, avidyā* does not exist any longer, nor the problems connected to it. Thus, since the expressive vehicle has disappeared, so do its existential problems. When in place of the snake you see the rope, according to the classical example of Gauḍapāda and Śaṅkara, of course the snake has disappeared for ever.

The reflection of *puruṣa*-consciousness has the power to move, to electrify *prakṛti*, which originates the body-forms with specific qualities (*guṇas*); the reflection can fall into identification with the second (*prakṛti*), and the source of such connection is *avidyā*; this implies the oblivion of the true nature (*svarūpa*) of the divine counterpart. But, as Plato says, this oblivion on the part of the reflection is not absolute, it is only toned down, dimmed. *Avidyā* is also the root of the *kleśas* and when it is defeated with the practice of *yoga*, i.e. through *viveka* and *vairāgya*, the incarnate *puruṣa* fuses with its divine counterpart and realizes *kaivalya*: i.e. the supreme isolation from what one is not or from the world of appearances (*māyā*).

26. The unceasing discrimination or discernment (viveka) is the means to abolish [avidyā.]

If ignorance, which is about the nature of *puruṣa*, is source of clouding and of false vision, *vivekakhyāti* of the *sūtra*, sattvic and conscious discernment is source of illumination and right vision.

Also *Vedānta* rests on the two pillars of realization: *viveka*, as factor of supra-conscious comprehension or consciousness of what is real and what real is not, and *vairāgya*, as consequent detachment from the non-real or appearance. By detaching from what one is not, as fruit of illumination, one comes to realize that which one really is. By now, we have comprehended what is not real: the visible, *prakṛti*-movement, the modification of the mother substance, the evanescent phenomena that appears and disappears and the world of names and forms. Instead, the real is the noumenon, the *puruṣa* eternally existent. It is the seer which, although immobile, generates movement, and which, although outside of time-space, determines space-time, and again, although without cause, generates cause.

27. Supreme knowledge is attained through seven defined degrees.

Prajñā, as supreme knowledge-consciousness is realized, according to Patañjali, in seven stages. These stages are experienced in different modalities for each *sādhaka* and it cannot be said that they are identical for everyone. Knowledge begins with the comprehension of *māyā-avidyā* and comes to an end with the realization of the supreme Lord, or *puruṣa*, in *nirbījasamādhi*. Along this way there are several stages of recognitions, of detachments and of fixations of consciousness.

28. Once the impurity is destroyed through the training of the yoga means, there is an irradiating comprehension that leads to full discernment [of the real.]

With the active practice of the eight means of *Yoga*, enumerated in the next *sūtra*, impurities disappear and supra-conscious knowledge, or illumination, unveils the supreme Reality of *puruṣa* devoid of veiling superimpositions.

29. The eight means [of Yoga] are: yama (self-control, prohibitions), niyama (observances), āsana (position), prāṇāyāma (control of breath), pratyāhāra (abstraction), dhāraṇā (concentration), dhyāna (meditation), samādhi (contemplation).

With this *sūtra* begins the description of the eight *aṅga* as practical means of realization.

We should not forget though, that also the other *darśanas*, like every authentic traditional Philosophy, are of a practical realizative order. The fact that some make of these Philosophies a speculation of the mind, or an exclusively literary-cultural fact, is unfortunately true, but this does not invalidate their finality, since they were born just to liberate the individual from the prison of *avidyā*.

> "This secret knowledge meant to fulfill the purpose of the soul (*puruṣa*)..."[10]

And the purpose of *puruṣa* is exactly its liberation and "Isolation" from all incompleteness.

To respect the supreme moral Law (*dharma*), to realize the ascesis (*sādhanā*), to detach from what we are not (*vairāgya*), to love knowledge (*vidyā*), to contemplate (*samādhi*) and to attain liberation from the cycle of deaths and births (*kaivalya*), is the duty of the *sādhaka* who practices *Yoga* or the other *darśanas*.

30. The prohibitions are: non-violence (ahimsā), non-falseness (satya), non-appropriation (asteya), continence (brahmacarya), non-possessiveness (aparigraha).[11]

31. [The prohibitions] not conditioned by social class (type of birth), place, time and circumstances, and extended to all stages, represent the great vow.

The first two *aṅgas* (*yama* and *niyama*) are about the attitude of consciousness and the moral position of the *sādhaka*. It is presupposed that whoever undertakes *Yoga* in order to attain freedom from the maculations already mentioned, must possess, to a degree, adequate qualities of ethical order. Should the qualifications required by these two means of *Yoga* be

---

[10] Īśvarakṛṣṇa, *Sāṁkhyakārikā*, with Gauḍapāda's Commentary, *sūtra* 69.

[11] Cp. Śaṅkara, *Vivekacūḍāmaṇi*, The Crest Jewel of Discernment. Translation from Sanskrit and Commentary by Raphael. *sūtra* 118. Op. cit.

missing, it would be preferable to abstain from proceeding, for many reasons. *Sūtra* 30 enunciates the principle of general order (flexible rule), while instead the subsequent one is of specific order (strict rule). To better understand the problem is necessary to know the social position of the candidate and the stage of life he belongs to.

In a traditional society there exist four orders or social classes: *brāhmaṇa* (sacerdotal order), *kṣatriya* (legislative-administrative-military order), *vaiśya* (entrepreneurial order in a broad sense), *śūdra* (worker's order).[12] Within the realm and in the practice of one's order, certain actions might be permitted. And so, a *kṣatriya* engaged in combat may even kill; a *vaiśya* may accumulate riches, and so on, but one who observes the great vow (*sūtra* 31) must abstain from them, even if they would be permitted under the order he belongs to.

This is also true for the stages of life (*āśrama*) which are also four: *brahmacārin* (student), *gṛhastha* (head of household), *vānaprastha* (hermit), *saṁnyāsin* (renouncing ascetic).

The prohibitions (*yama*) are: *ahiṁsā* (non-violence). Why *ahiṁsā*? The *Yogadarśana* has a unitary vision of life. If we recognize the unity of Being we cannot be in opposition with anybody. Physical science has discovered that the difference between the various atoms consists just in the quantity of the electronic number. Then, it is by the quantity of electrons alone that we know one atom from another atom, but both nuclei and electrons are identical, and of the same nature, in all compounds. If we transpose this datum in the ontological field we observe that the multiple expressions of life resolve in the all-pervading One. *Ahiṁsā* arises as resistance to the lack of comprehension that we are unity of life. It is not

---

[12] For further insight into the traditional social orders, cp. the Preface by Raphael in, *Bhagavadgītā*, The Celestial Song, Translated from Sanskrit and Edited by Raphael. Op. cit.

passiveness, or abandon; it is much more, underlying it is the knowledge of being unity, for which the other individual is ourself. Hence, it is the practicing of an *active* and *operative* universal love. Violence is the fruit of *avidyā* which makes unity appear as absolute multiplicity, whence the fighting of the ones against the others.

Non-falseness (*satya*); if lies is characteristic of *tamas* (darkness), *satya* is a quality of *sattva*. When gradually the tamasic *vṛttis*, imbued with falsity, irrationality, greed, and so on, are substitued by sattvic *vṛttis*, *satya* appears as a clear and luminous quality of consciousness.

Non-appropriation (*asteya*) is another fundamental element of *yoga*. Why? If *Yoga* leads to freedom from the "world of things", of whatever nature and level, appropriating of something means to be in contradiction. Furthermore, if *Yoga* means resolving both demerit (negative *karma*) and merit (positive *karma*), committing actions involving demerit again means not being in one's right place. Whoever follows the way of Liberation must be coherent with himself.

Continence (*brahmacarya*) is the abstaining from all sensory enjoyment. Here as well, one must be in accord with *yoga* that suggests that pleasure-attraction (*rāga*) and therefore repulsion (*dveṣa*) are cause of pain and sorrow (*duḥkha*); refer to the *kleśa* theory (II.3 and following). Jesus says that one cannot serve two masters.

Non-possessiveness (*aparigraha*) is one more indispensable condition of the disciple. Implied in possessiveness and greed is the "sense of ego"; now, this is the cause of individuation, of the assimilation of the embodied consciousness with the various vehicles and the *guṇas*; wanting to perpetuate the "sense of ego" (*ahaṁkāra*) means not doing *Yoga*, betraying the purpose for which the *sādhaka* has undertaken the way of return. *Yama* is an indispensable element of *sādhanā* because with it one begins to curb *tamas-rajas* to the advantage of *sattva*. With *yama* and *niyama* the *sādhaka* can measure to what extent he thirsts for liberation from *avidyā*, is coherent with himself, and committed to an effective *abhyāsa*.

32. The observances are: purity [internal and external,] to be content, ardent aspiration, study and abandon to Īśvara.[13]

Now we start listing the "observances" or *niyama*.

Purity (*śauca*) must regard primarily the mind; an impure mind causes our entire psycho-physical space to be maculated. A preliminary principle that renders the *manas* pure is *innocuousness* which, by favoring harmlessness toward everybody and all, makes the mind innocent; in its turn the mind acts positively on the vehicle of *prāṇa*, and consequently on the gross physical, which it renders more luminous (*sattva*).

To be content (*saṁtoṣa*) constitutes the fulfillment of the consciousness that is not ensnared by the disorderly movements of the *guṇas*. To cultivate the sense of equanimity[14] is an indispensable aspect in order to attain psycho-physical balance. And one must begin from it in order to carry out the other *yoga* means.

Ardent aspiration (*tapas*) is the firm self-discipline, the austerity that the *sādhaka* must have to crown the end of the *Yoga*. Without a firm unity of purpose, despite life circumstances, the *guṇas* cannot be slowed, dominated and transcended. To think that *Yoga* can be done in the bits of free time that social life is according us, means not having the comprehension of what

---

[13] See, *Bhagavadgītā*, The Celestial Song, Translated from Sanskrit and Edited by Raphael, XVI.1-3. Op. cit.

[14] *Ibid*. V.18.

Yoga demands from us. To underestimate the power of the *guṇas* implies, sooner or later, to find oneself faced with failure.

Study (*svādhyāya*) is another element involved in the *sādhanā*. It must be kept in mind that it is up to the *sādhaka* to do *Yoga*, and not to a possible Instructor, and therefore an active attitude is imperative. The *sādhaka* must study and meditate on the Doctrine because *Yoga* consists of theory and practice, since it is a pragmatic philosophy, and naturally this is meant in the operative, and realizative sense. He must assimilate the founding principles of the *darśana*, comprehend that *Yoga* is self-realization, or the science of discovering oneself, and that only he can attain this. He must exclude the attitudes of passive dependency vis à vis the *guru* and the Doctrine itself. The latter ones are just means and must not be considered as ends. Often the approach to one's own Instructor is wrong, although some of them might even favor a passive and dependent attitude. It is up to the disciple to take himself by the hand and cross ... the abyss. Event for which a possible passive and submissive behavior is counterproductive and misleading.

It is well to bring forth the condition of abandon to *Īśvara*. Because *Īśvara*, as we have seen before, is the God-person, the ontological aspect, the first cause of manifestation itself. And since *Īśvara* is also outside of time, space and caused cause, abandon to it entails resolving into It, transcending the phenomenal and contingent aspects.

Abandon must be conscious, intelligent and the fruit of maturity of consciousness and psyche; it is not the empirical ego, but the totality of consciousness to abandon itself, to avoid conflictual psychological dualisms. Offering and giving oneself to and elevating and fusing oneself with Transcendence is the natural state of the awakened embodied consciousness; *Īśvara* is nothing but our divine counterpart.

33. When one is troubled by harmful thoughts, one should foster opposing thoughts.

34. Harmful thoughts are violence and the like; they can be practiced personally, imposed or approved; they can be motivated by greed, anger or clouding; they are moderate, medium or strong, and as fruit they [all] give endless pain and ignorance; therefore it is necessary to foster the opposing [thoughts and inclinations.]

It is important to understand that if we are stimulated by qualifications that are discordant, impure or harmful, we must foster opposing qualities. This responds to a precise psychological technique. If, for instance, we are taken by anxiety, let us *evoke* serenity, and obviously not by just repeating the word at a pure verbal level. It is necessary to predispose oneself and persevere. We already are on a level of meditation with seed and of "technique of evocation". Thinking along a certain line we re-educate the substance or, better, *mould* the *prakṛti*.

Intentions and actions that bring harm to oneself and to others can have differing motivations. They can be, for instance, personally induced by the subject; imposed or approved by others, which makes them accomplices; they can be determined by psychological states such as greed and anger, or by the very clouding of the mind. Moreover, the intensity of these incompletenesses can be moderate, medium or strong, and this depends on the degree of passionateness, clouding or confusion in the mind of the entity. Their inevitable fruit are *duḥkha* and *ajñāna*: pain-suffering and ignorance. To be able to get out of these, it is necessary to foster the opposing qualities, as mentioned in *sūtra* 33.

35. In the presence of one who is firmly established in non-violence, hostilities cease.

36. [The yogi] firmly established in truthfulness determines the fruit of the action.

37. When [the yogi] is firmly established in non-appropriation, all gems manifest [to him.]

In these *sūtras*, and in the following ones, Patañjali expounds the results that one obtains when practicing the ten qualifications of *yama-niyama*. These qualities have to be developed to the utmost degree because they must mould the "substance" (*prakṛti*) and give the reflected consciousness a new orientation toward positions that correspond to *vidyā*. Many frustrations and failures could be avoided if the *sādhaka* were to use above all the lever of *yama-niyama*. Before exercising oneself in meditation (*dhyāna*) it is necessary to prepare both psyche and consciousness to the optimal conditions. What is the result of the practice of *ahimsā*? Abandoning and surmounting every hostility toward any aspect of life. When the *sādhaka* realizes to be in peace with himself and with all, he can agree that *ahiṁsā* has been stabilized. He *comprehends* the various expressions of life, as the fruit of the recognition that we are drops of the same ocean.

Due to the fact that consciousness is positioned in the supra-sensible, one who is stabilized in truth can recognize events that are in those spheres and must still manifest themselves on the sensible plane. One's word is truthful and so are the events that manifest themselves.

Sūtra 37 provides a truth which is disowned in the world of the ego; when an entity ceases to desire, all the treasures come to him: "Ask for the kingdom of Heaven and all the rest will be given to you."[15] To one who knows how to travel on the plane of non-resistance, life offers infinite graces without having to ask for them. This is a profound esoteric truth.

38. When [the yogi] is firmly established in sexual continence he acquires energy.

39. When [the yogi] becomes firm [in] non-possessiveness, he has knowledge of the why of re-birth.

Energy, be it sexual, emotional or mental, is always divine energy. During incarnation, the entity appropriates a *quantum* of energy which can be utilized for the various needs: it depends on the use one makes of it; then, in the *bardo*, one will have to answer to oneself and to others about one's own actions.[16]

When a disciple has resolved the attachment and possessiveness toward his own vehicles, the *guṇas* and the things of the world, and finds himself as consciousness in the state of *puruṣa*, he can understand the reason of his incarnation.

40. From the purification [of the external body] stems the disgust of one's own [body] form and for that of the others.

41. From [a mind or inner] purification of the sattva stems a joyful attitude, a one-point concentration, the control of the senses and the ability of seeing the ātmā.

Only one who has *comprehended* a body-form whatever, and therefore also the human gross body, can recognize the

---

[15] *Matthew*, VI.33.

[16] In Tibetan, *bardo* means, "intermediate state after death".

value of this *sūtra*. It is reported that Plotinus was ashamed to be in a body. It is also true, though, that to attain as much it is necessary to have experience of the intelligible world; only from those heights it can be agreed that physical forms are "shadows", simulacra, "masses" whose exhalations keep away... the Gods.

By purifying the mind, or the psychic state, we have a preponderance of *sattva*; this *guṇa* gifts higher intellective clarity, higher concentration (since the restlessness of the *vṛttis* have been eliminated), higher dominance over the senses, and the ability to perceive the transcendent *puruṣa* in a direct way.

42. By being content one attains supreme happiness.

43. Through ardent aspiration and with the removal of the impurities [one obtains] the power of the senses and of the body.

Fulfillment occurs when desires are transcended; until desire subsists it inevitably pushes toward forever experiencing new acquisitions and objective data. A pacified being is contented with himself and in himself because he has found fullness in himself. Every desire, craving and thirst for experiences has in itself a something of incomplete. Desire is longing for a forgotten happiness. Its condition is legitimate, since we are in "fall", but the direction it takes is in error. The fulfilled being does not desire because all desires have been resolved in one's own beatitude-fullness.

Sūtra 43 must be integrated with the *sūtras* 46-48 of Chapter III. By exercising *tapasya*, intelligent and austere ascesis, one attains perfection of the sense organs (*jñānendriya*) and of the body (*karmendriya*) and control over them. The various gross and subtle senses are just instruments, means at the service of consciousness, but often they become restless bosses. It is necessary to put them back in their right place so that they may perform only their specific function.

44. Through the study of oneself [one achieves] the union with the desired divinity.

45. With the abandon to Īśvara [one achieves] the realization of samādhi.

As a result of the study and comprehension of oneself as *puruṣa*, one enters in touch with the desired divine Principle. The *iṣṭadevatā* is the suprasensible principle selected for contemplation. The divinities, as *Īśvara* itself, are principles, states of consciousness that are also in us, and it is sufficient to respond to *sattva* in order to be in contact with them. We are on the manifest plane of *prakṛti*, and therefore on the plane of the individualized, universal and principial *qualities*; depending on the vibrations of specific *guṇas* we can be in contact with them.

Sūtra 45 must be integrated with *sūtras* 23-27 of Chapter I, and *sūtra* 1 of Chapter II. It is significant to note that Patañjali, not sectarian in the least, makes one comprehend that *samādhi* can be attained not only with the *aṣṭāṅgayoga* but also through the abandon to *Īśvara* (*īśvarapraṇidhāna*) characteristic of the *bhakta*. To abandon oneself to *Īśvara*, the supreme all pervasive and transcendent Principle, means to put into effect the *paravairāgya* (the total detachment from *prakṛti* and from its manifold appearances.) According to *Vedānta*, both essence and substance resolve themselves precisely into *Īśvara*, the unitary divine Principle. For *sūtra* 27 of Chapter I, the term designating it is *Om*, the *mantra* or word-sound, which resounded by pure consciousness leads directly to *That*.

46. The position [must be] steady and comfortable.

47. By way of relaxing of all [tension] and meditating on ānanta [one has a comfortable position.]

48. From this [right position,] no assault by the pairs of opposites.

Patañjali dedicates only three *sūtras* to the *āsanas*, while for the *Haṭhayoga* they constitute, together with the *prāṇāyāma*, the foundation and the premise.

Sūtra 46 simply suggests that the position must be comfortable and steady; whatever position or *āsana*, among the many, can be useful as long as it is suitable for our temperament and body. For instance, if one concentrates the mind on some principle, the attention gets free of physical reactions. The energy follows one's thought; if we pay attention to the gross reactive plane, it gives us tension and trouble. If we divert attention from the body, the energy can be available for other exercises, since it came out of any possible pair of opposites: pleasure-pain, attraction-repulsion or heat-cold.

Ānanta is the name of the serpent Śeṣa which, similarly to Vāsuki son of Kadrū, according to the Hindu mythology, encircles the whole world. By creating the image of a steady center and of external energy flows, that resolve themselves in a circle, or in a spiral, consciousness takes the center position that observes the movement without being influenced by it.

49. Having realized this, one has prāṇāyāma which is the suspension of the movement of inhaling and exhaling.

50. It is internal, external or steady; it is regulated by space, time and number; it is protracted or short.

51. A forth [stage] goes beyond both the internal and the external.

52. Thanks to it the screen of the light dissolves.

53. And [one reaches] the possibility of concentrating the mind.

Prāṇāyāma is a word composed by *prāṇa* and *ayāma* and means control of the *prāṇa*. *Prāṇa* is vital, supra-physical energy that permeates the physical body. The sheath that is right behind the physical sheath is called *prāṇamayakośa*, which means sheath "made of" *prāṇa*. This body feeds the gross body which is called *annamayakośa*, sheath "made of" food. The physical body is inert and that which animates and makes it lively is the very *prāṇa*. Automatically through the control of the *prāṇamaya* sheath one gains control of the body with all the implications this entails. The entire world of names and forms is animated and vitalized by *prāṇa*. Thus the material visible universe is permeated with another universe, invisible to the sensory eyes, which may represent an "antiworld" or antimatter.[17]

A corps becomes cold and inert because the prāṇic body which was animating it has withdrawn (together with the other subtle bodies.) The latter is sensitive to the breathing rhythm. Rather, it is the very *prāṇa* that determines the physiological breathing, the heart beats, etc. Hence the attention on the physiological breathing, primarily by the *Haṭhayoga*.

Through the *prāṇāyāma* one realizes the suspension of the respiratory movement to the point that the breathing becomes

[17] For the various bodies-sheaths, see *Bhagavadgītā*, II.30, and Śaṅkara, *Vivekacūḍāmaṇi*, The Crest Jewel of Discernment, *sūtra* 154 and following. For the *prāṇāyāma*, cp. *Bhagavadgītā*, V.27 and commentary, Ops. cit.

extremely subtle and imperceptible (with all the consequences this entails for metabolism.) The suspension of breathing can take place before the inhaling (external) or after (internal), i.e. with the air in the lungs or when they are empty, or the suspension can also take place at any point of the inhaling or exhaling. The *prāṇa* can be held in a particular point (space) of the body (for instance a *cakra*) and for a certain length (time).

Inhaling, or exhaling, can in its turn be made up by a determined number of respiratory cycles that can be prolonged or short; i.e. breathing of greater or lesser depth.

There is a fourth stage of *prāṇāyāma* that transcends the purely physiological breathing. Consciousness totally retires in the vital body, and from there breathing is actualized through the *prāṇa* directing the vital currents along determined centers or parts of the body. In this condition the physical body remains completely quiescent, rigid and in catalepsy, hence the screen that covers the light of the subtler planes is removed.

54. Pratyāhāra is when the senses are no longer in contact with the relevant objects. [Thus] one identifies with the mind's own nature [which remains steady and colorless.]

55. Hence, absolute (parmo = supreme, absolute) control over the senses.

With *pratyāhāra* (abstraction) the relationship with the external world is interrupted. Since this *sūtra* is very important we can pause and better elucidate the breath of its content.

Let us attempt to comprehend the various mechanisms with which both the psychical apparatus and the sensorial physical apparatus can condition us on the plane of *dhārāṇa* first and then on *dhyāna*. An external datum is received first of all by the senses. Through the prāṇic body, our five senses transmit their message to the awareness-consciousness. The transmission of the objects projected by the mind into our psychical space is provided for by the "internal organ" or *antaḥkaraṇa*.

At this point two more things occur. The discursive mind (*manas*) projects its interpretations on the sensorial data taking its cue from the knowledge-memory of the past, from what is stored in the subconscious, and tries to represent them, conceptualize them and define them within certain schemes. Hence the world of concepts projected onto the object. Also in the mind dwells the *ahaṁkāra* (sense of ego) which refers the experience to itself, thus creating the distinction. In addition to these projections-concepts another event occurs. The datum or object arouses a response on our part, response which is the effect of a *quality*, and therefore of a *guṇa*. One can refer to it as a "subjective sensation". As we know, the quality can be attractive (*rāga*) or repulsive (*dveṣa*, II.3), of pleasure or pain (II.15), or it can be neutral. Generally the mind (*citta*) evokes all the gross and subtle data. Hence it can be said that the world revolves around its representations-projections-illusions. Therefore, the external data goes through four phases: perception-sensation, awareness, interpretation-representation, and response of the *guṇa*.

Both the representation of the data and the response of the *guṇas* are the effect of *memory*, of the build-up of past experiences. This implies that along the horizontal line experience and memory are important, one can say that they are indispensable, while they are not so for the vertical line, rather, they become an obstacle. Up to this point we share the process with the animals, even if our *manas* is much more developed.

If the supra-conscious intuition (*buddhi*), which is not the fruit of the time-space experience, were not to enter into us, our knowledge would be limited, imprecise and not constant. It is well to reaffirm and remember that both the mental notion, or representational projection we make of things, and our qualitative response, stem from the senses and from the memory stored in our space or *citta* (I.2). This is a mechanical and automatic process. And, also, if we eliminated consciousness as a datum in itself and the other dimensions in life, the whole thing would resolve itself in a complex factor of mere conditioned reflex in front of which we would be completely powerless since it would effectively represent the individual as such.

From this perspective, the entity results in a portentous and extraordinary machine interacting with the external environment. Although it can express concepts, ideals, feelings, etc., still it is a machine, conditioned and limited by the senses, by the mind-thought, by the response-quality. There are materialistic notions that conceive the entity from this point of view.

Instead for *Yoga*, what we define as individual is nothing but the "shadow", the non-being, the factor that comes and goes, that appears and disappears, the reflection of a Reality that remains "behind". It is obvious that at a certain stage of awareness or of our *sādhanā*, this "shadow", this mechanical complex that becomes and then disappears, should not be fed, cultivated, or gratified because we would do nothing but perpetuate it.

Therefore, if we start from this principle, by experienced and not just theorized, *Yoga* drives us toward what stands behind the conditioned reflection-shadow, behind the senses (*indriya*), the mind (*manas*), and the very totality of the subconscious content (*citta*) in order to look for the Reality, the *puruṣa*, in that Being, which does not become, appear, or disappear because it is founded on its own *svarūpa* (I.3). *Puruṣa* represents the witness of any possible action by the body, the senses and the mind-thought. Thus, in all that which appears and disappears the *puruṣa* is the only permanent one, because it is pure consciousness (II.20).

The senses may or may not be there, they can be sick, altered, degenerated due to age, or quiescent. The mind does not produce absolute values and therefore interprets and reinterprets data over and over. The response by the *guṇas* may change, it can go from attraction to repulsion, from hate to love or vice versa. But in order to know these motor modalities, these polar alternatives, there must obviously be a witness, which is able to perceive both movements and which has to be *present*, for instance, in both pain and joy, hatred and love, and in right as well as false notions. In other words, in order to perceive duality there must be something which is always constant. This something, we have seen, is the witness-*puruṣa*. This statement is verifiable primarily through *pratyāhāra*. *Yoga* has also been able to understand that a part of the conditionings, or all of them, can be neutralized. The senses may be disconnected, hence no messages reach the witness-consciousness (*pratyāhāra*). Mind itself may be disconnected (the *vṛttis* are resting) hence it does not project anything on the sensory datum or perform any arbitrary interpretation. Also the qualitative response may be neutralized, hence there is a neutral state, thus beyond attraction-repulsion.

Therefore, *pratyāhāra* consists in resolving the five senses into the *manas* or, better, the *manas* under the impulse of consciousness collects in itself the five senses which represent its perceptive tools. If the *manas* performs this operation, it finds itself isolated from the objective data, and since in this abstraction it is no longer disturbed by internal or external factors, it may be available for *dhāraṇā* and *dhyāna*. It can be said that many *sādhaka* are unable to attain *samādhi* because they have not appropriately acquired the *pratyāhāra*, which represents the premise and the foundation of the *samādhi*.

We can summarize the five means (*aṅga*) presented so far. Through *yama* and *niyama* (first and second means) the emotional disorders are eliminated and the *aura* of the *sādhaka* gets purified. With *āsana* and *prāṇāyāma* (third and fourth means) the physical body and the *prāṇa* currents are dominated. Through *pratyāhāra* (fifth means or *aṅga*) one attains abstraction and the retiring of the *manas* from the identification with the activities of the senses and the external world. At this point the mind as well as the incarnate consciousness are finally available to proceed with the work of *dhāraṇa* and *dhyāna*. These are the sixth and seventh *aṅga* and they represent the central part, which is the most significant and unique of Patañjali's *Rājayoga*. Let us remember that it also goes by the names of *Dhyānayoga*, *Samādhiyoga* or *Yogadarśana*. It can be noted that the consciousness of the *sādhaka* goes, to say it in scientific terms, from the objective plane to the subjective plane, and finally, to the plane of *puruṣa*, which is the metaphysical foundation of both the objective and the subjective planes. The process takes place by going backwards along the way through which it developed. For whoever diligently follows these sequences, the result is assured, effective and without risk.

Chapter III

VIBHŪTI PĀDA

1. Concentration (dhāraṇā) is to fix the citta on one point.

2. To be fixed uninterruptedly on this point is meditation (dhyāna).

3. The same [meditation,] when it takes only the essential form of the object and not that of its mental representation, is called samādhi.

We saw that with *pratyāhāra* consciousness has detached from both the external and the internal stimuli arising from the movement of the *guṇas* and the subconscious content. In this abstraction the mind can finally be used to be fixed on a seed (*dhāraṇā*). When this univocal concentration is protracted for a long time one has the true meditation with seed (*dhyāna*). Anyhow, it can happen that during the practice contents (or *pratyaya*) extraneous to the selected seed, may still come in, and in that case one has to take the seed and bring it back to the attention of consciousness.

What is a *pratyaya*? In this context it is a specific content of *citta* operating at a certain point in time, it is an idea, a notion or seed which is the object of reflection, meditation or contemplation.

For instance, if we meditate for half an hour we can find how many times we have been diverted from the seed of meditation for a variety of reasons. In all likelihood we can agree that in that half hour exercise we meditated in all probably for a total of ten minutes or maybe five. Faced with the various contents of distraction we should not have a reaction of frustration, irritability or other, instead, with calm, bring the attention back on our seed. The whole thing must proceed with utmost relaxation and serenity. An act of reaction, or low spirit, implies introducing another *pratyaya*-seed in the field of the psychic space, and in this way one creates a never ending chain. The mental movement cannot be dominated with irritation, opposition, nervousness or discouragement.

Patañjali indicates that the mind has to be dominated and directed after long and constant exercise. Somebody may think that, in order to be realized, this event must involve a high degree of difficulty. We can answer that this is not true. We all have been concentrated even for hours on a single seed, but this seed forced itself onto our consciousness, and was of an attractive or repulsive nature, or we could say, it was motivated by sentiment. Rather, some people even developed a *fixation* to the point of creating a pathological state for themselves.

These *sūtras* propose to fix the mind in a conscious and deliberate fashion and outside of the attraction-repulsion perspective. In this way one has a solar and determined position as opposed to a sentimental motivation that *forces* us to concentrate on a specific *pratyaya*. There is an important difference here. We should make the mental stuff become the docile tool of the *puruṣa*, avoiding the opposite condition. Once the mind will be stabilized to the point of being available for as long as we want, we will be able to go on to the stage that Patañjali calls *samādhi*, or contemplation.

What is *samādhi*? With *dhāraṇā* and *dhyāna* our relationship is primarily with the mind and is related to any formal *pratyaya* (*rūpa*). On the other hand *samādhi* is fusing consciousness with the essence of the seed of meditation. This implies uniting with the noumenal state of a datum, eliminating the mental *rūpa* as well as the subject of perception itself, that is to say the *ahaṁkāra*, the sense or consciousness of ego. Every thing (body-object), of all orders and degrees, has two aspects: the formal and the essential. We are always with the two polar factors, essence and substance. The *rūpa* of the mind is the formal factor, conceptual, etc. Its *svarūpa*, in our case, is the more essential part, where the self-consciousness of the subject fixes itself. Now, the *samādhi* can be attained when both the subjective and the objective part of the mind are transcended. In other terms, it is attained when subject and object are integrated, hence consciousness fuses directly and unitarily with the subject, the object and knowledge; the three factors become unity. We can also say: when the phenomenon and the noumenon are integrated, the duality is transcended and we are in unity.

In order to further clarify: the *manas*-mind provides a *representation* of any object-datum, and not the reality in itself. Instead *samādhi* knows by direct way the "that which is". It results that *samādhi* is not a "trance", a hypnotic state, a catalexis or something of sorts. *Samādhi* is a precise and very advanced state of unitary consciousness. Normal thinking operates by association of ideas, and thus goes quickly from one content to the next. With *dhāraṇā* we have a beginning of concentration and fixing of the mind on a single objective. With *dhyāna* the fixing becomes more marked to the point of remaining for a long time on a *pratyaya*. With *samādhi* (especially the *nirbīja samādhi*) one has the reintegration of all duality into pure self-consciousness.

4. The three [applied] on a single object [form] the saṁyama.

5. Mastering it [one attains] the light of knowledge.

6. Its application is in stages.

Dhāraṇā, *dhyāna* and *samādhi* are the three stages of a single process, one more capable than the other of fixing the mind on a *pratyaya*. When taken together the three stages form the *saṁyama*. An advanced *yogi* enters into *samādhi* immediately, while for the beginner it is necessary to test himself with *dhyāna* or even with *dhāraṇā*. To master *saṁyama* means to illumine consciousness with knowledge, thus consciousness awakens to knowledge. As a matter of fact in traditional terms the *cit* is equated with knowledge-consciousness, or in Parmenidean terms, to know is to be.

7. The three taken together are more profound (internal) than the preceding ones.

The *saṁyama* (control of the three phases) is a mind-consciousness process, while the preceeding *yoga* means are of a more external order because they regard the preparation and propaedeutic preliminaries, although they form the basis of the interiorization process. Then, with *samādhi*, we have direct knowledge.

8. Nevertheless [in that sabījasamādhi] they are external when compared with the nirbīja [samādhi without seeds].

The *saṁyama* we dealt with, always refers to a seed of contemplation; that is a *sabījasamādhi* (*samādhi* with seed-*bīja*), hence it may regard a quality of the three *guṇas* of the *prakṛti*. Instead with *nirbījasamādhi* (*nir*: devoid of seed-*bīja*) one has the attainment of *kaivalya*, because it proposes the re-absorption or isolation of the *puruṣa* from any whatsoever seminal determination. With *nirbījasamādhi* one leaves all *pratyayas*: "Then the seer rests in its essential nature." (I.3) In other terms, one is outside of space-time-cause.

9. Between the moment when the mental impression enters and that in which one desires to suppress it, the mind is in the condition of nirodha (total cessation of thought).

10. Its flow (of nirodha) becomes stable when repeating the impression [with continued exercise.]

These two *sūtras* are very important because, we could say, of their topical scientific interest. Science suggests that light is made up of "quanta" that succeed one another. The universe is a continuum-discontinuum that can be interrupted at any moment. Since the speed of the "quanta", or of the continuum-discontinuum, is extremely high, man does not perceive it as a factor of discontinuity. The film of a movie is made up of many frames separated one from the other by a space or void. Since the film travels at a certain speed these gaps are not perceived. The mind operates in the same way because it, like any other existential *object*, is also *prakṛti*. Hence between one idea and the next, between one mental projection and the next there is a pause, a void, a "space" totally free, which the *yoga* tradition calls *nirodha*. *Yoga* already knew that the universe, including our own mind, is a continuum-discontinuum that can be interrupted at will, as we were saying earlier. So, we can suspend the flow of the *cittavṛtti* by implementing the *nirodha* and lengthening it as much as one pleases to the point of being masters of that original *source* whence our thoughts originate and into which they dissolve. The *puruṣa* instead is the constant, the *continuum.*

If *dhāranā* and *dhyāna* have been handled diligently, *nirodha* should prove easy to conquer and stabilize. On the other hand *sūtra* 10 indicates that by persevering in the exercise we will certainly attain the state of *nirodha pariṇāma* or modification (*pariṇāma*) of the suspension.

11. When the tendency of the mind to turn toward all objects (sarvārthatā) is eliminated and concentration arises, one has the modification of samādhi.

12. When the mental content coming in is the same as that arising [in the subsequent moment] one has the modification ekāgratā pariṇāma (perfectly concentrated attention).

The *samādhipariṇāma* consists in the gradual reduction of the mental distractions and the concentration on a single seed. Applying *saṁyama* on a specific seed all other objects directly or indirectly involved must be excluded. The process begins with *dhāranā* and is concluded with *dhyāna* until, with *samādhi*, one arrives at fusing oneself with the *svarūpa* of the seed itself, or at transcending it completely. Along this course one has a continuous transformation-modification (*pariṇāma*) of the mind.

One has the *ekāgratā pariṇāma* when the *pratyaya* appears, disappears and appears again, always in the same field of the mind. In this, as we touched upon earlier, the conviction that the micro as well as the macrocosmic universe is a continuum-discontinuum is implicit. *Ekāgratā* is the condition of *ekāgra*, i.e. the constant unification of the thinking on a single point.

13. Thus are explained also the modifications of property, character and state in the elements and in the sensory organs.

From the last four *sūtras* one deduces that the *pariṇāmas* demonstrated in reference to the mind or *citta* are true also for the *bhūtas* and for the *indriyas*, but obviously with different operative modes. As when applying *saṁyama* on a mental-ideal seed one arrives at the essence of the very seed (*svarūpa*), so when applying *saṁyama* on the *bhūta* and on the *indriya* (on the primary elements of the forms) one arrives at the ultimate essence of the *bhūta*. When science operates from the outside it transforms certain molecules and atoms in other molecules or atoms, while the *yogi* achieves the same result operating from within. Hence the various *siddhis* (psychic powers).

Applying *saṁyama* on a *bhūta*, or element of the substance, one reaches its informal origin, where it is born and established as element. From that condition the *yogi* operates to manipulate the *bhūta* and therefore matter. Every body-form is reducible to its primary atomic element. If one succeeds in penetrating that sphere, the properties (*dharma*), the specific character (*lakṣaṇā*) and the state (*avasthā*) of the body-form can be modified (*pariṇāma*). By applying *saṁyama* on the *indriya*, one traces the sensations up to their primary origin, and by so doing acquires the control over all sense organs (III.48). *Avasthāpariṇāma* means modification of state, of condition. With this and with the other two *sūtras* Patañjali proposes the basis for the comprehension and the operative action of the *siddhis*.

14. The substance-substratum (dharmī) is the one that is correlated with the properties that are latent, manifest or not [yet] manifest.

15. The sequential origin [natural law] is the cause of the evolutionary modifications.

All manifest or latent properties originate from a single substance (*dharmī*) which is nothing but *prakṛti*, or χώρα for Plato. Also, behind each natural phenomenon a law exists that justifies the external phenomenon.

16. From the saṁyama discipline on the three kinds of modifications [one has] the knowledge of the past and the future.

With this *sūtra* the theme of the *siddhis* is developed. We have nevertheless to convene that Patañjali proposes as the aim of his *darśana*, the attainment of the state of *kaivalya*, beyond *prakṛti* itself, which is the substance out of which all the specific qualities are born, including the *siddhis*.

If Patañjali wanted to insert this particular *pāda*, which in appearance contrasts with the aim of his *Yoga*, it is only in order to demonstrate that *prakṛti* is cause of modifications, properties, conditions, and so on, and that by drawing from that cause we can modify its effects. But to all this both physics and genetics have already arrived, as we touched upon when proposing the external approach. Science went from the objective to the subjective, the *yogi* instead operates in the opposite way and therefore does not need physical or mechanical tools to produce "phenomena".

One other thing to be borne in mind is that in this section Patañjali does not offer specific techniques. He limits himself to propounding just the modality of *saṁyama* on specific *pratyayas*.

In this way, by performing *saṁyama* on the three (*traya*) preceding kinds of *pariṇāma* – *nirodha*, *samādhi* and *ekāgratā* – one attains the knowledge of the flow of time, although without transcending it yet.

17. Due to their mutual superimposition, [there is] confusion between sound (śabda), meaning and idea; practicing saṁyama to distinguish them one has [instead] comprehension of the sounds of all the living beings.

If we do the *saṁyama* on sound, whichever it may be, we can go to its *svarūpa* and comprehend whence it is born and why. Thus one can, for instance, have knowledge of the profound motivations of the words the human beings utter.

18. From the direct observation of the impressions [one has] the comprehension of the previous births.

Through his experiences every human being stamps on his "aura" manifold impressions (*saṁskāras*), which solidify up to represent his "germinal body", seminal or causal. By doing *saṁyama* on the *saṁskāras* one comprehends the reason why we entered the world of *saṁsāra*.

19. [By directly perceiving] the content of somebody else's mind, one has knowledge of his citta.

By doing *saṁyama*, and therefore penetrating in somebody else's mind, one has knowledge of his content and his present *pratyaya (paracittajñānam)*.

20. Not, though, of the support of the content of the mind, because it is not its object (i.e. of the preceding saṁyama).

This last *sūtra* specifies the limit of the preceding *sūtra*. With that type of *saṁyama*, the *yogi* knows the object of thought, but not the motivations that prompted the person to formulate them.

Within their kind, the two earlier *sūtras* are important, and let us understand why. We will use an example in order to make it more evident.

In the "aura" of an individual, a person is able "see" a fairly clear and precise thought-form of a bleeding man and, not having knowledge of its origin, can give different interpretations. For instance, one can believe the bleeding man to be a member of the same family of the individual, or that sooner or later the individual himself will be wounded or still that is his desire is to kill somebody, and so on. All of these interpretations are false. The individual simply witnessed a man being wounded and the event remained impressed in his "aura", a thing which can stay on for quite some time. This example is useful in making us understand how many events, which are in our psychical space, are wrongly interpreted by unprepared and superficial "clairvoyants" or "sensitives".

21. By doing saṁyama on the form of the body (kāyarūpa) the perceiving of it ceases, as does the contact between the eye and light. Therefore [one attains] invisibility. It follows that also sound or other may disappear, and so on.

How can a body be made invisible? An object is visible when its luminosity hits the eye of a perceiving subject. If the light factor is missing, obviously the body is obscured. By applying *saṁyama* on the *tanmātra rūpa* the phenomenon of obscuring the object can be obtained. The *tanmātras* (measure, determination) define the specific range of a certain quality. On the following table the *tanmātras* are shown together with their corresponding "elements" (*bhūtas*) and sensory faculties (*indriyas*):

Tanmātra	*Bhūta*	*Indriya*
gaṅdha-smell	*pṛthivī*-earth	nose-odor
rasa-taste	*ap*-water	tongue-flavor
rūpa-sight	*tejas*-fire	eye-form
sparśa-touch	*vāyu*-air	skin-contact
śabda-hearing	*ākāśa*-ether	ear-sound

By mixing with each other in a given proportion, the *tanmātras* form the *mahābhūtas*, the objects of the gross world, or their constitution, the way it is perceived through the specific organs of knowledge (*jñānendriyas*). The *tanmātras*, therefore, correspond to the "sensation" a quality produces in the sensory organ and through which the object is recognized and experienced. In this way, it is a an intrinsic quality of consciousness, and directly derives from the principial qualities (*guṇas*). From what is reported above one can also argue that by applying *saṁyama* on the *śabdatanmātras* one can neutralize the ether or space (*ākāśa*) which makes operative the *śrotra* (the organ of hearing). Thus, by making it vanish, the *yogi* can control the phenomenon of sound. We saw earlier that by making *saṁyama* on the *tanmātra rūpa* one can neutralize *tejas*, the light that makes visible and activates the *indriya cakṣus* (the organ of sight), and hence make the physical body invisible.

As the various elements proceed from the ether-*ākāśa* and each one of them derives from the preceding one and contains the subsequent ones, likewise for the *tanmātras* each one develops from the preceding one, and so on. There is therefore a precise analogy between *tanmātra* (essence), *bhūta* (substance) and *indriya* (form).

22. *The karma can be immediate and future. By practising saṁyama or following certain signs [one has] the foresight of death.*

There are three types of *karma*: the *saṁcita* is the *karma* accumulated in the past but not yet matured or carried out, the *āgāmin* is the action that will be performed and will bear fruit in the future, and the *prārabdha* is the *karma* one already matured and impossible to neutralize, like for example that of having taken a physical body.[1]

In this context *karma* is the fruit of the action (*karmaphala*) that determines pain or happiness for the acting individuality, depending on the motive set in motion by the subject. One can therefore say that there are two kinds of *karma*: active *karma* (*prārabdha*) and non-active *karma* (*saṁcita*, which will have to mature but whose seeds have been set, and *āgāmin*, "future action" which might even not mature.) The *saṁcitakarma* and the *āgāmin* can be resolved with realization. The *prārabdha* can be rectified and directed.

By making *saṁyama* on the karmic "seeds" that dwell in the causal body (*karaṇaśarīra*) one can obviously become aware of the effects that can mature. But academic science already is able to know in advance on the physical plane even the sex of an unborn baby.

---

[1] Cp. Śaṅkara, *Vivekacūḍāmaṇi*, The Crest Jewel of Discernment. Translation from Sanskrit and Commentary by Raphael, *sūtra* 445 and following. Op. cit.

23. [By making saṁyama] on friendship and other [feelings] one gains the powers [of the corresponding force.]

24. [By applying saṁyama] on the strength of an elephant one gains the power [of the corresponding energy.]

For this *sūtra* suffices the maxim of the *Upaniṣad*: "One becomes what one thinks."[2] By exercising *saṁyama* on any quality of the *guṇas*, sooner or later, that quality will be an integral part of our life. This is very important because it gives the key to the rectification or transmutation of the energetic qualities within us.

25. The knowledge of subtle, hidden or remote things [is gained] by projecting the light in the suprasensible.

26. By doing saṁyama on the sun the knowledge of the worlds [is obtained.]

27. [By doing] saṁyama on the moon [one gains] the knowledge of the disposition of the stars.

28. [By doing] saṁyama on the north star [one gains] the knowledge of the motions [of the stars.]

If we consider that *Yoga* does not make use of material and objective instruments, but of the perception of the internal organs, then it is easy for us to understand that one can perceive the vital and subtle counterpart with which all the bodies are furnished. We have already scientifically es-

---

[2] *Maitry Upaniṣad*, VI.34, in, *Upaniṣad*, Edited by Raphael. Bompiani. Milano. (Italian Edition).

tablished that each particle has its counterpart, that there is matter and antimatter. Then by doing *saṁyama* on specific objects, whichever they may be, one even arrives at comprehending the noumenal-causal state of the phenomenon. What is hidden to the physical senses, becomes evident, the large becomes small in its essence and the future becomes present, because at certain levels the time-space is scaled down and then totally disappears.

29. [By doing saṁyama] on the center of the navel [one gains] the knowledge of the constitution of the body.

30. [By doing saṁyama] on the cavity of the throat [one gains] the cessation of hunger and thirst.

31. [By doing saṁyama] on the kūrmanāḍi nerve [one gains] immobility.

To adequately comprehend this section regarding the *siddhis* according to the *Yogadarśana*, it is necessary to have an overall picture about the integral constitution of the entity. Without this knowledge one will not be able to understand what it means to polarize oneself on the center of the throat, the navel, and so on, and why it is necessary to utilize those parts of the body to arrive at certain effects.

First of all the entity is formed of certain vehicles-bodies at the center of which is the embodied *puruṣa*. What makes the *puruṣa* say: "I am the physical body, or the mind body, and so on", is the fact of identifying with the body to the point of believing to be effect more than cause.

The embodied *puruṣa* is clothed with the following envelops or sheaths that are born, grow and die.

Mahāpuruṣa

↓

Ānandamayakośa
Buddhimayakośa
} Universal Person

Embodied *Puruṣa*
Reflection of
consciousness

◇ ← *Ahaṁkāra* (a "prism" that breaks up the principial unity)

Manomayakośa
Prāṇamayakośa
Annamayakośa
} Empirical individuality

We have seen that every sheath has its own instruments of perception and its fivefold vibratory expression that goes from *ākāśa* to *pṛthivī* as the solid gross element. Also, every sheath is conditioned by seven *cakras* (centers that gather and distribute energy and that are of great importance for what regards the *siddhis*.) However, it is necessary to point out that a *siddhi* is not the usual "psychic power" which is a secondary, though more striking, aspect. The true "power", if one wishes to call it so, is the awakening of those *cakras* that offer knowledge and enlightenment (*sūtras* 33, 34 and following). The Knowledge we are talking about is one of the highest powers that one can have, likewise for enlightenment itself and for the *samādhi*-vision of *sabīja* and of *nirbīja*. These are the true "powers".

The fact that an individual may "levitate" or be a simple healer through the *prāṇa*, and so on, does not mean that that individual is realized.

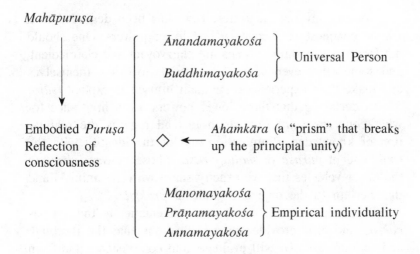

We can say that, at times, *Yoga* has been degraded to a simple conquest of secondary and lower powers. One should not forget that certain animals are clairvoyant and clairaudient, and some other even utilize ultrasounds to orient themselves and make their experiences. Patañjali himself is explicit (*sūtra* 37) in declaring that these lower powers are a hindrance for what concerns *samādhi*, which instead regards the realization of knowledge, illumination and of the identity with the transcendent *puruṣa* or *mahāpuruṣa*. Those powers inhere in the lower vehicles that we exactly share with the animals and that pertain to the objective plane of *prakṛti*.

Based on these premises, we can enumerate the various *cakras* and also provide some indications that the thorough and serious *sādhaka* will evaluate, and comprehend, and from which he will draw his own conclusions.

Let us begin by proposing some meaningful correspondences between the *cakras* and the endocrine glands for what regards the physical body, one of the bodies of the entity.

Cakra	Bīja	Gland	States of Consciousness
mūlādhāra	*lam*	suprarenal	fight for survival instinct
svādhiṣṭhāna	*vam*	gonads	procreative instinct
maṇipura	*ram*	liver-pancreas	sensorial consciousness
anāhata	*yam*	thymus	universal consciousness
viśuddha	*ham*	thyroid and parathyroid	empirical consciousness
ājña	*om*	pituitary or hypophysis	unitary consciousness
sahasrāra		pineal or epiphysis	consciousness of *puruṣa*

The *mūlādhāra cakra* is situated at the base of the spine. There the *kuṇḍalinī* energy, the "rolled up", the goddess *Śakti,* is collected. This is a concentrate of high potency energy which through the use of adequate techniques can be liberated, and raised along the *suṣumṇā*, the central *nāḍī* (the other two *nāḍīs* are *iḍā* and *piṅgalā*) and made connect with the *sahasrāra cakra* where the *Śiva* or *parapuruṣa* principle resides. The "opus", therefore, consists in making the *śakti* of the *mūlādhāra* spiritualized, and making the *Śiva* element or consciousness, corporeal or manifest on all existential planes, which in this instance include the gross physical plane as well.

The *ājña cakra* holds a special condition. It expresses the state of consciousness that corresponds to the location of the *puruṣa* that can determine itself in the world of *māyā* or resolve itself in the pure *puruṣa* reality (*sahasrāra cakra*). The *ājña cakra* thus represents the twofold possibility (it has in fact two petals like the two wings of a butterfly) available to the *puruṣa*, which are, the individual determination, as synthesis of all the other *cakras*, or the expansion into the universal stare, therefore shedding the individualized one.

If *ājña* is connected with the *viśuddhacakra*, which expresses the empirical consciousness, the embodied *puruṣa* is conditioned by the individualization process (*svādhiṣṭhāṇa* and *maṇipuracakra*.) If the *ājña* is connected with the *sahasrāra*, then it transcends the individualized state and is also connected with the *anāhatacakra*. There are some polar aspects related to the *cakras*. Therefore *viśuddha* is in polarity with the *svādhiṣṭhāṇa cakra* (higher intellective creativity and lower procreativeness) and *anāhata* is in polarity with *maṇipura* (universal love and egoic individualized love-feeling-desire.)

The opening of the *maṇipuracakra*, the solar plexus, puts consciousness in communication with the lower *taijasa* plane, or "astral plane", according to the Western esoteric tradition, which could be defined as world of "illusion".

The opening of the *svādiṣṭhāṇa cakra* exasperates and expands the instinctual consciousness, hence the so called "sexual magic". The *anāhata cakra* is the seat of the embodied *puruṣa* whose life thread is anchored in this center and whose expression of consciousness is universal and all-inclusive. This center expresses love rather than feeling, which is, instead, the expression of the *maṇipuracakra*.

The *sahasrāra cakra* and the *mūlādhāracakra* express the "sky" and the "earth" respectively and are joined to the "consciousness thread" called *sūtrātma* which passes through and integrates the various relative states of consciousness.

With regard to the phenomenal aspect of these *sūtras* one can say that doing *saṁyama* on the umbilical *cakra*, which is part of the solar plexus, one can gain knowledge of the physical vehicle. Why this? Because, from a higher and transcendent positioning, the vehicle can be comprehended in its integral composition. In order to comprehend the "illusory phenomena" of the subtle body, and therefore of the corresponding existential *plane* (lower *taijasa*), it is necessary to polarize oneself on the plane of the *manas* and therefore of the *manavaloka*, and so on. Moreover, by doing *saṁyama* on the *kūrma* nerve, a *nāḍī* which is more peripheral than the principal three already mentioned, one can have the physical body completely immobilized, rigid, and so on.

32. [By doing saṁyama] on light, at the top of the head, [one attains] the vision of the perfect beings.

33. Or from the power of pratibhā [one attains knowledge] of all things.

By concentrating under the skullcap (pituitary gland) a "hole" opens through which one can see the Masters of knowledge who are on the higher subtle plane (*hiraṇyaloka*), while by activating the solar plexus (*maṇipura cakra*) one is put in contact, as we have already mentioned, with the lower subtle plane, where the individualized entities reside.

With the power of illumination (direct knowledge, and not mediated by the mind tools) one has perfect knowledge. With the awakening of the buddhic body-vehicle (*buddhimayakośa*), of suprasensible order, one has this type of knowledge.

34. [By doing saṁyama] on the heart [one obtains] the awareness of the mind.

In the heart one finds the "city of the *jīva*", or embodied *puruṣa*, and doing *saṁyama* there one develops the "Intellect of Love". By opening the *anāhata cakra* one can comprehend the mechanism of cognition and, as we have seen earlier, the universality of the entity itself.

35. Experience derives from the inability to see puruṣa and sattva as separate. Since [sattva] exists for the sake of another, in order to know puruṣa it is necessary to do saṁyama on what represents its own end.

It is necessary to remember that to a great extent *Yoga* utilizes as its support the *darśana Sāṁkhya* which posits, on the one hand, a plurality of *puruṣas* and, on the other hand, the *prakṛti* whose qualitative factors are constituted by the three *guṇas*: *sattva, rajas* and *tamas*. Compared with the other two *guṇas*, *sattva* is the purest in quality, the most luminous, and harmonic and given the fact that it is the highest condition, which in *Vedānta* terms can be compared to the *ānanda*, the reflection of consciousness can be assimilated to it (the *asmitā* of *sūtra* 6, Chapter II.) But, we can express ourselves: "I am pain, suffering, good, bad, etc.", likewise we can say: "I am happiness, beatitude, etc.". Then, if *saṁyama* is directed to the fact that the *guṇas* express themselves for the sake of someone else, one goes looking for the other, the beneficiary of the enjoyment of the *guṇas*. A quality is always inhering in something. If one deepens the *saṁyama*, one discovers that between *puruśa* and *prakṛti*, with its own constituent elements, there is a fundamental distinction in their specific natures; one belongs to the nature of the Being and the other to that of becoming; the first one is *causa sui*, the other is caused.

It is also necessary to consider that the transcendent *puruṣa* is pure consciousness (*caitanya* or *citiśakter* of *sūtra* 34, Chapter III,) while its embodied reflection, anchored to the heart, is conditioned consciousness (*citta-saṁvit* of *sūtra* 34, Chapter III.) What is involved in the movement of *prakṛti* is a "ray" of awareness-consciousness originating from the absolute and pure *caitanya*. There is always in us a purely transcendent datum which represents an absolute, and to which all our references lead; our very "anxiety" to know ourselves and to transcend ourselves is a "motion" toward *That*. See *sūtra* 24, of Chapter IV.

36. Hence are born intuition, hearing, touch, sight, taste and smell.

37. These are obstacles to samādhi, but are powers in the [ordinary] objective experience.

By doing *saṁyama* on certain aspects of the entity, as we have seen, one obviously acquires paranormal powers (although these are not always the effect of yogic perfection, above all if one bears in mind that the psychic powers-*siddhis* are "gifts" of *prakṛti*.) Therefore, one can master those *tattvas* which pertain more to the psychic senses than to the physical senses, which are just the gross physical participants of the former.

Sūtra 37 explicitly states that the *siddhis* are obstacles to knowing and realizing *puruṣa*. And in a perfect *kaivalya* there are no more *siddhis*.

38. The mind can penetrate the body of others through the weakening of the cause of bondage and through the knowledge of the passages.

By thoroughly practicing *pratyāhāra* or by realizing *vairāgya* (detachment) from the physical body, the embodied consciousness is freed from it, and can move away and fix itself elsewhere. These events are by now known to the Western parapsychology.

39. In mastering udāna [one has] levitation and absence of contact with water, mud, thorns and so on.

Udāna is one of the five vital breaths of the *prāṇa*. It represents the ascending flow with which the entity leaves the physical body upon death, or through *saṁyama* can exit from the body and transfer himself in the formal subtle (*prāṇamayakośa*) and be free from the earth gravitational force and from the obstacles that can be found at the gross physical level (*annamayakośa*).

40. By subjugating the samāna [one has] radiance.

By mastering the *samāna* (another vital breath of the *prāṇa* that oversees the correct assimilation of nourishment and the energy distribution of the organism) one can develop and increase the gastric fire, which makes the digestion of food possible and produces a heightened acceleration of the entire pranic process in the body. *Prāṇa* is hyperphysical luminous energy.

41. By doing saṁyama on the relationship between ākāśa and the organ of hearing [one obtains] a supra-conscious hearing.

By doing *saṁyama* on the *ākāśa* related to the ear (*śrotram*) one obtains the audition of subtle sounds, supraphysical or hypersonic. By accelerating the *tattva* that corresponds to it, hearing has the capability of grasping sound frequencies non-perceivable by the physical ear. Between *ākāśa*, ear-sound and hearing there is a precise correspondence, as we have seen earlier (III.21).

42. By doing saṁyama on the relationship between body and ākāśa, similar to a cotton flake, one travels in space.

The gross physical body has its foundation in the *ākāśa* and as consciousness finds itself in this *tattva* (*quiddity* or *ipseity* of a datum; and according to the *Yogadarśana* there are 26 *tattvas*), by way of an act of will (and on the subtle plane will is act) it can bring the *mass* back to its own *energy*-essence to then convert it back into its objective condition, like a cotton piece of cloth can be brought back to its simple essence of a flake. It is important not to break the archetypal structure of the body that resides in the state of *ākāśa*, otherwise the mass-body disintegrates in its molecular components whereby the vehicle is lost as an instrument of contact with the gross physical plane. Therefore, by doing *saṁyama* on the relationship between the *ākāśa* and its gross physical precipitate (body) one obtains the possibility of transcending the material space and "fly" in the all-pervading ether of the Being.

43. [By doing saṁyama] on the imaginable external modification of the mind one has mahāvideha; with this the screen of light is destroyed.

Gauḍapāda would say: when Ether (the *ātman* within the body) leaves the vase in which it is contained it fuses with the universal Ether outside the vase (*bahir*: outside, external to something.) For the consciousness that comprehends itself as its original nature, the body (*deha*) is a "prison".[3] Together with the Orphics,[4] Plato confirms that the body is a "prison". A *yogi* able to leave, not only the physical body, but also the empirical-mental body (the experience of this *sūtra*) can discover by himself how much these, and especially the gross physical vehicle, are "prisons", little "cells" from which to escape as soon as possible.

Patañjali, as we saw earlier, is not giving operative techniques that enable the aspirant *yogi* to gain these *siddhis*, he only points out the possibilities that one can realize by carrying out certain *saṁyamas*.

---

[3] Cp. Gauḍapāda, *Māṇḍūkyakārikā*. Translation from Sanskrit and Commentary by Raphael. Aurea Vidyā. New York.

[4] Cp. Raphael, *Orphism and the Initiatory Tradition*. Aurea Vidyā. New York.

44. By doing saṁyama on the gross, subtle and pervasive states, on the real form and on the finality [one has] the mastery of the pañcabhūta.

45. From this derive the perfections like that of obtaining the utmost smallness, the perfection of the body and the liberation from all the obstacles.

46. Grace of form, beauty, strength and adamantine compactness constitute the perfection of the body.

In the *Sarvavedāntasiddhāntasārasaṅgraha* (*sūtra* 396-400 and 409) Śaṅkara maintains:

"And so the *Śāstras* have described the coming into manifestation of the subtle world and its structure. Let us now go on to illustrate the generation-production of the gross elements"

"The gross-physical world [together with its elements] derives [from the subtle world and] from the subtle or primordial elements, i.e. the *ākāśa*, and so on, according to a precise order of forming and the rigorous law of quintuplication"

"Each subtle element is divided first into two equal parts, one of which remains unvaried while the other is subdivided further into four parts [eighths of the entire]"

"And then, each eighth of each element combines with the eighths of the other elements and, finally, every compound obtained in this way combines with the elements halves that had remained unchanged and free"

"In this way the gross elements have their origin; each one of these contains within itself [besides the part of its corresponding subtle one] also the other [subtle] elements. Such is the process [ontological and not "chemical"] of the generation-creation of the gross elements and of their distribution and quantification through quintuplication"

"It is, therefore, clear now the reason for the different properties and qualities of the [subtle] elements [that are reflected in those of the gross elements, of the senses and of the forms of the "material" world.] Ether has only one property, that which inheres in the quality of sound; air possesses two qualities which inhere in the two qualities of sound and contact."

We have given this sequence of *sūtras* regarding the exteriorization of the elements from the subtle to the gross because it is synthetic and very indicative. Whoever meditates on them can derive indications for a correct *saṁyama*.

We perceive the external world through the sense organs (*jñānendriya*), the *ākāśa*-ether through hearing, the air through touch, the fire through sight, the water through taste and the earth through smell. The *pañcabhūtas* (which in final analysis have as their ontological substratum the three *guṇas* of the *prakṛti*) influence the *indriyas*, which translate the objective data into sensations; we could say that these are the various *pratyayas* on which the *manas* (formal mind) elaborates concepts, but the *manas* would be inert (*jaḍa*: inanimate object) if it did not have behind itself the *buddhi*, which gives it the intelligent comprehension and the discriminating activity.

The control over a "thing" can come to pass through the knowledge of its structure and of the stages through which it determines itself as thing. So *Yoga*, through the power of *saṁyama*, has discovered one and the other. Consciousness escaping from *pṛthivī* (earth), crossing over the element *ap* (water) and *tejas* (fire), fixing itself on the element *vāyu* (air), has mastery over fire, water and earth, as many *yogis* have demonstrated. Consciousness is anchored to the various elements by the law of *attraction*; if it were to apply the corresponding opposite law, that of *repulsion*, the elements, which are kept united by attraction, would loosen to the point of breaking up completely.

Then, if consciousness, after having detached itself from the force of attraction, but without annulling it completely, fixes itself in *ākāśa* of the *viśva* plane (gross sphere), it can dematerialize and rematerialize the body-form. And why this? Because on the subtle plane the law that will is act is in force, as the elements, having extreme "lightness" (zero mass), can be driven by the power of *intent* of the consciousness. The object (element) can be influenced by the subject (Heisenberg's principle of determination.) Man's gross physical body contains the five elements at the gross, subtle and pervasive states, and consciousness, through the yogic power, can go from one element to the next, and can go even further and transcend the entire fivefold structure of the gross plane and gross body to enter in a deeper and wider dimension. Rather, if consciousness, being in the *ākāśa* of the gross, does not have the ability of *fixing* itself in order to overcome the attractive power of the *taijasa* plane, it is sucked in by it. As an analogy, if when half asleep one does not have the ability of fixing consciousness in that intermediate state, one can be either brought back to waking or sucked into slumber.

47. Control over the sensory organs [is obtained] by doing saṁyama on their power of apperception, on their own nature, egoity, immanence and purpose.

What was said with regard to the *bhūtas* also applies, to a certain extent, to the *indriyas*. The first stage, for what concerns the *indriyas*, is the apperception (*grahaṇa*), which is given by the transmission of the information of the *bhūtas*; this has been explained earlier (for the *yoga* tradition also the *manas* is a "sense", and can therefore be considered the sixth sense, after the five *indriyas*.) Then comes the nature itself of the sensory organ, which consists of its peculiar sensory feeling (the *svarūpa* of the organ.) Then the sense of ego (*asmitā*). Then the immanent factor responding to the three *guṇas*, the all (*bhūtas* and *indriyas*) starts from them, as it has already been stressed. Finally, the purpose (*arthavattva*) that the organ fulfills which is instrumental to the embodied *puruṣa*. By doing *saṁyama* on the various sensory factors, gradually one reaches control of the *indriyas*, as it was done for the *bhūtas*.

48. Hence swiftness of action similar to that of the mind, independence with regard to the [corporeal] instruments and mastery over nature.

With the mastery of the *jñānendriyas* and the *karmendriyas* (the five senses and the five organs of action or mechanical organs), the *puruṣa*, obviously, has the direct and instantaneous perceptive knowledge without any aid on the part of the *indriyas* and the *bhūtas*. Consciousness is of the nature of knowledge-*cit* without resorting to mediated instruments of perception. Any instrumental means of perception is always a limitation for the *puruṣa*. In order to be, the *puruṣa* does not need the *prakṛti* and its related *guṇas*. In fact, its natural state is exactly that of *kaivalya*.

49. With the discernment of the difference between puruṣa and sattva omnipotence and omniscience arise.

Although one can acquire powers of various nature, one has to consider that, and we want to repeat it, these belong to the *prakṛti* in any case, hence we are still in duality: a subject holder of a power which can be exercised only with regard to an object that belongs to the *pradhāna*. After having recognized the distinction of the *puruṣa* even from the luminous *sattva*, one can have elevated faculties of omniscience through which to comprehend the operative mechanism of the *pradhāna* or *prakṛti* and then one is able exercise every power.

50. From the non-attachment even to it [power of the preceding sūtra] the seed of the bond vanishes and kaivalya is attained.

And yet, however lofty those powers may be, in order to attain *kaivalya*, the *puruṣa* will have to utilize *paravairāgya*, the supreme detachment, so as to completely transcend *prakṛti*.

There are great *yogis* who are able to have no *siddhis*, precisely because they have risen beyond the *pradhāna*, the original universal substance.

51. When one is invited by the heavenly powers, [one must] avoid pleasure and pride because there is the possibility of an unwelcome relapse.

This *sūtra* is to be meditated upon in depth because many *sādhaka*, if the complete *kaivalya* is not yet attained, may fall, and this not due to their lack of sincerity in their practice (*abhyāsa*), nor their negative impulses in them, but because they have given in to proposals by others, be they human entities, *devas* of an individual order, and so on.

For a *yogi* who is not in *kaivalya*, life is a continuous challenge. One needs to keep always alert because the "enemy" is always behind the door. Money, psychic powers, control over beings and things, and so on, are tentacles that can seize and compromise the individual devoted to the *yoga* Realization. The higher the initiatory level of the *yogi* the more his *dharma* is that of having a spiritual resonance in the world and the more he will be tempted in various ways. On the other hand, all the great ones, including Jesus, had temptations. Some *yogis* ran aground in front of great apparent opportunities, like the one of carrying out a mission of salvation. The "messiah complex" must be overcome and transcended if one wants to attain *kaivalya*. Anyhow, it is not money or political power that are noxious, but our erroneous relationship with them and the erroneous use we may be making of them. Patañjali devotes an entire section to the "powers", yet he puts the *sādhaka* on guard against both the *saṁskāras* not yet resolved and the enticing temptations, which may come even from the entities of the individualized plane. It would appear that he has classified the various powers precisely to enable us to recognize them and stay away from them.

Suffices to consider this *sūtra* to realize this. A great number of these powers: levitation, lower clairvoyance, telepathy, going out from the gross physical body, breaking some objects with the power of thought, healing by psychical way, and so on, are common to many individuals, more than one would think; moreover, they are the object of study of Western parapsychology as well. But it is also true that it is not easy to have the majority of those individuals turn to the realizative way, and even less so to *kaivalya*. *Vairāgya* is for them a great and painful problem.

52. Knowledge coming from discernment [is obtained] by doing saṁyama on the instant and on its succession.

Kṣaṇa: instant, temporal moment, *krama*: succession, process of becoming. This *sūtra* would have to be related to *sūtra* 33, Chapter IV. The *yoga* science, already in times far gone, had taken into consideration the question of time, but also those of space and of cause, and from what we can learn has anticipated certain scientific lines of formulation of modern times.

As a real succession, time is a product of our mind, it is enough to do *saṁyama* on this concept to be convinced of it. The light of the sun is not a *continuum* because the photons are waves-corpuscles which appear and disappear. Only *kṣaṇa*, the instant, exists; the mind represents "continuity" (*krama*) to itself because it is unable to perceive *kṣaṇa* as such. It is like in the movies where, although the film is formed by frames that are separate from one another, because the eye does not have the capability to grasp their distinction, it has the sensation of continuity. Time, the way we conceive of it (and likewise for space), is one of the many false concepts of which the *sādhaka* must learn to get rid in order to enter that *kaivalya* where becoming totally disappears. Only what *is not* becomes, while what *is* cannot become other from what it is. Therefore the *continuum* is only the *Puruṣa*.

Because this *sūtra* is quite significant, also to the end of the realization, we could stop a little and study it in more detail. In various dictionaries time is defined as "duration of what has a beginning and an end," "measure of such duration," or "time is a succession of instants;" and in the latter case the instant is taken as the elementary measure of time, similar to what the point is in geometry.

Following these definitions, which can certainly be taken into consideration, we can note that time, or the instant by itself, is an abstract concept. Time is not cause, but is the effect of something behind it. It is the declension of two points or a distance; and according to the given definition, it is the duration between a beginning and an end; it measures two events or two happenings; it is the delimitation of a "movement", which extends from a point A to a point B. And from this, reflections of a practical philosophical order cannot but arise. Let us examine some of them:

1. Time taken by itself is an abstraction
2. Time is the result of movement
3. Time is description of a circumference
4. Time is the succession of "temporal units", similar to light which is a succession of photons and to the line which is a succession of points

It can be noted, and we touched upon it earlier, that these things offer matter of great reflection and meditation.

Time when taken by itself, is an abstraction, and when we try to classify, define or turn it into something concrete we are forced to refer it to something. We will obviously have to experience this proposition in a conscious way. In perfect immobility there is no time because we have no points of reference, we have no beginning or end; in other terms, we have no movement from which to draw coordinates. If we start with an ideation, or a mental picture, and we terminate it, we will have to have two precise points of reference: the *end* of a preceding movement of the mind, which represents the beginning of our time, and the *beginning* of a further movement, which in its turn represents the closing. These two precise points of reference represent the distance within which our time is located. But, by what is the content between the two points of reference represented?

We can say that it is represented by a "movement of thought"; i.e. the mind *moved* describing a line going from point A to point B. This line constitutes the distance, and consequently the quantity; that is to say the space.

Therefore, with its thought, the mind describes a movement, a space, a time. To render these data objective, we resorted to some measures in an arbitrary way, inventing the hour and the meter respectively, or the millimeter and the second; these are the unities of time-space, the factors that render our frame of life intelligible.

Time like space, is the *representation* of a psychological movement. But, as it is referred to a movement-process-event, which in its turn is the resultant of "points of event", if we could (and we can) interrupt the sequence of points of these instants-moments, then movement, time and space will all disappear: i.e. *māyā* would disappear. Although some may think that it is impossible to stop the instant, we – within us – should try it. Our perception is used to grasp a range of measures into which generally the infinitesimally small does not fit because the mind is not trained. We should then gradually learn how to slow the "movement" in us to the point of reducing it to the unity of the instant, to the infinitesimal portion of the event (*kṣaṇa*). Then we will be able to annul it because *māyā*, which is time-space-movement, can be annulled and transcended with *silence* or perfect immobility of consciousness. According to Plato, time is the "moving image of eternity."[5]

---

[5] Plato, Timaeus, 37.

In geometry a plane, or a form (and an event itself is a form), is the effect of the succession of points one after the other. If in the process we stop our hand in a certain point "x" and we put ourselves in the without-movement, the form-plane cannot come true. It cannot be born because the time-space, or *māyā*, has been transcended. Parmenides negates the movement in terms of absoluteness and he thus negates time. For the Eleatic the Being "is now altogether" because "Goddess Dike granted to it neither to be born nor to perish."[6] From this perspective time becomes simple *appearance*; that is to say *māyā*. Therefore, in the supreme Being time and space do not enter.

The metaphysical reality can emerge only when we have liberated ourselves from this kind of process. The universe, as was said, is a continuum-discontinuum, thus between one discontinuum time and the other is the without-time, out of which time can resurface. If things stand in this way, and science itself has by now confirmed it, then we can interrupt the temporal discontinuum and fix ourselves in the atemporal condition of the "continuum", annulling the mental photonic sequence and this, obviously, if we thirst for transcendence.

53. Hence the comprehension of the difference between two similar things even if they are distinct by species, character and position.

We know certain things because there always is a distinction by class, character and position; the conceptual mind needs these categories to be able to define a datum; but when the distinctions happen to be lacking because two data find themselves to be co-instantaneous and perfectly identical in

---

[6] Parmenides, *On the Order of Nature*, Fr. 8.5, 13, 14. Op.cit.

their essential nature and quality, how can they be distinguished? How can two *kṣaṇas* be distinguished? *Pratipatti* means comprehension, perception and, in this context, the ability to distinguish two things which have been fused, conjoined or superimposed.

From the previous *saṁyama*, we could then have the ability to comprehend the distinction of the two *kṣaṇas* which appear and disappear in alternate order maintaining the same position. We can say that to comprehend time, one has to put oneself out of time, as to comprehend the universal manifestation itself, one needs to put oneself in the *nirbījasamādhi*.

54. The knowledge one has from the discernment-discrimination is liberating, simultaneously it extends to all objects, comprehends all means and includes, past, present and future.

The knowledge one is talking about is the fruit of that immediate discernment that gives the possibility to "comprehend in order to be", is supreme knowledge as opposed to the empirical one concerning the world of becoming, which means it is relative knowledge. That knowledge unveils the *puruṣa* which *is*, and which is to be found outside of the phenomenal world and multiplicity; and therefore beyond space-time. Only this Knowledge is liberating, transcendent and resolving.

55. Kaivalya is attained by an equal purity of puruṣa and sattva.

When the *sattva* predominates uncontested vis à vis *rajas* and *tamas*, it made itself completely pure so that it reflects the very purity of the *puruṣa*. The fact that the *mahapuruṣa* is the supreme reality distinct from the three *guṇas*, and therefore from *sattva* itself, has been expounded in *sūtra* 50 of this *pāda*.

Chapter IV

KAIVALYA PĀDA

1. The siddhis are obtained by way of birth, chemical means, mantras, with tapas and samādhi.

Some powers are there already with birth because they have been acquired in other lives, and therefore there is a ripened fruit, although sown in another time-space. Also some drugs confer possibilities, but they are dangerous, they are not reliable and offer lower *siddhis*; rather, the least that can happen is to be taken into a hospital, and at times even a psychiatric one.

The particular sounds of the *mantras* can for sure contribute to the acquisition of *siddhis* if consciousness is predisposed and the vehicles are responsive. One has to have a certain sensibility for sound and talent of intonation. The *siddhis* can also be obtained through *tapas*, ascesis or austerity, and with that particular fire that determines the ripening of spiritual events. And finally, through *samādhi*. Except for the drugs, which are venom for the body and for the spirit, the other means are valid, especially that of *samādhi*, which was spoken about in the previous *pādas*.

2. The transformation of a type-species in another happens with the fluidity-movement of prakṛti.

If an element is transformed into another it is because it has in itself the potential of becoming it, otherwise this would not be able to take place. The *prakṛti* has within itself the virtuality to change into manifold aspects because it possesses this fluidity of possibilities.

3. On the other hand they are not the accessory elements to directly start the movement of prakṛti. They remove the obstacles, the same way that it happens to a farmer [watering a field.]

By removing the obstacles from the free flow of life it runs easily: whatever action, the way it happens for an acquired merit, gives the possibility just of giving the direction to the event. Knowledge itself does not create Liberation, but offers the means to eliminate those obstacles that interfere with its attainment.

4. The generated minds [come down] solely from the sense of "I am".

5. A sole mind directs the activity of the different minds.

6. Of them [minds] only the one generated by meditation is exempt from [karmic] impressions.

The *yogi* can generate "minds" by simple projection. The individuality – active in *viśva*, gross physical plane – might find it impossible to accept such a statement;

yet the entity during dream generates other individuals with precise qualifications, structured in a certain way, with whom he entertains dialogues. Only that this process is generated in an unconscious fashion, while the *yogi* does it in a conscious way. As in a dream, not just one but many entities can manifest themselves, likewise the conscious *yogi* can project manifold "minds", born from that substratum which is obviously the *I am*. This possibility is self-evident for those who had experiences in the subtle plane, but it can also take place in the gross physical plane.

A sole mind, even though it remains same to itself, causes manifold minds, as precisely in dream, in which a sole mind, even though it does not suffer impoverishment or other, projects innumerable entities.

An advanced *yogi*, free from *karma*, can project the "minds" naturally free of maculations, that which does not happen with a mind already impregnated with *saṁskāras* and *vāsanās*. This is obvious: one projects one's own completeness or incompleteness, it depends on the degree of realization achieved.

7. The action (karma) of the yogi is neither white nor black, while it is threefold in the others.

This *sūtra* talks about *karma* in relationship with the fruits, and so there are three possible fruits of *karma*: one is positive, the other one is negative and the last one is mixed (the type of *karma* of the majority of common individuals.) The *yogi* is free from *karma*, why? Because he is universal consciousness, and has therefore transcended the *asmitā*, he does not act for the sake of the fruits; his action is *innocent*, spontaneous, and free from whatsoever expectation; it is an action that stands on itself, not motivated by desire or will, and is not intentional either, like the scent of a flower which is not motivated but by its reality of being. The individuality, or sense of ego, is only moved by desire, expectation and acquisition, and magnetically attracts to itself the fruits of its desires and expectations.

8. From this are manifested only the tendencies [or potential desires: vāsanās] in accordance with their nature.

The three types of *karmas* listed earlier can manifest themselves in space-time and in the opportune conditions, and the quality of the *karma* is determined by the type of *saṁskaras* or *vāsanās*. The effect is of the nature of the cause.

9. [As there is] identification between memory and impressions (vāsanās) there is created a succession [of them] even when they are separated by class, place and time.

In the preceding *sūtras* it was mentioned that the ripening of certain karmic seeds can only occur when the right conditions are there, and thus the cause of *karma* does not perish until it is resolved, and it extends beyond a simple incarnation of the reflection of consciousness. Moreover, in a specified incarnation only determined seeds can ripen because if all the residual *karma* had to come down, the individuality would be completely an-nihilated. This can be extended to an entire humanity of a particular space-time. The karmic deposit of the entity, in *Vedānta* terms, is called *kāraṇaśarīra*: causal body. It is this body (*śarīra*) that needs to be resolved in order to leave the world of *māyā*. In which way can *karma* or, in other terms, the cause and the effect, be neutralized?

First of all it has to be said that in the world of *māyā* this is a law of general order (also Jesus states that we reap the fruits of what we have sown); there is no God who punishes us for our actions; these absolve or condemn themselves by themselves, it depends on the nature of the action and on the intent that makes the event move. It is stated in physics that a moving body can be neutralized by applying to it an equal and opposing force. In order to neutralize *karma*, which is the law of cause effect, one needs to promote a cause equal and opposing, i.e. that has the same expressive intensity and an opposing energetic quantity. *Karma*, like everything that regards *māyā*, is not absolute, and therefore a passive attitude or one of resignation is neither intelligent, resolving or right. Consequently *karma* can be resolved by taking into consideration the sequence of the three types of *karma* of *sūtra* 7: the negative-black *karma* can be transformed by promoting positive causes (*sattva*), and these (as they also "bind") by way of the attitude of the *yogi* mentioned earlier.[1] Once this state is attained, one is beyond good-ill, the way these terms are understood by the individual, and not because the Realized does not do good, but because he is free even from the fruits good may give. And this for a simple aspirant is an extremely difficult thing.

10. They [impressions] are without beginning because the desire of life is permanent.

---

[1] See the comment to *sūtra* 7 of this chapter.

It is opportune to dwell a little on this *sūtra* because it can give rise to misunderstandings. Some commentators go as far as saying that the process of accumulation of the *saṁskāras* is, in a few words, eternal, and in fact the *sūtra*, when taken by itself, could lend itself to this understanding. But Patañjali could not contradict himself, and this is why we believe that those who contradict themselves are these commentators. Why? First of all, one has to reaffirm that the *Rajayoga* is one of the six Hindu *darśanas* whose authority are the *Vedas* and the *Upaniṣads* that is to say the *Śruti*, and, therefore, Tradition which has always talked about Liberation, release from the bondage of *māyā-avidyā*, conflict, pain, and so on. Patañjali is obviously not the lesser, and has therefore posited the problem of *kaivalya*, the release from the becoming of *prakṛti*. *Kaivalya* can mean: isolation from *prakṛti*, absoluteness, isolated unity, isolation from the threefold world, independence from any possible thing and total and integral detachment from the *avidyā*. It also represents the dissolution of the constituting elements (the three *guṇas*.) *Sūtra* 32 in *pāda* IV recites: "Therefore, having the three *guṇas* achieved their purpose, the process [in them] of the modifications reaches its end."

Therefore, Patañjali poses the problem of Liberation, and accordingly the overcoming of the three *guṇas*, the cessation of desire, the fruition of the *karma* and the solution of the *kleśas*. If this were not this way, his *darśana* would truly be useless, and even a hoax on the aspirant *yogi*.

Some commentators translate *nitya* as eternal, but this meaning does not seem acceptable in this context because it conveys the idea that desire, being eternal, has no beginning nor end. Besides, as desire is a characteristic of the individuality, we would have to deduce that this could never resolve, transcend or release itself. Absolute eternity is on the other hand the characteristic of *puruṣa*, not of the *guṇas* and of appearances. The modifications of the *guṇas* and therefore of *prakṛti* (time-space-cause), come to an end (IV.32).

Nityatva has been translated, in our context, with "permanent" in the sense of "capable of lasting or persisting in time", to "go on in time", and this effectively corresponds to truth when considering that unresolved desire has the theoretic capability to continue for an entire *manvantara*. In fact *nitya* in mythology corresponds to the "Eternals", which is also a synonym of *mahāvidyā* (the great Ignorance).

And why are the *saṁskāras* without a beginning although they have an end with *kaivalya*? We can see that the *sūtra* talks only of without beginning, but not of without end. A temporal beginning[2] implies a datum with which to confront oneself because the phenomenal time to define itself must have two terms of comparison; and this is so also true of space. Time for its description, presupposes relational coordinates. Now, we cannot establish the "ontological beginning" because we do not have a prior term of comparison; and it is without ontological beginning because it proceeds from the "without relationship", which is the characteristic of the causal body or *mahāvidyā*. But even though it is without ontological beginning it has an end precisely because it is a beginning, a first temporal beginning, and this cannot but have an end. If the *sūtra* is comprehended under this perspective,

---

[2] With regard to temporal beginning, see, Parmenides, *On the Order of Nature*, Notes to the Fragments. 23. Op. cit.

then it is coherent with Patañjali's vision who, as it was touched upon, propounds the problem of *kaivalya*, the *ceasing* of the *saṁskāras-vāsanās* or, in other words, of *avidyā* as first factor of the production of the *kleśas*. The theme, this one, which has been developed by all the other *darśanas* which, under this perspective, are perfectly coherent with that of Patañjali's. And so, the following *sūtra* talks about the causal relationship whose effect (*vāsanā*) disappears with the removal of the first cause; that is to say, as it was already mentioned, of *avidyā*. Moreover, space-time and cause belong to the *prakṛti* and not to the embodied *puruṣa*.

Only with a purely pantheistic vision could we have an impossibility of solution because the very nature of the Being would in that case be becoming and movement from which the living one would never be able to escape, as he would be integral part of the divine essence. But Patañjali's *darśana* is not pantheistic, to the contrary. The *puruṣa* is completely beyond the world-substance-*prakṛti*; rather, it does not even touch it if not by induction. See *sūtra* 13 hereafter.

11. [But] as [the impressions] are tied together by cause and effect, by the sustenance and by the object, also their extinction derives from the disappearance of those.

The *saṁskāras* are supported by cause and effect, which in their turn promote the world of *saṁsāra*, and the first origin of this, let us repeat it, is the *avidyā*; the disappearance of this primordial nescience resolves all the rest. The *avidyā* is the oblivion of oneself, of one's own nature, is a forgetting, a losing of oneself in other from oneself, it is the ignorance concerning precisely one's own essence (it is, therefore, not the ignorance regarding the world of names and forms.) We are not the physical body, nor the mind body, we are not our profession and not even this world, we are something more; the former ones can be considered just "accidents", attributes which can be or not be there, while the *puruṣa* is what it is, beyond the process of becoming.

12. The past and the future exist in their own nature; the difference [of the temporal conditions depends] on the properties (dharma) [inherent in prakṛti.]

13. They [properties,] be they manifest or non-manifest, participate of the nature of the guṇas.

The past and the future, and therefore the world of temporal phenomena, are the expressions of *prakṛti*; that is to say that time has *prakṛti* and not *puruṣa* as its foundation. The difference in temporal conditions still depends on the properties of *prakṛti*, and these participate of the nature of the *guṇas*. The flow of events, manifest or not yet manifest, in that they are still in latency, find their principle in *prakṛti* and in the diverse modification possibilities of the *guṇas*. This *sūtra* has to be correlated to *sūtra* 10, as it is complement.

14. An object is such due to the uniqueness of the modifications [of the guṇas.]

Every object (quality) that we perceive is just a particular modification of the three *guṇas*. The world of names and forms is a combination of their indefinite expressive possibility, like the infiniteness of the molecules depends on the atomic combination.

15. The same object [seems different] due to different minds: these two (object and mind) are in different conditions.

An object of perception, although identical to itself, can be seen by two observers under different aspects, because their minds place themselves in different positions, and at times even opposed.

16. An object does not depend on a single mind, [if it were to depend on it] what would happen [to it] if it were not known?

17. An object is known or ignored due to the coloration that the mind assumes.

An object can be known if it stimulates the mind through the senses, and "colors" it in more or less depth, so that it becomes possible for the mind to receive the object in itself. Then the mind "reaches out" and absorbs the object making an act of knowledge, according to the various types of *saṁyama*. *Sūtras* 15 to 17 respond to the concept of opinion (δόξα) of ancient Greece (Parmenides, Plotinus, etc.).

18. The modifications of the mind [are] always known to their Lord, the puruṣa, because it does not change.

The *puruṣa* is the unalterable witness of the modifications of the body and of the mind. The change as such can be perceived only if there is a non-changeable background, otherwise it would be impossible to perceive it. The movement of our own planet is not perceived by us because we are integral part of it.

The object of the preceding *sūtras* can be perceived by the mind because behind the object and the mind itself there is the *puruṣa*, which is precisely the witness of one and the other.

This *sūtra* is very important from a philosophical point of view; it poses the problem of the Being, in that it *is* and does not become, and of the changeable becoming which, as such, appears and disappears from the horizon of the state of *puruṣa*.

19. It [mind] does not shine of its own light due to its perceptibility.

20. [The mind] cannot know at the same time both [perceiver and perceived.]

21. If one [opined] the possibility for the mind to be known by another [mind] there would be cognition of the cognition and a regressio ad infinitum [besides the confusion of memories.]

Mind itself is movement, becoming, and a simple object of perception. In that *puruṣa*, we are conscious of the *vṛttis* of our thoughts, instincts and of the emotions. Moreover, as the mind is not *ipseity*, or reality in itself, it cannot contemporaneously be the perceiver and the perceived. Nor can we advance the hypothesis that the mind might have another mind as the perceiver because such a hypothesis would lead us to a *regressio ad infinitum*, without then resolving the problem.

22. The consciousness that does not pass from one to the other [citta level] is known through self-unveiling.

Consciousness is self-knowing in a direct way and not through the reflection of a mirror (mind).

When the *puruṣa* rests on itself for itself and with itself, it then self-unveils itself in its essential nature (I.3).

Sūtras 19 to 22 respond to a philosophical vision. The "know thyself" propounded by these *sūtras* (as also by the Pythia referred to by Plato) self-unveils itself automatically and naturally with the removal of the darkening and veiling obstacles (*kleśas*, *vāsanās*, etc.). Hence Patañjali's eight *aṅgas* that diligently and constantly followed take us to the attainment of *kaivalya*, i.e. "that which one is". See all the *sūtras* to the end of the chapter.

23. The mind colored by the knower and the known comprehends everything.

In order to perceive and know, the mind needs two conditions: first it has to be stimulated and "colored" (IV.17) by the object of cognition, and secondly, it has to receive "light" from the consciousness of the *puruṣa*. Why this? Because the mind, in itself and for itself, is a simple inert and non-conscious object. It is a body-vehicle of manifestation like the gross physical body, albeit with a different function.

24. Although colored by innumerable vāsanās, it [the mind] exists for another because it acts in association.

The mind, as we have underlined, is just a means, an instrument whose purpose is to serve another from itself. Although colored by innumerable *saṁskāras*, the mind is a *medium* to perceive and know the phenomenal world. Both the body-instrument and the *guṇas* themselves are always vehicles mediated by the embodied *puruṣa*. See *sūtra* 35, III *pāda*.

25. For he who sees the distinction there is the complete cessation of the reflection upon the consciousness of the ātmā.

26. Then the mind turns to the discernment and leans toward the kaivalya.

For one who, at the consciousness level, has clear the distinction between *puruṣa* and mind, or whatever vehicle of manifestation, the interest to turn toward the object world, be it gross or subtle, ceases, thus consciousness becomes fit to reach the attainment of *kaivalya*.

In this way the mind, which at the beginning was inclined to turn toward sensory and transitory data, is now ready to make a true "conversion" of direction and lean toward the *puruṣa*.

These last *sūtras* represent the essence of the *Rājayoga*. It begins with the study of the mind, of both the conscious and subconscious psychic movements, and ends with their solution and with becoming aware of the *mahāpuruṣa* as absolute and permanent reality. While *Haṭhayoga* takes as its support the vital (*prāṇa*) sheath and considers it as "object" of perception, which enables it to control it and master it, *Rājayoga* makes contact with the sphere of the mind and arrives at detaching from it, then masters it and finally transcends it.

This *sūtra*, and we could say the whole *Rājayoga*, have a parallel expression in the Alchemical and Western Hermetic tradition (let us always remember that the spiritual or initiatic Tradition is one.) The Alchemical phases of realization are: separation of the consciousness-Mercury from the body-Salt compound, fixation of the Mercury onto itself, and finally reuniting of the Mercury with the transcendent Sulphur.[3]

The phases of the *Rājayoga* are identical: separation of the reflection of the *puruṣa* from the formal compounds (sheaths) and their qualities (*guṇas*), fixation of the reflection of the *puruṣa* onto itself (I.2-4); and finally reuniting of the reflection with its transcendent source or *parapuruṣa*, the supreme *puruṣa* (or *mahāpuruṣa*.)

27. At intervals [during discrimination] other impressions (pratyaya) appear, caused by the saṁskāras.

28. The solution of these [impressions] correpsonds to that of the kleśas already described.

In the intermediate state of actualization of the *kaivalya*, *pratyayas* may arise, which are the fruit of ancient *saṁskāras*, but that can be resolved and transcended in the way it was done with regard to the *kleśas* (II.10-11) and primarily with the solution of the *avidyā* whence the *kleśas* arise.

---

[3] For the Alchemical terminologies, see, Raphael, *The Threefold Pathway of Fire*, ch. I, "Fire of Life", Aurea Vidyā, New York.

29. One who has no more attachments, not even to the fruits of meditation (illumination), and trains in the conscious discernment, attains the dharma-megha-samādhi (the cloud of virtue).

30. Therefore [one has] liberation from the kleśas and from karma.

Those who are able to stay detached even from the highest realizations offered by the world of becoming and to exercise the most conscious discernment (therefore *viveka* and *vairāgya*) attain the *dharma-megha-samādhi*, the *samādhi* that brings a cloud of fullness.

With the attainment of this last *samādhi*, the bondage that was tying us to the *karma* and the *kleśas*, is broken and Liberation attained.

Kleśas and *karma*, after all, are nothing else but cause and effect, thus also time and space. With the final illumination one can comprehend that space-time-cause is a fiction of the mind and of the *ahaṁkāra* in order to perpetuate themselves, because in the state of *puruṣa* they are nothing but pure illusion.

31. Then knowledge, bereft of impurities and of the veil that distorts it, due to its infiniteness [turns] the knowable (of the mind) [into] a small thing.

Having attained the fullness of one's own state, one can also comprehend that, in front of one's own self-illuminating absoluteness, the world of phenomenal relativity is nil in value. Having known the splendor of the sun, who would ever dare to turn to the feeble rays of the moon?

32. Therefore, the [three] guṇas having achieved their purpose,[4] *the process of modifications [in them] reaches its end.*

The *gūnas* themselves, in their indefinite modifications, having achieved their purpose, and seen for what they really are (cause of duality), lose their fascination, and therefore their action is annulled.

33. The change related to the moments (kṣaṇas), and which is knowable at the end [of the modification,] is the succession (kramaḥ).

Kṣaṇa, we have seen in Chapter III.52, is the indivisible unit of time; *kramaḥ* is the continuos-discontinuos process of moments-points (*kṣaṇas*) that form the event. The vital phenomena are precisely a continuum-discontinuum, but their succession is so fast that our *individualized* perception cannot grasp it; moreover, every phenomenon is changeable and never the same, although even in this case the perception of the entity does not grasp the circumstance. We realize the changes when they reach their final condition, their end; thus we are aware of a succession of ideas only when it stopped, and so we are conscious of the memory. The *yogi* can comprehend such an event when he is outside of it; when he sees no longer with the eye of the senses, but with that of pure Consciousness, then he can know the becoming for what it is and not the way he had imagined it.

---

[4] Īśvarakṛṣṇa, *Sāṁkyakārikā*, with Gauḍapāda's Commentary, *sūtra* 60.

34. Kaivalya follows the reabsorption of the guṇas [or of the three constituent elements] as devoid of purpose for the puruṣa; [there is kaivalya] when consciousness is founded on its own essence.[5]

When the qualified *prakṛti*-becoming loses its interest because it is recognized that, in front of the *puruṣa*, it *is not*, then the *puruṣa*-consciousness is "isolated" from the *avidyā* and it rests on its own nature.

[5] Cp. Śaṅkara, *Vivekacūḍāmaṇi*, The Crest Jewel of Discernment, *sūtra* 344-354 and related commentary Op. cit.

SANSKRIT TEXT

yogasūtram ||

samādhipādam |

atha yogānuśāsanam || 1 ||

yogaścittavṛttinirodhaḥ || 2 ||

tadā draṣṭuḥ svarūpe 'vasthānam || 3 ||

vṛttisarūpyamitaratra || 4 ||

vṛttayaḥ pañcatayyaḥ kliṣṭā akliṣṭāḥ || 5 ||

pramāṇaviparyayavikalpanidrāsmṛtayaḥ || 6 ||

pratyakṣānumānāgamāḥ pramānāṇi || 7 ||

viparyayo mithyājñānamatadrūpapratiṣṭham || 8 ||

śabdajñānānupatī vastuśūnyo vikalpaḥ || 9 ||

abhāvapratyayālambanā vṛttirnidrā || 10 ||

anubhūtaviṣayāsaṁpramoṣaḥ smṛtiḥ || 11 ||

abhyāsavairāgyābhyāṁ tannirodhaḥ || 12 ||

tatra sthitau yatno 'bhyāsaḥ || 13 ||

sa tu dīrghakālanairantaryasatkārāse vito dṛḍhabhūmiḥ || 14 ||

dṛṣṭānuśravikaviṣayavitṛṣṇasya vaśīkārasaṁjñā vairāgyam || 15 ||

tatparaṁ puruṣakhyāterguṇavaitṛṣṇyam || 16 ||

vitarkavicārānandāsmitārūpānugamātsaṁprajñātaḥ || 17 ||

virāmapratyayābhyāsapūrvaḥ saṁskāraśeṣo 'nyaḥ ll 18 ll

bhavapratyayo videhaprakṛtilayānām ll 19 ll

śraddhāvīryasmṛtisamādhiprajñāpūrvaka itareṣām ll 20 ll

tīvrasaṁvegānāmāsannaḥ ll 21 ll

mṛdumadhyādhimātratvāttato 'pi viśeṣaḥ ll 22 ll

īśvarapranidhānādvā ll 23 ll

kleśakarmavipākāśayairaparāmṛṣṭaḥ puruṣaviśeṣa īśvaraḥ ll 24 ll

tatra niratiśayaṁ sarvajñatvabījam ll 25 ll

sa pūrveṣāmapi guruḥ kālenānavacchedāt ll 26 ll

tasya vācakaḥ praṇavaḥ ll 27 ll

tajjapastadarthabhāvanam ll 28 ll

tataḥ pratyakcetanādhigamo 'pyantarāyābhāvaśca ll 29 ll

vyādhistyānasaṁśayapramādālasyāviratibhrāntidarśanālabdha-bhūmikatvānavasthitavāni cittavikṣepāste 'ntarāyāḥ ll 30 ll

duḥkhadaurmanasyāṅgamejayatvaśvāsapraśvāsā vikṣepasahabhuvaḥ ll 31 ll

tatpratiṣedhārthamekatattvābhyāsaḥ ll 32 ll

maitrīkaruṇāmuditopekṣāṇāṁ sukhaduḥkhapuṇyāpuṇyaviṣayāṇāṁ bhāvanātaścittaprasādanam ll 33 ll

pracchardanavidhāraṇābhyāṁ vā prāṇasya ll 34 ll

viṣayavatī vā pravṛttirutpannā manasaḥ sthitinibandhanī ll 35 ll

viśokā vā jyotiṣmatī ll 36 ll

vītarāgaviṣayaṁ vā cittam ll 37 ll

svapnanidrājñānālambanaṁ vā ll 38 ll

yathābhimatadhyānādvā ll 39 ll

paramāṇuparamamahattvānto 'sya vaśīkāraḥ ||40||

kṣīṇavṛtterabhijātasyeva maṇergrahītṛgrahaṇagrāhyeṣu tatsthatadañjanatā samāpattiḥ ||41||

tatra śabdārthajñānavikalpaiḥ saṁkīrṇāsavitarkā samāpattiḥ ||42||

smṛtipariśuddhau svarūpaśūnyevārthamātranirbhāsā nirvitarkā ||43||

etayaiva savicārā nirvicārā ca sūkṣmaviṣayā vyākhyātā ||44||

sūkṣmaviṣayatvaṁ cāliṅgaparyavasānam ||45||

tā eva sabījasamādhiḥ ||46||

nirvicārāvaiśāradye 'dhyātmaprasādaḥ ||47||

ṛtambharā tatra prajñā ||48||

śrutānumānaprajñābhyāmanyaviṣayāviśeṣārthatvāt ||49||

tajjaḥ saṁskāro 'nyasaṁskārapratibandhī ||50||

tasyāpinirodhesarvanirodhān nirbījaḥ samādhiḥ ||51||

sādhanapādam ।

tapaḥsvādhyāyeśvarapraṇidhānāni kriyāyogaḥ ॥1॥

samādhibhāvanārthaḥ kleśatanūkaraṇārthaśca ॥2॥

avidyāsmitārāgadveṣābhiniveśaḥ kleśāḥ ॥3॥

avidyā kṣetramuttareṣāṁ prasuptatanuvicchinnodārāṇām ॥4॥

anityāśuciduḥkhānātmasu nityāśucisukhātmakhyātiravidyā ॥5॥

dṛgdarśanaśaktyorekātmatevāsmitā ॥6॥

sukhānuśayī rāgaḥ ॥7॥

duḥkhānuśayī dveṣaḥ ॥8॥

svarasavāhī viduṣo 'pi tathā rūḍho 'bhiniveśaḥ ॥9॥

te pratiprasavaheyāḥ sūkṣmāḥ ॥10॥

dhyānaheyāstadvṛttayaḥ ॥11॥

kleśamūlaḥ karmāśayo dṛṣṭādṛṣṭajanmavedanīyaḥ ॥12॥

sati mūle tadvipāko jātyāyurbhogāḥ ॥13॥

te hlādaparitāpaphalāḥ puṇyāpuṇyahetutvāt ॥14॥

pariṇāmatāpasaṁskāraduḥkhairguṇavṛttivirodhācca duḥkhameva sarvaṁ vivekinaḥ ॥15॥

heyaṁ duḥkhamanāgatam ॥16॥

draṣṭṛdṛśayoḥ saṁyogo heyahetuḥ ॥17॥

prakāśakriyāsthitiśīlaṁ bhūtendriyātmakaṁ bhogāpavargārthaṁ dṛśyam ‖ 18 ‖

viśeṣāviśeṣaliṅgamātrāliṅgāni guṇaparvāṇi ‖ 19 ‖

draṣṭā dṛśimātraḥ śuddho 'pi pratyayānupaśyaḥ ‖ 20 ‖

tadartha eva dṛśyātmā ‖ 21 ‖

kṛtārthaṁ prati naṣṭamapyanaṣṭaṁ tadanyasādhāraṇatvāt ‖ 22 ‖

svasvāmiśaktyoḥ svarūpopalabdhihetuḥ saṁyogaḥ ‖ 23 ‖

tasya heturavidyā ‖ 24 ‖

tadabhāvātsaṁyogābhāvo hānaṁ taddṛśeḥ kaivalyam ‖ 25 ‖

vivekakhyātiraviplavā hānopāyaḥ ‖ 26 ‖

tasya saptadhā prāntabhūmiḥ prajñā ‖ 27 ‖

yogāṅgānuṣṭhānādaśuddhikṣaye jñānadīptirā vivekakhyāteḥ ‖ 28 ‖

yamaniyamāsanaprāṇāyāmapratyāhāradhāraṇādhyānasamādhayo 'ṣṭāvaṅgāni ‖ 29 ‖

ahiṁsāsatyāsteyabrahmacaryāparigrahā yamāḥ ‖ 30 ‖

jātideśakālasamayānavacchinnāḥ sārvabhaumā mahāvratam ‖ 31 ‖

śaucasaṁtoṣatapaḥsvādhyāyeśvarapraṇidhānāni niyamāḥ ‖ 32 ‖

vitarkabādhane pratipakṣabhāvanam ‖ 33 ‖

vitarkā hiṁsādayaḥ kṛtakāritānumoditā lobhakrodhamohapūrvakā mṛdumadhyādhimātrā duḥkhājñānānantaphalā iti pratipakṣabhāvanam ‖ 34 ‖

ahiṁsāpratiṣṭhāyāṁ tatsaṁnidhau vairatyāgaḥ ‖ 35 ‖

satyapratiṣṭhāyāṁ kriyāphalāśrayatvam ‖ 36 ‖

asteyapratiṣṭhāyāṁ sarvaratnopasthānam ‖ 37 ‖

brahmacaryapratiṣṭhāyāṁ vīryalābhaḥ ‖ 38 ‖

aparigrahasthairye janmakathaṁtāsaṁbodhaḥ ||39||

śaucātsvāṅgajugupsā parairasaṁsargaḥ ||40||

sattvaśuddhisaumanasyaikāgryendriyajayātmadarśanayogyatvāni ca ||41||

saṁtoṣādanuttamaḥ sukhalābhaḥ ||42||

kāyendriyasiddhiriṣṭadevatāsaṁprayogaḥ ||43||

svādhyāyādiṣṭadevatāsaṁprayogaḥ ||44||

samādhisiddhirīśvarapraṇidhānāt ||45||

sthirasukhamāsanam ||46||

prayatnaśaithilyānantasamāpattibhyām ||47||

tato dvandvānabhighātaḥ ||48||

tasminsati śvāsapraśvāsayorgativicchedaḥ prāṇāyāmaḥ ||49||

bāhyābhyantarastambhavṛttirdeśakālasaṁkhyābhiḥ paridṛṣṭo dīrghasūkṣmaḥ ||50||

bāhyābhyantaraviṣayākṣepī caturthaḥ ||51||

tataḥ kṣīyate prakāśāvaraṇam ||52||

dhāraṇāsu ca yogyatā manasaḥ ||53||

svaviṣayāsaṁprayoge cittasyavarūpānukāra ivendriyāṇaṁ pratyāhāraḥ ||54||

tataḥ paramā vaśyatendriyāṇam ||55||

vibhūtipādam ।

deśabandhaścittasya dhāraṇā ॥1॥

tatra pratyayaikatānatā dhyānam ॥2॥

tadevārthamātranirbhāsaṁ svarūpaśūnyamiva samādhiḥ ॥3॥

trayamekatra saṁyamaḥ ॥4॥

tajjayātprajñālokaḥ ॥5॥

tasya bhūmiṣu viniyogaḥ ॥6॥

trayamantaraṅgaṁ pūrvebhyaḥ ॥7॥

tadapi bahiraṅgaṁ nirbījasya ॥8॥

vyutthānanirodhasaṁskārayorabhibhavaprādurbhāvau nirodhakṣaṇacittānvayo nirodhapariṇāmaḥ ॥9॥

tasya praśāntavāhitā saṁskārāt ॥10॥

sarvārthataikāgratayoḥ kṣayodayau cittasya samādhipariṇāmaḥ ॥11॥

tataḥ punaḥ śāntoditau tulyapratyayau cittasyaikāgratāpariṇāmaḥ ॥12॥

etena bhūtendriyeṣu dharmalakṣaṇāvasthāpariṇāmā vhyākhyātāḥ ॥13॥

śāntoditāvyapadeśyadharmānupātī dharmī ॥14॥

kramānyatvaṁ pariṇāmānyatve hetuḥ ॥15॥

pariṇāmatrayasaṁyamādatītānāgatajñānam ॥16॥

śabdārthapratyayānāmitaretarādhyāsātsaṁskārastatpravibhāgasaṁyamātsarvabhūtarutajñānam ॥ 17 ॥

saṁskārasākṣātkaraṇātpūrvajātijñānam ॥ 18 ॥

pratyayasya paracittajñānam ॥ 19 ॥

na ca tatsālambanaṁ tasyāviṣayībhūtatvāt ॥ 20 ॥

kāyarūpasaṁyamāttadgrāhyaśaktistambhe cakṣuḥprakāśasaṁprayoge 'ntardhānam[etena śabdādyantardhānamuktam] ॥ 21 ॥

sopakramaṁ nirupakramaṁ ca karma । tatsaṁyamādaparāntajñānamariṣṭebhyo vā ॥ 22 ॥

maitryādiṣu balāni ॥ 23 ॥

baleṣu hastibalādīni ॥ 24 ॥

pravṛttyālokanyāsātsūkṣmavyavahitaviprakṛṣṭajñānam ॥ 25 ॥

bhuvanajñānaṁ sūrye saṁyamāt ॥ 26 ॥

candre tārāvyūhajñānam ॥ 27 ॥

dhruve tadgatijñānam ॥ 28 ॥

nābhicakre kāyavyūhajñānam ॥ 29 ॥

kaṇṭhakūpe kṣutpipāsānivṛttiḥ ॥ 30 ॥

kūrmanāḍyāṁ sthairyam ॥ 31 ॥

mūrdhajyotiṣi siddhadarśanam ॥ 32 ॥

prātibhādvā sarvam ॥ 33 ॥

hṛdaye cittasaṁvit ॥ 34 ॥

sattvapuruṣayoratyantāsaṁkīrṇayoḥ pratyayāviśeṣo bhogaḥ parārthātsvārthasaṁyamātpuruṣajñānam ॥ 35 ॥

tataḥ prātibhaśrāvaṇavedanādarśāsvādavārttā jāyante ॥ 36 ॥

te samādhāvupasargā vyutthāne siddhayaḥ ॥ 37 ॥

bandhakāraṇa śaithilyātpracārasaṁvedanācca cittasya paraśarīraveśaḥ ||38||

udānajayājjalapaṅkakaṇṭakādiṣvasaṅga utkrāntiśca ||39||

samānajayājjvalanam ||40||

śrotrākāśayoḥ saṁbandhasaṁyamāddivyaṁ śrotram ||41||

kāyākāśayoḥ saṁbandhasaṁyamāllaghutūlasamāpatteścākāśagamanam ||42||

bahirakalpitā vṛttirmahāvidehā | tataḥ prakāśāvaraṇakṣayaḥ ||43||

sthūlasvarūpasūkṣmānvayārthavattvasaṁyamādbhūtajayaḥ ||44||

tato 'nimādiprādurbhāvaḥ kāyasaṁpaddharmānabhigataśca ||45||

rūpalāvaṇyabalavajrasaṁhananatvāni kāyasaṁpat ||46||

grahaṇasvarūpāsmitānvayārthavattvasaṁyamādindriyajayaḥ ||47||

tato manojavitvaṁ vikaraṇabhāvaḥ pradhānajayaśca ||48||

sattvapuruṣānyatākhyātimātrasya sarvabhāvādhiṣṭātṛtvaṁ sarvajñātṛtvaṁ ca ||49||

tadvairāgyādapi doṣabījakṣaye kaivalyam ||50||

sthānyupanimantraṇe saṅgasmayākaraṇaṁ punaraniṣṭaprasaṅgāt ||51||

kṣaṇatatkramayoḥ saṁyamādvivekajaṁ jñānam ||52||

jātilakṣaṇadeśairanyatānavacchedāttulyayostataḥ pratipattiḥ ||53||

tārakaṁ sarvaviṣayaṁ sarvathāviṣayamakramaṁ ceti vivekajaṁ jñānam ||54||

sattvapuruṣayoḥ śuddhisāmye kaivalyam ||55||

kaivalyapādam |

janmauṣadhimantratapaḥsamādhijāḥ siddhayaḥ ||1||

jātyantarapariṇāmaḥ prakṛtyāpūrāt ||2||

nimittamaprayojakaṁ prakṛtīnāṁ varaṇabhedastu tataḥ kṣetrikavat ||3||

nirmāṇacittānyasmitāmātrāt ||4||

pravṛttibhede prayojakaṁ cittamekamanekeṣām ||5||

tatra dhyānajamanāśayam ||6||

karmāśuklākṛṣṇaṁ yoginastrividhamitareṣām ||7||

tatastadvipākānuguṇānāmevābhivyaktirvāsanānām ||8||

jātideśakālavyavahitānāmapyānantaryaṁ smṛtisaṁskārayorekarūpatvāt ||9||

tāsāmanāditvaṁ cāśiṣo nityatvāt || 10 ||

hetuphalāśrayālambanaiḥ saṁgṛhītatvādeṣāmabhāve tadabhāvaḥ || 11 ||

atītānāgataṁ svarūpato 'sti adhvabhedāddharmāṇām || 12 ||

te vyaktasūkṣmā guṇātmānaḥ || 13 ||

pariṇāmaikatvādvastutattvam || 14 ||

vastusāmyecittabhedāttayorvibhaktaḥ panthāḥ || 15 ||

na caikacittatantraṁ vastu tadapramāṇakaṁ tadā kiṁ syāt || 16 ||

taduparāgāpekṣitvāccittasya vastu jñātājñātam ॥ 17 ॥

sadā jñātāścittavṛttayastatprabhoḥ puruṣasyāpariṇāmitvāt ॥ 18 ॥

na tatsvābhāsaṁ dṛśyatvāt ॥ 19 ॥

ekasamaye cobhayānavadhāraṇam ॥ 20 ॥

cittāntaradṛśye buddhibuddheratiprasaṅgaḥ smṛtisaṁkaraśca ॥ 21 ॥

citerapratisaṁkramāyāstadākārāpattau svabuddhisaṁvedanam ॥ 22 ॥

draṣṭṛdṛśyoparaktaṁ cittaṁ sarvārtham ॥ 23 ॥

tadasaṁkhyeyavāsanābhiścitramapi parārthaṁ saṁhatyakāritvāt ॥ 24 ॥

viśeṣadarśina ātmabhāvabhāvanāvinivṛttiḥ ॥ 25 ॥

tadā hi vivekanimnaṁ kaivalyaprāgbhāraṁ cittam ॥ 26 ॥

tacchidreṣu pratyayāntarāṇi saṁskārebhyaḥ ॥ 27 ॥

hānameṣāṁ kleśavaduktam ॥ 28 ॥

prasaṁkhyāne 'pyakusīdasya sarvathā vivekakhyāterdharmameghasamādhiḥ ॥ 29 ॥

tataḥ kleśakarmanivṛttiḥ ॥ 30 ॥

tadā sarvāvaraṇamalāpetasya jñānasyānantyājjñeyamalpam ॥ 31 ॥

tataḥ kṛtārthānāṁ pariṇāmakramasamāptirguṇānām ॥ 32 ॥

kṣaṇapratiyogī pariṇāmāparāntanirgrāhyaḥ kramaḥ ॥ 33 ॥

puruṣārthaśūnyānāṁ guṇānāṁ pratiprasavaḥ kaivalyaṁ svarūpapratiṣṭhā vā citiśakter iti ॥ 34 ॥

INDEX

RAPHAEL

Unity of Tradition

Having attained a synthesis of Knowledge (with which eclecticism or syncretism are not to be confused), Raphael aims at "presenting" the Universal Tradition in its many Eastern and Western expressions. He has spent a substantial number of years writing and publishing books on spiritual experience and his works include commentaries on the *Qabbālāh*, Hermeticism and Alchemy. He has also commented on and compared the Orphic Tradition with the works of Plato, Parmenides and Plotinus. Furthermore, Raphael is the author of several books on the pathway of non-duality (*Advaita*), which he has translated from the original Sanskrit, offering commentaries on a number of key Vedantic texts.

With reference to Platonism, Raphael has highlighted the fact that, if we were to draw a parallel between Śaṅkara's *Advaita Vedānta* and a Traditional Western Philosophical Vision, we could refer to the Vision presented by Plato. Drawing such a parallel does not imply a search for reciprocal influences, but rather it points to something of paramount importance: a sole Truth, inherent in the doctrines and teachings of several great thinkers, who although far apart in time and space, have reached similar and in some cases even identical conclusions.

One notices how Raphael's writes from a metaphysical perspective in order to manifest and underscore the Unity of Tradition, under the metaphysical perspective. This does not mean that he is in opposition to a dualistic perspective, or to the various religious faiths, or "points of view".

A true embodied metaphysical Vision cannot be opposed to anything.

Writing in the light of the Unity of Tradition, Raphael's works, calling on the reader's intuition, present precise points of correspondence between Eastern and Western Teachings. These points of reference are useful for those who want to approach a comparative doctrinal study and to enter the spirit of the Unity of Teaching.

For those who follow either an Eastern or a Western traditional line these correspondences help us comprehend how the *Philosophia Perennis* (Universal Tradition), which has no history and has not been formulated by human minds as such, "comprehends universal truths that do not belong to any people or any age." It is only for lack of "comprehension" or of "synthetic vision" that one particular Branch is considered the only reliable one. Such a position can but lead to opposition and fanaticism. What can degenerate the Doctrine is either a sentimental, fanatical devotion or condescending intellectualism, which is critical and sterile, dogmatic and separative.

In Raphael's words: "For those of us who aim at Realization, our task is to get to the essence of every Doctrine, because we know that just as Truth is one, so Tradition is one even if, just like Truth, Tradition may be viewed from a plurality of apparently different points of view. We must abandon all disquisitions concerning the phenomenal process of becoming, and move onto the plane of Being. In other words: we must have a Philosophy of Being as the foundation of our search and of our realization."[1]

Raphael interprets spiritual practice as a "Path of Fire". Here is what he writes: "...The "Path of Fire" is the pathway each disciple follows in all branches of Tradition; it is the Way of Return. Therefore, it is not the particular teaching of an individual nor a path parallel to the one and only Main Road... After all, every disciple follows his own "Path of Fire", no matter which Branch of Tradition he belongs to."

---

[1] See, Raphael, *Tat tvam asi*, That thou art, Aurea Vidyā, New York.

In Raphael's view, what is important is to express through living and being the truth that one has been able to contemplate. Thus, for each being, one's expression of thought and action must be coherent and in agreement with one's own specific *dharma*.

After more than thirty-five years of teaching, both oral and written, Raphael is now dedicating himself only to those people who wish to be "doers" rather than "sayers", according to St. Paul's expression.

Raphael is connected with the *maṭha* founded by *Śrī Ādi* Śaṅkara at Śṛṅgeri and Kāñcīpuram as well as with the Rāmaṇa Āśram at Tiruvannamalai.

Founder of the Āśram Vidyā Order, he now dedicates himself entirely to spiritual practice. He lives in a hermitage connected to the *āśram* and devotes himself completely to a vow of silence.

* * *

May Raphael's Consciousness, expression of Unity of Tradition, guide and illumine along this Opus all those who donate their *mens informalis* (non-formal mind) to the attainment of the highest known Realization.

PUBLICATIONS

Aurea Vidyā Collection

1. Raphael, ***The Threefold Pathway of Fire***, Thoughts that vibrate.
ISBN 978-1-931406-00-0

2. Raphael, ***At the Source of Life***, Questions and Answers concerning the Ultimate Reality.
ISBN 978-1-931406-01-7

3. Raphael, ***Beyond the illusion of the ego***, Synthesis of a Realizative Process.
ISBN 978-1-931406-03-1

4. Raphael, ***Tat tvam asi***, That thou art, The Path of Fire According to the Asparśavāda.
ISBN 978-1-931406-12-3

5. Gauḍapāda, ***Māṇḍūkyakārikā****, The Māṇḍūkya Upaniṣad with the verses-*kārikā* of Gauḍapāda.
ISBN 978-1-931406-04-8

6. Raphael, ***Orphism and the Initiatory Tradition***
ISBN 978-1-931406-05-5

7. Śaṅkara, ***Ātmabodha****, Self-knowledge.
ISBN 978-1-931406-06-2

8. Raphael, ***Initiation into the Philosophy of Plato***
ISBN 978-1-931406-07-9

9. Śaṅkara, ***Vivekacūḍāmaṇi****, The Crest-jewel of Discernment.
ISBN 978-1-931406-08-6

10. ***Drigdriśyaviveka****, Discernment between *ātman* and non-*ātman*. Attributed to Śaṅkara.
ISBN 978-1-931406-09-3

11. Parmenides, ***On the Order of Nature***, Περί φύσεως*, For a Philosophical Ascesis.
ISBN 978-1-931406-10-9

12. Raphael, ***The Science of Love***, From the desire of the senses to the Intellect of Love.
ISBN 978-1-931406-12-3

13. Vyāsa, ***Bhagavadgītā****, The Celestial Song.
ISBN 978-1-931406-13-0

14. Raphael, ***The Pathway of Fire according to the Qabbālāh***, Ehjeh 'Ašer 'Ehjeh (I am What I am).
ISBN 978-1-931406-14-7

15. Patañjali, ***The Regal Way to Realization****, Yogadarśana.
ISBN 978-1-931406-15-4

16. Raphael, ***Beyond Doubt***, Approaches to Non-duality.
ISBN 978-1-931406-16-1

17. Bādarāyaṇa, ***Brahmasūtra****
ISBN 978-1-931406-17-8

18. Śaṅkara, ***Aparokṣānubhūti****, Self-realization.
ISBN 978-1-93-140619-2

Related Publications

Raphael, ***Essence and Purpose of Yoga***
The Initiatory Pathways to the Transcendent.
Element Books, Shaftesbury, U.K.
ISBN 978-1-852308-66-7

Raphael, ***The Pathway of Non-duality***, Advaitavāda.
Motilal Banarsidass, New Delhi.
ISBN 81-208-0929-7

Forthcoming Publications

Śaṅkara, ***Brief Works****, Treatises and Hymns.

Five Upaniṣad*, Īśa, Kaivalya, Sarvasāra, Amṛtabindu, Atharvaśira.

Raphael, ***Fire of Ascesis***

Raphael, ***Fire of Awakening***

Raphael, ***Fire of the Philosophers***

* Translation from Sanskrit or Greek and commentary by Raphael

Aurea Vidyā is the Publishing House of the Parmenides Traditional Philosophy Foundation, a Not-for-Profit Organization whose purpose is to make Perennial Philosophy accessible.

The Foundation goes about its purpose in a number of ways: by publishing and distributing Traditional Philosophy texts with Aurea Vidyā, by offering individual and group encounters and by providing a Reading Room and daily Meditations at its Center.

* * *

Those readers who have an interest in Traditional Philosophy are welcome to contact the Foundation at: parmenides.foundationșearthlink.net.

CPSIA information can be obtained
at www.ICGtesting.com
Printed in the USA
BVHW080419220322
632033BV00001B/25

9 781931 406154

Shining Stars: Family and Astrology

Astrology studies the heavens—the stars and planets. It is a quite complex and ancient science; we simplify some of its main concepts in this
chapter. We use birth or natal charts throughout this book. A birth
chart is a map of the heavens at the time of your birth—if you know
your exact time of birth, this chart is very specific to you; if you don't,
not to worry—many people have this problem. If you can't narrow
your time of birth down at all, an astrologer will use noon on the day
of your birth as your birth time. When we use noon as the birth time
in this book, the chart is labeled a noon birth chart rather than simply
a birth chart, to distinguish the two. What else does an astrologer need,
besides your time of birth? The obvious, of course: the day, month, and
year of your birth. The place of your birth is necessary, as well. You
may want to collect some of this information for yourself and your
family members now, so that you can have birth charts done—this will
be very useful in some of the exercises we do in later chapters.

Arlene used the computer software program Solar Fire 5, published by Astrolabe, Inc., to generate the birth charts we've adapted as examples throughout this book. Charts are cast using the Geocentric view, Tropical Zodiac, Placidus house system, and True Node because these are the most common in modern Western Astrology. To use your birth chart with this book, you need to be sure to specify these parameters when generating your own astrological birth chart. You can order a birth chart online or from your local metaphysical bookstore; there's more information on how to order a birth chart in Appendix A at the back of this book. We've provided a sample birth chart with highlighted family connections in Appendix A, as well.

The Zodiac

You probably know your own Sun ☉ sign: This is determined by the position of the Sun when you were born. The path the Earth follows in its orbit around the Sun is called the *Zodiac*. There are 12 signs of the Zodiac, indicating the position of the Sun during the Earth's orbit; we've included a *Zodiac wheel*, so you can find your Sun sign (if you don't already know it) simply by finding your birthday.

Introduction

Claim your brightest destiny and fulfill your own essential nature.

More than ever, we are searching for an inner awareness that brings outer confidence, joy, and direction. *The Intuitive Arts* series, with volumes on *Family, Health, Love, Money,* and *Work,* gives readers looking for answers to questions of daily living tools from the esoteric arts that help them look deeply, see, and make real changes affecting their futures. In each problem-solving volume, curious querents are presented exercises in the Intuitive Arts of Astrology, Tarot, and Psychic Intuition that examine, instruct, illuminate, and guide. In essence, you get three books for one—but also so much more!

An understanding of the interplay of the Intuitive Arts of Astrology, Tarot, and Psychic Intuition is something most people gain slowly over time, or with the aid of a professional Intuitive Arts practitioner who already has the knowledge to give in-depth readings that link the arts together.

In *The Intuitive Arts* series, expert author Arlene Tognetti shares her deep knowing of the arts of Astrology, Tarot, and Psychic Intuition to give you the best opportunity to work out solutions to life's problems and challenges with the benefit of the sophisticated relationships between the arts Arlene reveals chapter by chapter. By combining the Intuitive Arts together throughout each chapter's exercises, you'll gain insights that link the arts together—how, for example, Astrology's Moon ☽ signs are personified in Tarot cards that represent family archetypes. Or use your Psychic Intuition to create a family mandala harnessing the power of your Elemental Family Signature.

Arlene Tognetti and New Age book producer Lee Ann Chearney at Amaranth Illuminare created this series for Alpha Books to respond to the public's growing fascination with all things spiritual. People (like you!) want to know how they can use the Intuitive Arts to solve everyday challenges, plan for the future, and live in the present, with hands-on advice and techniques that will make things better for them. We want to help you improve the issues surrounding your unique life situation by providing a multi-art approach that gives you multiple pathways to personal growth and answers your questions about family, health, love, money, and work.

Using Tarot's Major and Minor Arcana cards and spreads; Astrology's birth charts and aspect grids, sign, planets, and houses; and Psychic Intuition's meditations, affirmations, and inner knowing exercises, the innovative *Intuitive Arts* series provides a truly interactive, solution-oriented, positive message that enriches a personal synergy of mind, body, and spirit!

Read on to further your knowledge and understanding of how the Intuitive Arts work together to reveal deep insights. In this series volume, *The Intuitive Arts on Family,* learn how Astrology, the Tarot, and Psychic Intuition reveal your future family harmony through the generations!

Are *you* ready to manifest the family that nurtures and inspires you?

chapter 1

Father and Mothe
Sister and Brothe

What are the Intuitive Arts?
Shining stars: Family and Astrology
It's all in the cards: Family and Tarot
What do your instincts say? Family and Psychic Intui
Your family tree (or shrub, or garden)
What's next?

Singer-songwriter James Taylor may have had it right in a so fans love, "Shower the People." When you give love to the p care about most—your family—conditions can only improve increase. Every family has its joys and challenges, and this ch explores the nature of family bonds, from a psychological an viewpoint, in popular culture (past and present), and through of the Intuitive Arts: Astrology, Tarot, and Psychic Intuition. these Intuitive Arts, and how do they look into and reveal h shapes our lives? Let's find out!

What Are the Intuitive Arts?

Why did you pick up this book? Maybe you're already inter the Intuitive Arts. You might have some family relationships want to work on, or perhaps you're trying to create your ow Whatever your place, we think the Intuitive Arts can help yo where you want to go. When we speak of the Intuitive Arts i book, we mean these three practices: Astrology, Tarot, and P Intuition. Each of these areas requires something of you: You basic concepts of Astrology, and you need to have your astro birth chart in hand; for the study of Tarot, you need your ow deck; and for Psychic Intuition, all you need is your open mi

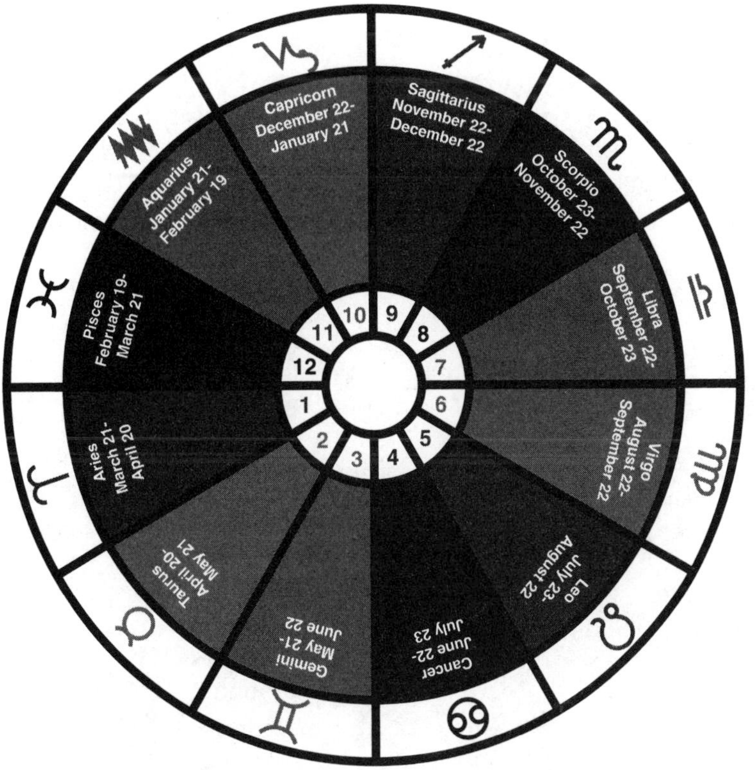

To find your Sun ☉ sign, simply find your birth date and see which sign it corresponds to.

Your Sun sign is very important in Astrology. It represents your self, your will, and your creativity. Each Sun sign is associated with certain characteristics and parts of the body. We've charted each Sun sign, its symbol, its inclusive dates, keywords, and associated bodily parts in the following table.

Astro Sign	**Symbol**	**Dates**	**Keywords**	**Body Part**
Aries	♈	March 21 to April 20	Energetic, take-charge, pioneering	Head, face
Taurus	♉	April 20 to May 21	Sensual, grounded, down-to-earth	Neck, throat

Astro Sign	Symbol	Dates	Keywords	Body Part
Gemini	♊	May 21 to June 22	Resourceful, quick-witted, mercurial	Head, arms, shoulders, lungs
Cancer	♋	June 22 to July 23	Empathetic, nurturing, emotional	Stomach, breasts
Leo	♌	July 23 to August 22	Charismatic, fun-loving, confident	Back, spine, heart
Virgo	♍	August 22 to September 22	Resourceful, practical, analyzing	Intestines, gall bladder, liver, bowels, pancreas
Libra	♎	September 22 to October 23	Principled, balanced, harmonious	Kidneys, lower back
Scorpio	♏	October 23 to November 22	Passionate, powerful, profound	Genitals, reproductive organs
Sagittarius	♐	November 22 to December 22	Adventurous, fun-loving, enthusiastic	Liver, hips, thighs
Capricorn	♑	December 22 to January 21	Serious, hard-working, responsible	Bones, teeth, joints
Aquarius	♒	January 21 to February 19	Idealistic, humanitarian, persistent	Ankles, circulation
Pisces	♓	February 19 to March 21	Spiritual, compassionate, dreamy	Feet, immune and hormonal systems

Each astrological sign is associated with a quality, which relates to activity, and also the season in which the astrological sign falls. The three qualities are Cardinal, Fixed, and Mutable. The first sign of each season is *Cardinal;* these are independent signs of beginnings. The second sign of each season is *Fixed,* and these are determined, powerful signs. The final sign of each season is *Mutable,* and these are flexible and adaptable signs. A chart of the qualities of each sign follows.

Cardinal	**Fixed**	**Mutable**
Aries ♈	Taurus ♉	Gemini ♊
Cancer ♋	Leo ♌	Virgo ♍
Libra ♎	Scorpio ♏	Sagittarius ♐
Capricorn ♑	Aquarius ♒	Pisces ♓

Houses and Planets

Before we see what a birth chart reveals, let's look at the energies of the planets and at the 12 houses in the Zodiac. Each Zodiac house relates to an area of life. The 4th house, for example, is the house of home, family, and foundations. A wheel with each of the 12 houses and the areas to which they relate follows.

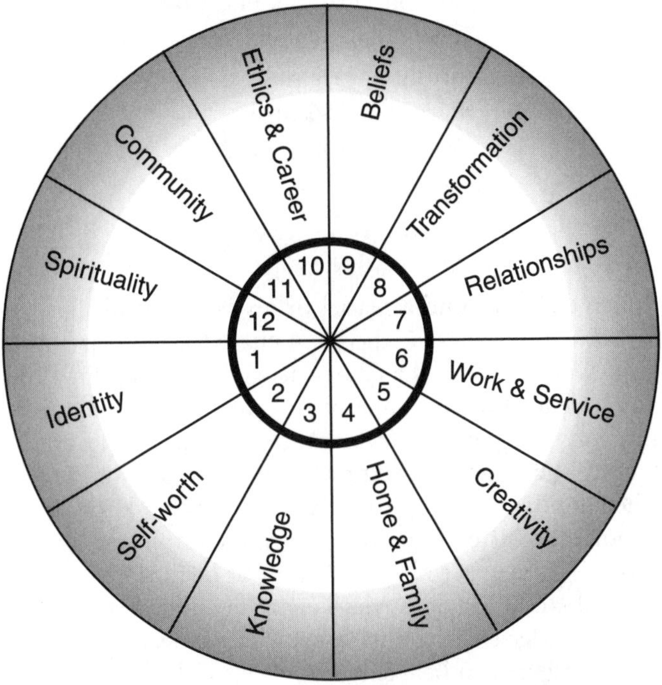

Each of your birth chart's 12 houses represents an area of your life.

We look at a number of planets and asteroids in the birth charts throughout this book. We begin by introducing you to the inner or personal planets, the social planets, and the outer planets. The personal planets are the Sun ☉, Moon ☽, Mercury ☿, Venus ♀, and Mars ♂. The social planets are Jupiter ♃ and Saturn ♄; and the outer planets are Uranus ♅, Neptune ♆, and Pluto ♇. The Sun and Moon aren't actually planets, we know, but we call them planets to simplify matters. Following is yet another table, this one listing each of these planets and some of the keywords we associate with them.

Planet	Keywords
Sun ☉	Self, will, creativity
Moon ☽	Emotions, unconscious
Mercury ☿	Intelligence, communication
Venus ♀	Love, resources, harmony
Mars ♂	Ego, energy, desires
Jupiter ♃	Wisdom, growth, education
Saturn ♄	Discipline, responsibility
Uranus ♅	Intuition, originality
Neptune ♆	Spirituality, idealism
Pluto ♇	Transformation, power

Birth Charts

Within a birth chart, to find a planet or an astrological sign, you need to look for its symbol. Here is the birth chart for celebrity family man Mel Gibson. Working with the charts of well-known public figures is a great way to learn how to make birth chart interpretations that resonate intuitively to a person's true nature. And we suspect as you read this book you'll be eager to interpret birth charts not only for yourself, but for other family members, too. Even before you know the meaning of the symbols in a birth chart, you can relate intuitively to the map of the heavens at the exact time and place of birth the chart represents for that individual. What does Mel's chart say, intuitively, to *you?* The triangular grid under the chart wheel is Mel's aspect grid and it shows the relationships between heavenly bodies in Mel's birth chart.

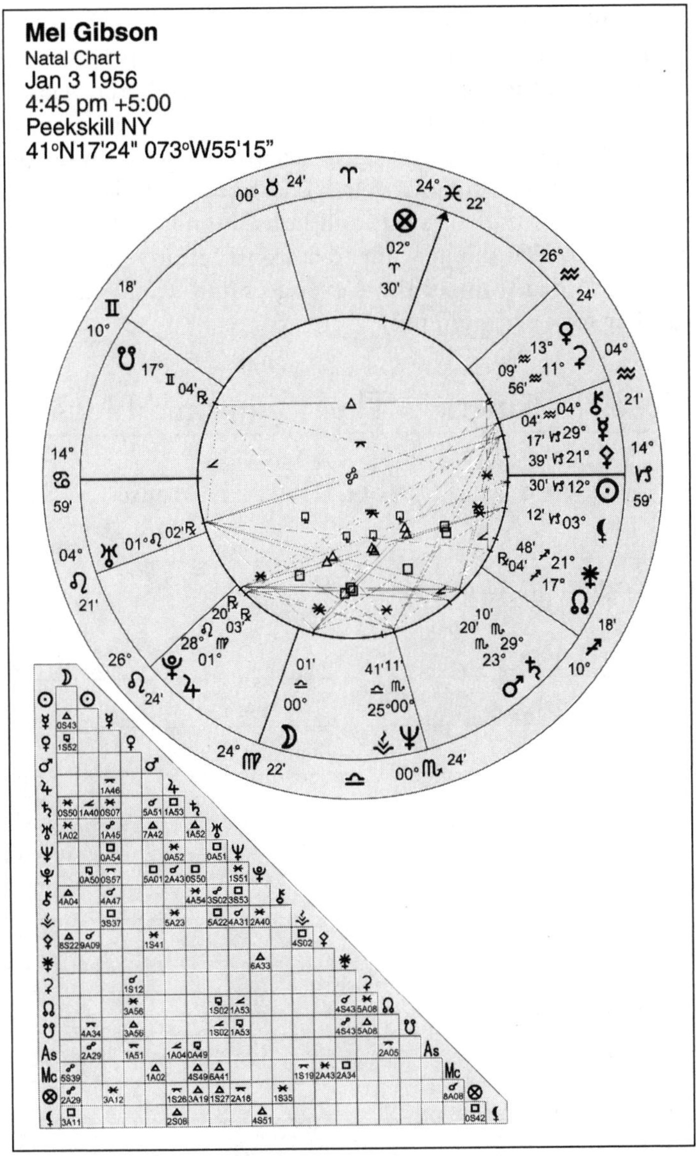

Mel Gibson's astrological birth chart and aspect grid.

Let's begin our exploration of Mel's birth chart. Look inside each of the houses on Mel's chart and find the symbol for the planets we introduced earlier. Do you see the Sun ⊙ sign symbol with the planet? This is the sign the planet is in. Now record the house and sign for each of these planets in the following table. You might also want to look back at the keyword lists for the planets, signs, and houses, and record them, as well, just to familiarize yourself with this information. Mel's Moon ☽, for example, is in Libra ♎ in his 4th house of home and family. When you have your own birth chart on hand, do this exercise for your own planets in their signs and houses (and for your family members, as well). You might want to start an Intuitive Arts notebook, where you can record some of these exercises and keep your birth charts together for easy reference.

Mel Gibson's Planets in Their Signs and Houses

Planet	Planet Keyword	Astro Sign and Symbol	Astro Sign Keyword	House	House Keyword
Sun ☉	________	________	________	________	________
Moon ☽	*Emotion*	*Libra* ♎	*Harmony*	*4th*	*Home and family*
Mercury ☿	________	________	________	________	________
Venus ♀	________	________	________	________	________
Mars ♂	________	________	________	________	________
Jupiter ♃	________	________	________	________	________
Saturn ♄	________	________	________	________	________
Uranus ♅	________	________	________	________	________
Neptune ♆	________	________	________	________	________
Pluto ♇	________	________	________	________	________

Retrogrades and Eclipses

Retrogrades ℞ and eclipses are normal parts of planetary cycles. When a planet is retrograde rather than direct, it seems to be moving backward through the Zodiac when viewed from the Earth; this is an illusion caused by our view of the planets from Earth as they orbit the Sun. (The Sun ☉ and Moon ☽ are never retrograde.) Ancient astrologers, who thought the planets revolved around the Earth, saw retrograde planets as ill omens. These days, however, we believe retrograde planets represent a change in the planet's influence. We think of retrograde influence as "stuck" energy, and interpret the energy of a retrograde planet as reversed, or internalized. Retrograde periods represent the need and opportunity to become more introspective and to review past experiences—if we don't learn from history, we're likely to repeat it.

Hanged Man R, World R: being stuck in retrograde energy.

There are two types of retrogrades: birth chart retrogrades and transiting retrogrades. Natal retrogrades are those in your birth chart, from your date, time, and place of birth; these retrogrades affect only you. Transiting retrogrades are retrograde planets that affect everyone at the same time.

The retrograde symbol ℞ in your birth chart beside a planet's symbol indicates the planet is retrograde. Look back at Mel Gibson's birth chart. What retrograde planets do you see? There are three:

Jupiter ♃ retrograde ℞
Uranus ♅ retrograde ℞
Pluto ♇ retrograde ℞

A natal retrograde ℞ suggests you might have more challenges in the area of the planet's influence. At the same time, you're likely to be more motivated and have an extra drive—an obligation—to overcome them.

Transiting retrogrades can be charted in advance, and some people adjust their lives because of transiting retrogrades. Mercury ☿ and Venus ♀ retrograde more frequently than the other planets; their orbits are between the Earth and the Sun. When Mercury is retrograde (which it is three times each year for about three weeks each time), we notice glitches in the areas of communication, technology, and transportation.

You could find your flight delayed or your hotel reservation misplaced. When Venus is retrograde, relationship issues come into focus. A transiting Venus retrograde might also stimulate you to rethink your values.

We've listed keywords for the planets in their direct and retrograde motions. You can't do anything about retrogrades—they just happen—but a little preparation for their influences can be a helpful thing.

Planet	**Direct Keyword**	**Retrograde Keywords**
Mercury ☿	Communicates	Stalls communications, rethinks
Venus ♀	Enjoys	Reconsiders, reevaluates love
Mars ♂	Engages	Power thwarted, suppressed aggression
Jupiter ♃	Benefits	Exceeds limits, exceeds potential growth
Saturn ♄	Cooperates	Restructures, lessons revisited
Uranus ♅	Innovates	Reforms, reinvents
Neptune ♆	Dreams	Reexamines, seeks truth
Pluto ♇	Transforms	Reviews, considers societal change

While the Sun and Moon do not have retrogrades, they do have eclipses. Solar and lunar eclipses manifest as energy focused in particular areas of your birth chart. Eclipses tend to affect us for cycles of one year (solar eclipse) and six months (lunar eclipse). Their effect may be immediate, and can also set up a longer cycle of revealing (awakening us to major changes in ourselves as well as worldly change). A solar eclipse occurs when the Moon is between the Earth and the Sun and the Moon blocks some portion of the light from the Sun. In a lunar eclipse, the Earth is between the Moon and the Sun, and the Earth blocks the light of the Full Moon. All eclipses bring awareness to areas we need to understand better. Eclipses have the potential to open us up to truths and illusions—they bring the truth to light.

It's All in the Cards: Family and Tarot

The Tarot is a storehouse of information for you and your family. Once you spend some time with the cards, and become familiar with their imagery and their nuances, you'll be more comfortable with them and able to reach into this great reserve to help you learn about yourself, family members, and relationships. There are many Tarot decks to choose from, and when purchasing one, you should select one that appeals to you. In this book, we use the Universal Waite Tarot Deck published by U.S. Games Systems, Inc. Appendix B contains images of all the Tarot cards in this deck and a brief description of their family meanings.

The Fool and the World: the cycle of life.

A Tarot deck includes 78 cards; 22 of these are called Major Arcana cards, and the remaining 56 are Minor Arcana cards. What's the difference? Major Arcana cards are numbered from 0 to 21, and are archetypal cards that portray the karmic journey of life and life lessons, from the Fool to the World. The Minor Arcana or everyday cards comprise four suits: Wands, Pentacles, Swords, and Cups. Cups is the suit associated with family, so it has special importance for us. Each suit includes royal cards (King, Queen, Knight, Page) and numbered cards (Ace–10) for a total of 14 cards per suit. Some Tarot readings use only the Major or the Minor Arcana, but most use the entire deck.

Each suit of the Minor Arcana has a particular focus and energy, and each is also associated with one of the four Elements and three astrological signs:

Suit	**Wands**	**Cups**	**Swords**	**Pentacles**
Element	Fire	Water	Air	Earth
Energy	*Yang*	*Yin*	*Yang*	*Yin*
Focus	Beginnings, action	Creativity, emotion	Communication, the mind	Abundance, material issues
Astro sign	Aries ♈, Leo ♌, Sagittarius ♐	Cancer ♋, Scorpio ♏, Pisces ♓	Gemini ♊, Libra ♎, Aquarius ♒	Taurus ♉, Virgo ♍, Capricorn ♑

How Do We Use Tarot Cards?

While the science of Astrology may seem very complicated, Tarot cards simply require you to use your intuition—an equally difficult task for many of us! Generally, one person asks a question and a second person (an experienced intuitive professional like Arlene) interprets the cards. The person asking the question is called the *querent*. Once you have a deck and have familiarized yourself with it, you can do lots of general readings on your own—this is great practice! We provide many sample readings in this book, and guide you through them so you can do them yourself. Once you've read the entire book, you'll feel a lot more comfortable with your Tarot deck—and with your own intuition. We want you to see the Tarot as a tool to help you understand your family life, and to help you tune in to your own unconscious mind.

Let's take a look at a few Tarot cards, so you can begin to familiarize yourself with them. We've selected two Major Arcana cards and one card from each of the four Minor Arcana suits.

The Empress, the Sun, the Ace of Wands, the 6 of Cups, the 6 of Swords, and the 5 of Pentacles.

What do you think of the cards? The impressions you receive from each card immediately are what you should note—this is your intuitive response. When you're ready to record your impressions, use the spaces provided to do so (or you may choose to record these impressions and all of your exercises for this book in your Intuitive Arts notebook).

The Empress: ______________________________

The Sun: ______________________________

Ace of Wands: ______________________________

6 of Cups: ______________________________

6 of Swords: ______________________________

5 of Pentacles: ______________________________

There aren't any right or wrong responses—each Tarot card has multiple meanings. Which meanings are relevant depends on the question asked, the other cards in the reading, and the conditions around the querent at the time of the reading.

The meanings of the cards are altered when the cards come up reversed or upside down—indicated with an "R," as in The Empress R. The reversed meaning is not necessarily the opposite of the upright meaning—and the reversed meaning is also not necessarily negative. Reversed cards may signify lessons to be learned, and they may also indicate delays. Like Astrology's retrogrades, reversed cards ask you to look at things in a different way, to understand a different energy. A reversed card contains the same lesson as the upright card but with a need to work on the lesson at a deeper level. Like retrograde planets, reversed Tarot cards are telling us to go back and review something we missed, perhaps something from our past that now reappears.

After you've looked over these six Tarot cards, consider some of the possible meanings that follow. It's best to remember that the meanings of these cards will change depending on the reading—what question did you ask, and what other cards appear?

The Empress

- ☯ Upright meanings: abundance, fertility, nurturing, prosperity
- ☯ Reversed meanings: poverty, insecurity, infertility, family difficulty, dysfunction, or loss

The Empress is the archetype of the mother! She's the mother we all want to have and might wish to be, and this card can represent your mother or you as a mother, and also indicates a happy home, solid marriage, and fertility and abundance of home and hearth.

The Sun

- ☯ Upright meanings: contentment, success, a peaceful life, happy unions
- ☯ Reversed meanings: delay, doubt, dissatisfaction

The Sun upright lets us know that we will be healthy and content! It indicates a positive outcome in life, work, or love. Regarding the family, home and relationships are stable and ease of movement between family members is certain when this card appears. The Sun indicates blessings bestowed upon a happy couple, with a new birth, a new home, or simply welcoming energy. When the Sun reversed appears, there is a situation in which the cloudy skies make for some doubt in life. Family relationships may be tense and stressed, and the family may need to regroup and begin to communicate their needs and perceptions better. Seeking help from wise counsel and support from close friends can help with this uncertainty in family life.

Ace of Wands

- ☯ Upright meanings: new energy, renewed courage and self-esteem, creative upsurge
- ☯ Reversed meanings: low self-esteem, time to regroup, something missing

The Ace of Wands indicates new beginnings of all kinds, and in relation to family, this card can indicate the birth of a child or signify a new attitude toward your family situation. When this card is reversed, energy may be spent in a direction that could prove to be a loss. Family dynamics may also not be organized in such a way as to prevent arguments and misunderstandings.

6 of Cups

- ☯ Upright meanings: happy memories, family reunion, gift or inheritance
- ☯ Reversed meanings: unhappy memories, disappointment with family

The 6 of Cups is usually called "happy childhood memories," making its family connection pretty clear. You could be meeting up with an old friend or reuniting with family members if this card appears in your reading. It often relates to family values and to siblings. Children are in this card, which depicts a loving and giving relationship. Reversed, the card indicates nostalgia and possibly living in the past, wishing for someone or something to return, and not taking emotional responsibility within the family.

6 of Swords

- Upright meanings: moving away from difficulty, journey over water, harmony in the future
- Reversed meanings: being stuck, shelving of plans, postponement, delay

Family meanings of the 6 of Swords include loss from which the family is recovering. (The mother and child are hovering as the father leads them into calmer waters.) The family will begin recovering from difficulty or sorrow, and will begin to be in harmony again. The family will move across the rocky waters of life and begin anew. There will be renewed hope and understanding between members as well as a desire to reconcile. Reversed, the card indicates apprehension and anxiety due to the delays and roadblocks. The family may have trouble navigating these rocky waters and needs relief or rest.

5 of Pentacles

- Upright meanings: financial or spiritual difficulty, impoverishment, abandonment
- Reversed meanings: reversal of bad luck, return of courage and hope

The 5 of Pentacles has a traditional connection to fear of abandonment. In the context of family, this card can indicate that the events and emotions of your life have left you with this fear. This can be as literal as your feelings of abandonment by a parent or a spouse, or can have to do with feelings of emotional abandonment that have left you needy and untrusting. This card may also signify the family's loss of property or their values. Family members may not see eye to eye. Reversed, this card indicates a renewed ability of the family to rise above all difficulties no matter how difficult or traumatic.

Tarot and Timing

Tarot cards also reveal time frames as part of their meanings. The royal cards and numbered cards have certain associations, as does each Tarot suit. The cards indicate the time frame during which your question will be answered or the indicated action will take place.

Tarot Cards	**Tarot Timing**
Ace through 10	1 to 10 days, weeks, or months (depending on the card)
Page	11 days, weeks, or months
Knight	12 days, weeks, or months
Queen and King	Unknown time—it's up to you!

Tarot Suits	**Tarot Suit Timing**
Wands	Days to weeks/spring
Cups	Weeks to months/summer
Swords	Days, fast!/fall
Pentacles	Months to years/winter

The numbers on the Tarot cards also have symbolic meaning. The Minor Arcana cards, after the royal cards, are number Ace (or 1) through 10.

Number	**Symbolic Meaning**
1	Drive and determination
2	Balance and union
3	Creative enthusiasm
4	Practical planning
5	Impulsive spontaneity
6	Nurturing concern
7	Serene contemplation
8	Powerful achievement
9	Spiritual completion

What Do Your Instincts Say? Family and Psychic Intuition

Do you listen to your hunches? Do you follow your instincts? Have you ever felt a sense of déjà vu, or had a strong response to someone you've just met? You probably picked up this book because you want to learn more about family, particularly your own family. Intuitive exercises are ways of getting in touch with your inner self to discover what you're really thinking. In this first intuitive exercise, we help you build your family intuition. You need to do this exercise with at least one other family member. You can do this exercise with as many people as you like, but start with two at a time.

Here's the question: *Do you and your family members share an intuitive link?* You're a family, after all, which means you have a strong bond (whether it be blood or not). Perhaps you always know when your sister is calling, or when your husband is upset, or when your best friend is worried and trying to conceal it. Maybe you have a stronger intuitive sense than this, but this is a good place to start, and this exercise will help you strengthen the intuitive bond you share with family, and make it work for you.

1. Get together with another family member, and decide on something you want to communicate. You can select something very simple—a color, an animal, a shape. Just decide on the category, and then decide which one of you will be the *sender* and which will be the *receiver.*
2. After you've made these decisions, one of you (the receiver) should leave the room and sit quietly elsewhere in the house. For a specified amount of time (three to five minutes, for instance), the sender focuses on the image of her choice within the agreed-upon category. If the category was shape, the sender might focus on the circle shape, perhaps envisioning a circle and repeating the word in her mind.
3. The receiver, of course, is in another room, trying to free her mind—not trying to select an image, but opening her mind to receive the image being sent by the sender. If the receiver becomes focused on an image of her own, she won't be able to pick up on the image sent by her family member.
4. After the allotted time, the two parties should come together again, and the receiver will say what she feels the sender was trying to tell her.

Did she guess correctly? If not, this doesn't mean that your family is doomed to misunderstand one another, or that one or both of you have no Psychic Intuition—we all have it! Honed intuition doesn't guarantee family harmony, of course (though it may help you foresee it), but it can help you heighten your awareness of your family members, and make you much more attuned to their thoughts and feelings.

Try this exercise with other family members, and repeat it with the same family members, recording the results in your Intuitive Arts notebook. You might just be surprised to find that, just as exercise builds strength, practice can hone your Psychic Intuition. Later you might try this exercise with Tarot cards (the sender selects a card and focuses on it, while the receiver tries to envision the card the sender is holding). At this stage, however, your family members might not be familiar with the Tarot, and wouldn't know which card you were holding, even if they could see it (though if their intuition is well honed, they might be able to describe the card!).

Your Family Tree (or Shrub, or Garden)

Sometimes it's like that adage ... you can't live with 'em and you can't live without 'em. Families come in all shapes and sizes, and include the families we're born into, and perhaps were raised in, as well as the families we create for ourselves, joining spiritually and emotionally with friends and lovers, children, and extended blood relations.

A Short History of Family

Today we tend to think of family in terms of the *nuclear* family—mother, father, and their children—and *extended* family—all the relatives of the nuclear family (grandparents, aunts, uncles, cousins, and so on). Most people in the United States live in nuclear families, though these families may not include a mother and a father, and though there are a number of other kinds of families in the modern United States, including families with single parents, stepparents and stepsiblings, two mothers or two fathers, and so forth. The nuclear family has long been the heart of family, even when the household more often included extended family members, such as grandparents. Family once was the identifying unit within society, responsible for the care and education of children and for the care of the elderly. Today the individual is the focal element of society, and there are institutional services providing for education and eldercare. The role of family has definitely changed—both its societal role, and what we as individuals expect from our family.

Multigenerational success.

Until very recently, within the family, the father was the head of household, and the primary job of the mother was the care of the household and the children. This has changed, but only in the past 50 years or so. Earlier than this, prior to the 1800s, marriage was less likely to be based on love and affection than to be an arrangement, and children were seen as an economic resource for the family. Today, on average, women have fewer children at a later age, and the role of family is to nurture those children and prepare them for adulthood. The change in women's roles and the advent of birth control also means that children may now be a choice for a woman or a couple—a fundamental change in family construction. Family is no longer defined as individuals related by blood or marriage, nor is marriage necessary to the creation of family.

Struggles, loss, and deceit.

The divorce rate still hovers at about 50 percent today, and cohabitation without marriage has become acceptable in our society. Many defer marriage until their late 20s or 30s, and more and more elderly live on their own or in an elder community. These changes and others in our society have made the nuclear family in the United States increasingly diverse in recent decades; family now includes all kinds of people—those related by blood or by marriage, those who are adopted, and those who choose to combine themselves into a family. Family refers to those people who see us at our best and our worst, and who, in the best of circumstances love, accept, and support us through both.

Coming home to approval.

Today we expect much from our family, most of it not material, though a certain level of material comfort is also desired (food, clothing, shelter, video games). Families are the nexus of socialization for children, and the early, formative years within family are seen as responsible for everything from an individual's self-esteem and ability to succeed to their ability to function in society, and particularly in other relationships. We have a tendency to expect these things from our family of origin, and conversely, family is blamed for our failure in relationships, in work, actually in all aspects of our lives. Before Sigmund Freud and the advent of psychoanalysis, perhaps we might have wished to blame our mothers for being overprotective; we just didn't know how to verbalize it, and if we did, it certainly would not have been an acceptable sentiment to verbalize.

Success in family, marriage, and love.

We don't want to think about blame, though. We're interested in where you and your family are right now, and where you'd like to be. Whether you have a family that is tight-knit and harmonious or one that's less than supportive, we all have family, and most of us always will. How do we make the most of these relationships?

Why Do We Need Family?

Do we *need* family? Most psychologists would insist that we do. Family, or those close bonds associated with family, is considered essential to human development. Infants deprived of physical contact with an adult caregiver often fail to thrive. Obviously, early in life, family is essential to existence. It is usually family members who are responsible for our care and well-being. For children, the basic necessities of life (food, clothing, shelter), as well as emotional needs, are most often met by family. We learn much about who we are and how to interact with others from the interactions within our family of origin. We learn to bond and connect, to form that necessary energy that makes us know we are alive and human. Through the interactions of our family, we learn how to make these connections, and we then use this knowledge as, in adulthood, we create yet another generation.

The Stages of Life

Erik Erikson (1902–1994) was a child psychologist who expanded on Freud's psychoanalytic theory. Erikson defined psychoanalytic stages of human life based on the characteristics of a "healthy" personality. His stages are described in the following table.

Erikson's Psychoanalytic Stages

Stage	Age	Crisis
Infancy	Birth to 1 year	Trust vs. mistrust
Early childhood	2 to 3 years	Autonomy vs. shame/doubt
Play age	4 to 5 years	Initiative vs. guilt
School age	6 to 12 years	Industry vs. inferiority
Adolescence	13 to 18 years	Identity vs. identity diffusion
Young adult	Young adulthood	Intimacy vs. isolation
Adulthood	Middle adulthood	Generativity vs. self-absorption
Mature age	Late adulthood to death	Integrity vs. disgust/despair

Erikson focused on the conscious mind and the emergence of identity. He believed that identity resulted from conflict faced at each stage of development. One's personality, then, is the result of one's response to the conflict in that stage, and the emotional developments made due to this conflict. You might be able to learn a bit about yourself by looking at this table and seeing where you are—and where you've been—in life. We don't want to get too technical here, but if you think about yourself at age 9 or 11, you might see some of the conflict of this stage in your life. The positive outcome of the conflict between industry and inferiority would be a sense of productivity and ability—good self-esteem. If you don't have the resources to handle this conflict well, you may feel inferior and unproductive. Much of the influence on children at this age comes from within the school environment, but your family played a role, as well: Were you praised as a child and made to feel talented and special? Even if your parents didn't respond negatively, calling you "stupid" or otherwise belittling you, if they didn't help you feel like you could do *anything* (and do it *well*), you might have had a very difficult time with this stage. (It's a conflict, after all.) According to Erikson, how you dealt with this conflict would affect your attitude toward work and achievement (and your abilities in these areas) throughout your life.

Notice that for the later stages, no ages are given. Where do you fall? Think about your family members. You can use the ideas Erikson presents to gain insights into your family and how it functions, as a unit and as individuals. One of the interesting things about Erikson's stages is that *they continue throughout life.* According to Erikson, we are working on creating ourselves until we die! This may seem depressing to some of you, particularly if you think of adulthood as the time when you're in control and you have the answers. We find it refreshing, this ability we have to continue to grow and change. And frankly, where families are concerned, it gives us hope. Even your parents aren't finished learning yet! (Of course, they may not admit to this!)

Father, mother, young adult, child: What stages might these cards represent?

What's Next?

Before moving on, think about what you'd like to learn and accomplish using this book and the Intuitive Arts. Do you want to repair a family relationship? Learn to be a better parent to your children? Perhaps you simply want to gain some insight into your family members, learning more about them and yourself in the process. We're ready to begin working with you to use the Intuitive Arts to make your family all you want and need it to be (and to discover what that is!). Remember to keep an open mind, and get ready to open up a whole new experience of family relationships.

chapter 2

Celebrating Family Re-Union

The duality of opposites
Astrology's *yin* and *yang*
What's your balance? Looking at *yin* and *yang* in your family birth charts
The *yin* and *yang* of the Tarot
What the cards show for your family's *yin* and *yang* dynamics
Psychic Intuition reverses polarity

How balanced is your family? No, we don't mean that way! We mean in terms of the energies of your interactions. Are you like the north and south poles of a magnet, smoothly connecting with each other to form strong bonds? Or are you preventing connections and pushing each other away? This chapter explores the yin *and* yang, *the balance, of family relationships. The premise of balance is at the core of the Intuitive Arts of Astrology, Tarot, and Psychic Intuition. This is a dynamic balance, continually in a push-and-pull exchange. When it comes to your family relationships, you might feel there's too much push or too much pull. This doesn't have to result in confrontation and conflict. You can use the flow of your energy—your* yin *and* yang *balances—to relate and react with one another in supportive, complementary ways.*

My Pole or Yours? The Opposing Forces of Life Energy

The polarity of energy keeps the universe in balance. The ancient Chinese concept of *yin* and *yang* symbolizes this polarity, showing how opposites both separate and complete each other. What do you notice when you look at this *yin* and *yang* symbol? Do you see contrast or complement? We like to think of it as duality—opposites that must coexist for either to exist.

Yin *and* yang *represent the balance of energy that is the essence of all existence.*

The *yin* and *yang* symbol represents the classic balance between opposites that both attract and repel. We look at the energies of *yin* and *yang* as the push and pull in family relationships, the give-and-take of family dynamics. Here are some of the common characteristics we attribute to *yin* and to *yang* energies.

Yin Characteristics	**Yang Characteristics**
Feminine	Masculine
Negative	Positive
Indirect	Direct
Cool	Warm
Dark	Bright
Internal	External
Receptive	Assertive
____________________	____________________
____________________	____________________
____________________	____________________

Are there others that come to mind for you? You can add them to their respective lists if you like; we left some extra room for you to do that. Just as polarity helps us to explain and understand the natural world in which we live, it provides insights into the dynamics of family relationships.

The Yin and Yang of Astrology

Each astrological sign is either *yin* or *yang*. The ways these signs appear in your birth chart influence the *yin* and *yang* of your actions and behaviors. Six signs are *yin*, and six signs are *yang*.

Yin Astro Signs	**Yang Astro Signs**
Taurus ♉	Aries ♈
Cancer ♋	Gemini ♊
Virgo ♍	Leo ♌
Scorpio ♏	Libra ♎
Capricorn ♑	Sagittarius ♐
Pisces ♓	Aquarius ♒

Everyone's astrological birth chart contains all of the signs. What we look for to understand family relationships are the combinations of signs *between* birth charts, which show complements and challenges among family members. This is what creates the push and pull of your family dynamic. Although certain combinations are inherently more challenging, this doesn't mean the relationship is destined for struggle! The *potential* for discord is there, but you can learn to accommodate each other's needs and differences—and even celebrate them—when you understand what they are.

The Push and Pull of Sibling Matchups

Comparing birth charts lets us see how *yin* and *yang* affect family relationships. We start by identifying the *yin* and *yang* of each person's ascendant, or rising sign, and six of the planets: the five personal planets (Sun ☉, Moon ☽, Mars ♂, Mercury ☿, Venus ♀) and Jupiter ♃, the planet of personal wisdom and growth. Your ascendant is the astrological sign that was rising on the horizon at the time of your birth, and in your birth chart it is the sign on the cusp of your 1st house, the house of identity and self. Your ascendant influences your persona, or the way you present yourself to others. The six planets influence how we develop bonds in interpersonal relationships like family.

We'll look at the *yin* and *yang* balance of some famous siblings to explore what this can show: Michael Jackson and Janet Jackson, Shirley MacLaine and Warren Beatty, and Julia Roberts and Eric Roberts. First up: the Jacksons.

Here's the *yin* and *yang* balance we find among these seven personal signs for this brother and sister. As we don't know the birth times for Janet or Michael, Arlene cast noon charts for them. This means their Moon ☽ signs and ascendant signs could be different than what their noon charts show, depending on how far from noon their birth times are.

Astro Planet	**Michael Jackson in Astro Sign**	**Yin or Yang**	**Janet Jackson in Astro Sign**	**Yin or Yang**
Sun ☉	Virgo ♍	*Yin*	Taurus ♉	*Yin*
Moon ☽	Pisces ♓	*Yin*	Aries ♈	*Yang*
Mercury ☿	Leo ♌	*Yang*	Taurus ♉	*Yin*
Venus ♀	Leo ♌	*Yang*	Aries ♈	*Yang*
Mars ♂	Taurus ♉	*Yin*	Taurus ♉	*Yin*
Jupiter ♃	Libra ♎	*Yang*	Cancer ♋	*Yin*
Ascendant	Scorpio ♏	*Yin*	Leo ♌	*Yang*

Although there's an overall *yin* and *yang* balance for Michael and Janet, there is little harmony between the signs. Both have four *yin* and three *yang* signs. Michael and Janet have their Moon ☽ (emotions), Mercury ☿ (communication), Jupiter ♃ (abundance and wisdom), and ascendant in *yin/yang* balance—each balancing the other sibling's energy. The other three signs—Sun ☉ (self), Venus ♀ (money and art), and Mars ♂ (action and ego)—share the same polarity. This sharing can create a dynamic that may seem either unchallenged or "too easy" or overly competitive, and lead to disharmony and tension in the areas the signs influence.

Michael and Janet both have a lot going on in the 10th house, which controls career and ambition, social roles, and what others think of you. (Both have their Suns ☉ in the 10th house.) They are both very career-oriented, with little room for much else—this is something they definitely have in common! Both have Mars ♂ in Taurus ♉, which makes them extremely persistent and determined.

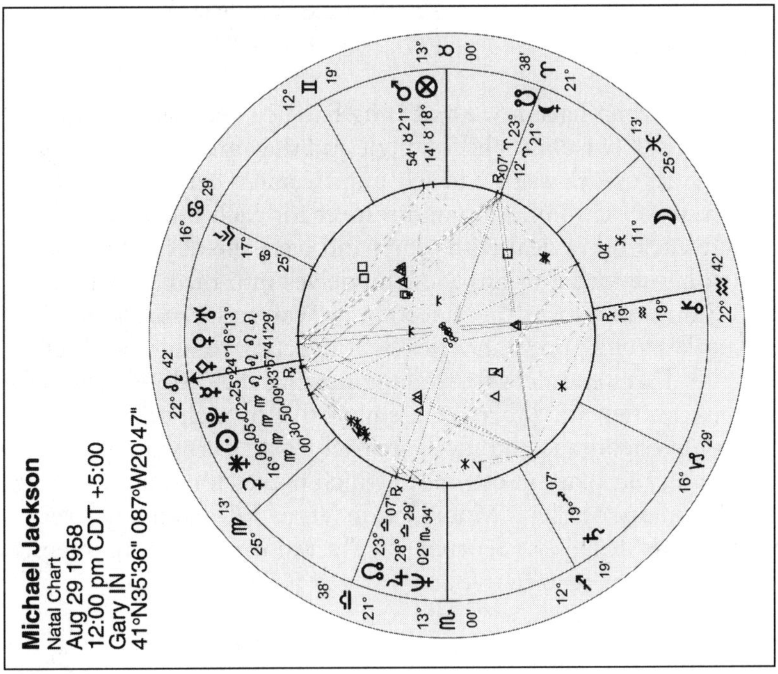

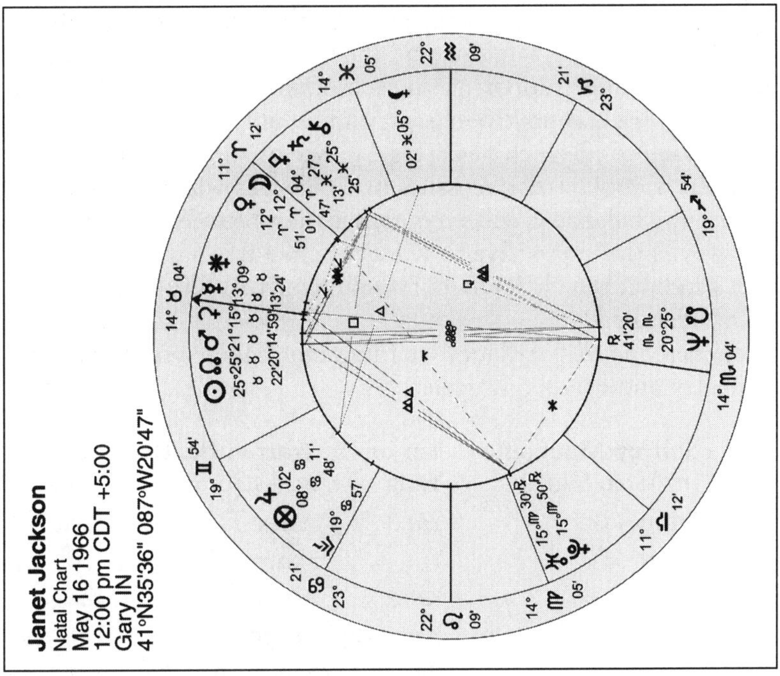

Birth charts of Michael Jackson and Janet Jackson.

The balance of *yin* and *yang* signs between their charts creates the possibility of mutual understanding and the ability to share in ideas and vision, and be helpful or supportive to each other during difficult times. They also have some competitive energy, and would need to accept the different approach to life each has. This balance of *yin* and *yang* can afford them the ability to resolve issues or challenges with mutual respect; because the balance is collective rather than between each set of signs, however, they may have to work to make this happen.

Now let's look at the birth charts for sibling actors Shirley MacLaine and Warren Beatty.

Here's the *yin* and *yang* balance we find among these seven planets for sister Shirley and brother Warren.

Astro Planet	**Shirley MacLaine in Astro Sign**	**Yin or Yang**	**Warren Beatty in Astro Sign**	**Yin or Yang**
Sun ☉	Taurus ♉	*Yin*	Aries ♈	*Yang*
Moon ☽	Virgo ♍	*Yin*	Scorpio ♏	*Yin*
Mercury ☿	Aries ♈	*Yang*	Aries ♈	*Yang*
Venus ♀	Pisces ♓	*Yin*	Taurus ♉	*Yin*
Mars ♂	Taurus ♉	*Yin*	Sagittarius ♐	*Yang*
Jupiter ♃	Libra ♎	*Yang*	Capricorn ♑	*Yin*
Ascendant	Virgo ♍	*Yin*	Virgo ♍	*Yin*

Shirley and Warren have a *yin* and *yang* balance between Mars ♂ (ego) and Jupiter ♃ (wisdom, philosophy), and they are both Virgo ♍ ascendants, which makes work and self-improvement very important to them—they have great admiration and respect for each other's work. They can help each other deal with fame, and have the desire to protect each other from the media or anyone who delves into their private lives.

Shirley's Sun ☉ in Taurus ♉ connecting to Warren's Venus ♀ in Taurus ♉ and Warren's Sun ☉ in Aries ♈ connecting to Shirley's Mercury ☿ in Aries ♈ are excellent for communicating their ideals, drives, and ambitions. Shirley and Warren are supportive of each other's life goals and would encourage and motivate each other's growth. They also have Mercury in Aries in common, which makes for spontaneity as well as stubbornness. Shirley's Moon ☽ is in Virgo ♍, making her very practical; with his Moon ☽ in Scorpio ♏, Warren is much more intense and emotional, as well as intuitive.

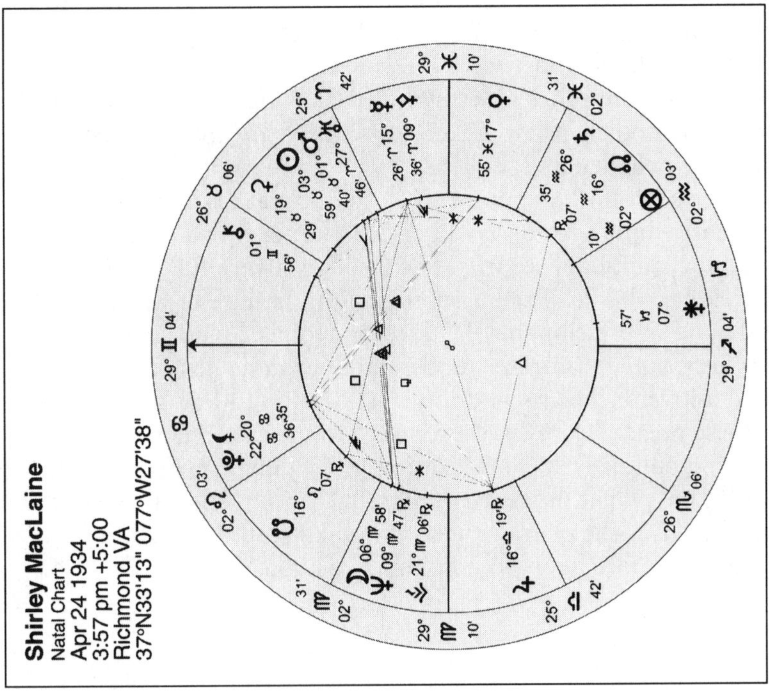

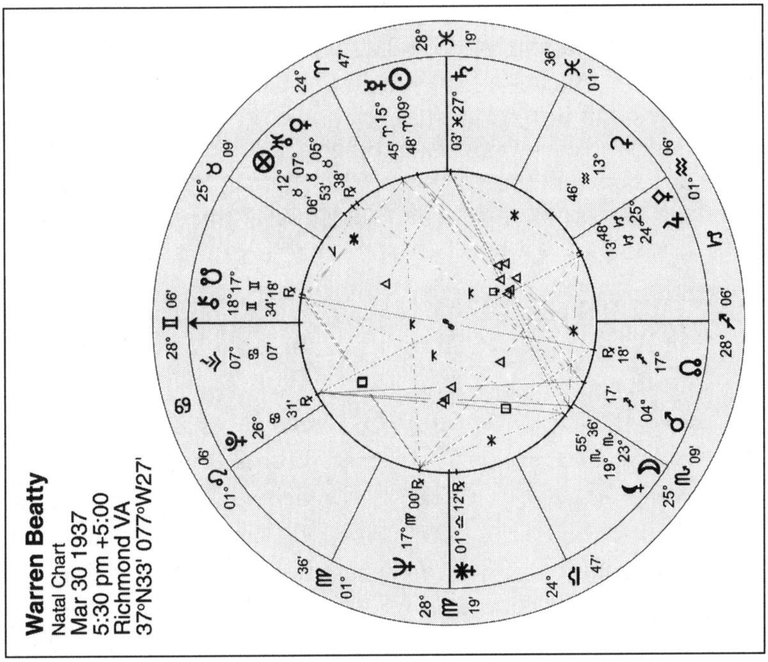

Birth charts of Shirley MacLaine and Warren Beatty.

Their Mars ♂ may present some difficulty in their relationship. Shirley's *yin* Taurus ♉ Mars may not relate well to Warren's *yang* Sagittarius ♐ Mars, surfacing differences in lifestyle approaches. But they likely have enough respect in their relationship to agree to disagree! Shirley and Warren support each other's career endeavors and have the type of balance that many successful partners or couples have.

Finally, take a look at the birth charts of siblings Julia Roberts and Eric Roberts. Eric's chart is a noon chart.

Astro Planet	**Julia Roberts in Astro Sign**	**Yin or Yang**	**Eric Roberts in Astro Sign**	**Yin or Yang**
Sun ☉	Scorpio ♏	*Yin*	Aries ♈	*Yang*
Moon ☽	Leo ♌	*Yang*	Leo ♌	*Yang*
Mercury ☿	Scorpio ♏	*Yin*	Taurus ♉	*Yin*
Venus ♀	Virgo ♍	*Yin*	Gemini ♊	*Yang*
Mars ♂	Capricorn ♑	*Yin*	Aquarius ♒	*Yang*
Jupiter ♃	Virgo ♍	*Yin*	Leo ♌	*Yang*
Ascendant	Cancer ♋	*Yin*	Leo ♌	*Yang*

Julia is nearly all *yin,* and Eric is nearly all *yang*. How harmonious does that make this matchup? When you look again at the list of qualities associated with *yin* and *yang,* you can see that in just about every way these two are opposites. Although these siblings can balance and complement each other in important ways, their *yin/yang* polarity can also create some challenges for them.

They share a Moon ☽ in *yang* Leo ♌, which makes them emotional and charismatic. Julia's Moon is in her 2nd house, which gives her a strong need for emotional security. She also has a very full 3rd house, which represents siblings. Eric's Moon is in his 1st house, which makes him moody and impressionable. With their Moons connecting in that theatrical, fiery sign of Leo, they understand a shared passion for their careers and a love of the arts and the craft of acting—and desire recognition in these areas. However, those two Moons can inflame each other as well—Leo is full of pride and wanting to do things its own way. Eric's Sun ☉, the planet of identity and self, in *yang* Aries ♈ suggests he's more objective—he doesn't sweat the small stuff. Julia's Sun ☉ in *yin* Scorpio ♏ is more likely to take things personally.

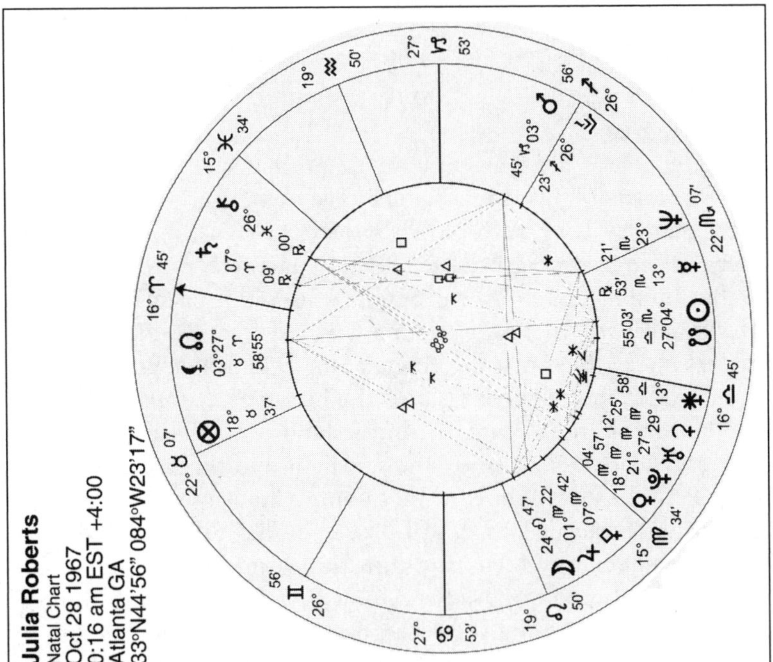

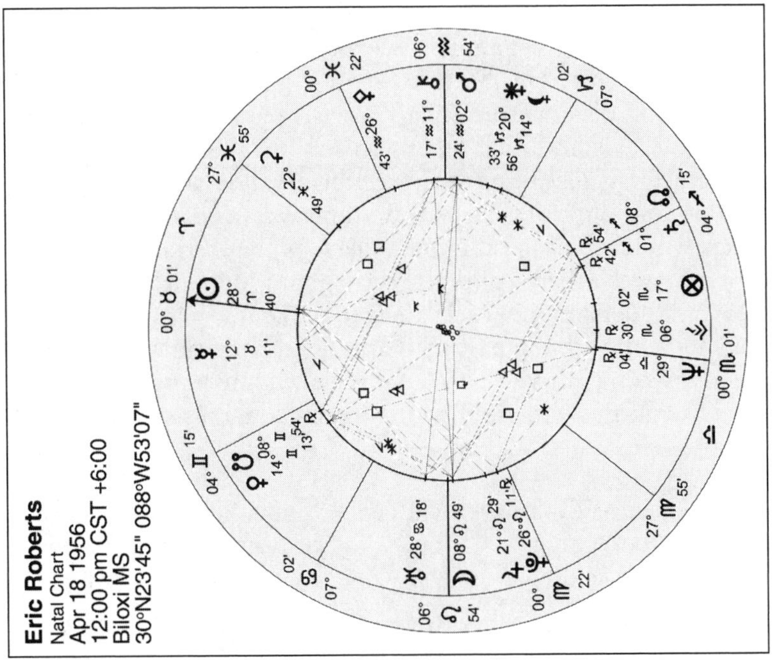

Birth charts of Julia Roberts and Eric Roberts.

We call their Sun sign combination "fire and water." *Yang* Aries embodies the Element of Fire, and *yin* Scorpio is a Water sign (more about the Elements in Chapter 3). Eric's strong independent nature can seem a bit short and distant from Julia's intense, passionate, emotional nature. Do they understand each other's volatile, passionate, and humorous characters? Yes! Eric is the extreme of *yang,* and Julia is the extreme of *yin*—and opposites attract. But opposites can also *repel.* These siblings will teach each other many lessons that certainly can keep the bond between them continual throughout life, but they will have to work at understanding each other to make this happen.

Now let's look at a sibling pair who appear to be in tune—though they are intensely competitive—and see if their *yin* and *yang* balance supports this harmony. Here are the birth charts of tennis star sisters Serena Williams and Venus Williams.

Astro Planet	**Serena Williams in Astro Sign**	**Yin or Yang**	**Venus Williams in Astro Sign**	**Yin or Yang**
Sun ☉	Libra ♎	*Yang*	Gemini ♊	*Yang*
Moon ☽	Virgo ♍	*Yin*	Leo ♌	*Yang*
Mercury ☿	Libra ♎	*Yang*	Cancer ♋	*Yin*
Venus ♀	Scorpio ♏	*Yin*	Gemini ♊	*Yang*
Mars ♂	Leo ♌	*Yang*	Virgo ♍	*Yin*
Jupiter ♃	Libra ♎	*Yang*	Virgo ♍	*Yin*
Ascendant	Taurus ♉	*Yin*	Libra ♎	*Yang*

Like the Roberts siblings, these sisters have a *yin* and *yang* balance in their inner planets. They both have *yang* Sun ☉ signs, but every other planet is a *yin* and *yang* balance for this pair. The difference is, of course, that unlike Julia and Eric, Serena and Venus each have a balance of *yin* and *yang* themselves (three *yin* and four *yang*).

Both sisters have *yang* Suns ☉. Venus's Sun ☉ is in her 9th house of beliefs and philosophy—which is also the house of distant or foreign travel. Whether across the "pond" or in the land down under, her *yang* Gemini ♊ energy leads her to enjoy the spotlight and other cultures. Venus's *yang* Leo ♌ Moon ☽ bolsters her competitive spirit with emotion and charisma. Serena's Sun ☉ in Libra ♎ in her 6th house of work gives her *yang* energy focus and direction. And look at that packed 6th house! There, too, are her Moon ☽, Mercury ☿, and Jupiter ♃ to lead the celestial cheering squad supporting her efforts. The 6th house is also the house of health, making this an outstanding alignment of planets for an athlete.

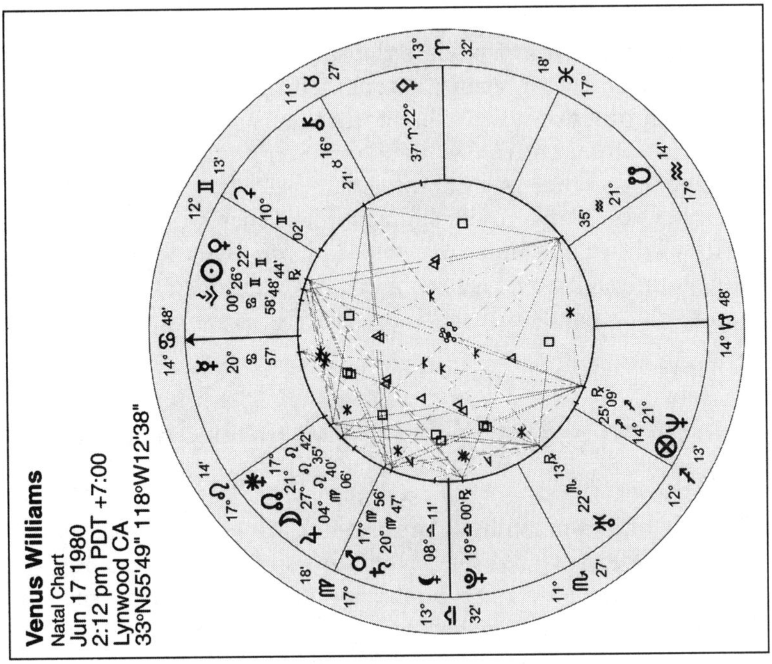

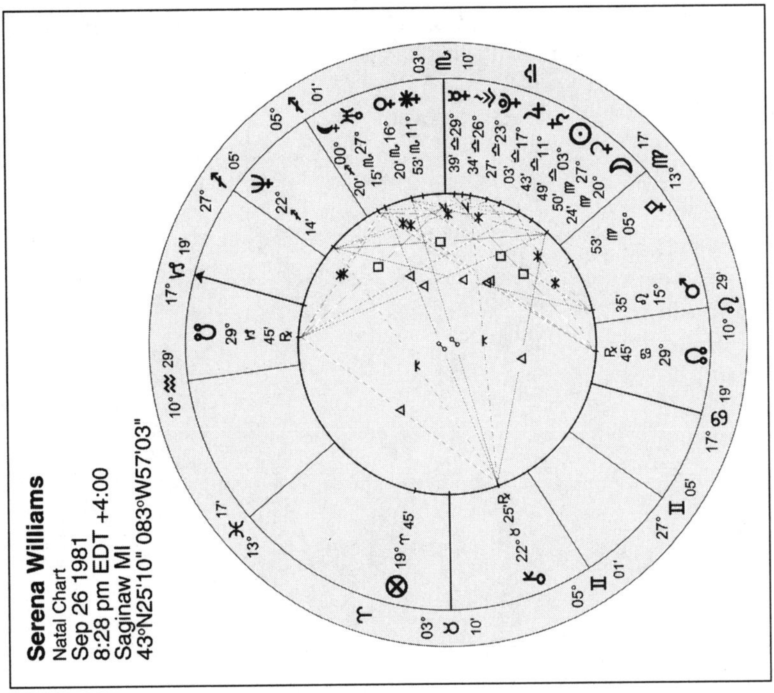

Birth charts of Serena Williams and Venus Williams.

Interestingly, Venus and Serena are also a winning doubles tennis team. Their *yang* natal Suns also share the same Element, Air (Libra ♎ for Serena and Gemini ♊ for Venus), strengthening the mutual respect they have for each other's individuality and at the same time allowing them to focus their competitiveness on shared goals. These two sisters can certainly work together as a good team.

We come back to some of these siblings' birth charts throughout this book. After all, it takes more than *yin* and *yang* balance to make a harmonious family relationship. But as you can see, it's a great start. When *yin* and *yang* balance is there, the relationship seems to have a solid bond.

Reading the Signs of Yin and Yang Balance in Your Family

How "balanced" are *your* family relationships? You can uncover your *yin* and *yang* balance as we did for our famous siblings. All you need is your astrological birth chart and a birth chart for the family member whose relationship with you you want to explore. Although we chose sibling pairs for our examples, you can choose *any* family member.

Here's a table of the symbols for the astrological signs, to help you identify them quickly and easily in your birth chart.

Astro Sign	Astro Symbol
Aries	♈
Taurus	♉
Gemini	♊
Cancer	♋
Leo	♌
Virgo	♍
Libra	♎
Scorpio	♏
Sagittarius	♐
Capricorn	♑
Aquarius	♒
Pisces	♓

Here's a table for you to record the personal signs for you and your family member. Go through your birth chart to identify the signs of the planets and your ascendant. Remember, your ascendant is the sign on the cusp of your 1st house. When you find the planet, write down its sign, and then look at the table earlier in the chapter to identify whether this sign is *yin* or *yang* and write that as well. Do this for each of you.

Astro Planet	**You in Astro Sign**	**Yin or Yang**	**Family Member in Astro Sign**	**Yin or Yang**
Sun ☉	___________	______	_____________	______
Moon ☽	___________	______	_____________	______
Mercury ☿	___________	______	_____________	______
Venus ♀	___________	______	_____________	______
Mars ♂	___________	______	_____________	______
Jupiter ♃	___________	______	_____________	______
Ascendant	___________	______	_____________	______

When you've filled in your table, take a look at the number of *yin* and *yang* signs you each have. What is your overall *yin/yang* balance? Write the totals here:

Family Members	**Number of Yin Signs**	**Number of Yang Signs**
You:	__________	__________
Family member:	__________	__________
_________________	__________	__________
_________________	__________	__________
_________________	__________	__________
_________________	__________	__________

Now, take a look at how each sign matches up. What is the *yin/yang* balance? Are you mostly opposites, like sister and brother Julia and Eric? Or are you both predominantly *yin* or predominantly *yang*?

Each planet's energy influences you in characteristic ways. In Chapter 1, we identified these characteristics with keywords. Here are the keywords for the six personal planets you're looking at in this exercise:

Planet	Keyword
Sun ☉	Explores
Moon ☽	Senses
Mercury ☿	Communicates
Venus ♀	Enjoys
Mars ♂	Engages
Jupiter ♃	Benefits

As you look at these keywords and the *yin* and *yang* balance you have with your family member for each planet, can you see how the *yin* or *yang* of the planet's sign influences each of you in how you relate to one another? Someone with Mercury ☿ in a *yang* sign like Gemini ♊ or Sagittarius ♐ is likely to be direct and assertive in communicating with others, for example, and someone with Mercury ☿ in a *yin* sign like Cancer ♋ or Capricorn ♑ is likely to be indirect and subtle.

Of course, many other astrological factors shape and influence you and your relationships. Your *yin* and *yang* balance is a starting point for understanding how you and your family members relate and get along. Identifying imbalances is the first step toward learning to accommodate them.

Tarot and the Yin and Yang of Family Dynamics

The cards of the Tarot can represent either *yin* or *yang* energy, depending on their positions in your readings and their relationships to the questions you ask. Major Arcana cards often represent people, in which case they take on the *yin* or *yang* of the person and his or her corresponding role. You might find that the Empress or the Emperor frequently show up in your readings to represent the Mother or the Father role that you play in your family—the Empress then takes on the *yin* characteristics we associate with Mothers and mothering and the Emperor the *yang* characteristics we connect with Fathers and fathering. Certain cards will feel *yin* or *yang* to you, too, which will influence how you interpret their presence in your readings.

Let's explore the *yin* and *yang* of the Tarot. Get your Tarot deck and separate it into the Major Arcana and Minor Arcana cards. There are 22 Major Arcana cards numbered 0 (the Fool) to 21 (the World). For this exercise, we work just with the Major Arcana cards, so you can set aside the Minor Arcana cards. You can do this exercise by yourself or with family members.

From the Fool to the World, the cards of the Tarot's Major Arcana often represent people. Which one of the 22 Major Arcana cards represents you?

Spread out the 22 Major Arcana cards so you can see them all. Look at the cards, each in turn. Let your Psychic Intuition explore the images and connections the cards evoke for you. Don't think about the cards in any analytical or logical way—just experience them. Choose one card that you feel represents you, right now in this particular moment of time.

Now study this card. Again, let your Psychic Intuition take the lead. Does this card feel *yin* or *yang* to you? Why? If other family members are participating in this exercise with you, how do their cards feel? Do you agree with each other's assessment that a card is *yin* or *yang*?

Cassandra did this exercise with her dad, Lawrence. Cassandra chose Strength; Lawrence selected Justice.

"I was drawn to this card immediately," Cassandra said. "I see a balance of *yin* and *yang* in Strength, and I see this kind of balance in myself. I'm compassionate and receptive, and I'm also positive and strong."

To represent themselves, Cassandra picked Strength and Lawrence chose Justice.

Cassandra made a list of the *yin* and *yang* words she associated with the Tarot card Strength:

Yin Associations with Strength	Yang Associations with Strength
Flowers	Positive
Woman	Strong
Compassion	Light
Animal	Warm
Receptive	Aggressive
Fecund	Virile

Although these words are not necessarily in contrast or opposition to one another, you can see that they capture the essence of the *yin* and *yang* energies that the Strength card embodies. Cassandra perceives a *yin* and *yang* balance within herself, and selected a Major Arcana card that represents that balance.

Her father, Lawrence, chose the card Justice. "There is a desire in me to be balanced and weigh all things before I ever make a final decision," Lawrence said. "I have had a tough time in my past with making decisions. Now, I am always weighing what is the best way to get to a goal or the best way to work with a family member, friend, or client."

Lawrence identified his *yin* and *yang* associations with the Tarot card he selected to represent himself. Although he listed both *yin* and *yang* words, he felt the card Justice was overall a *yang* energy, symbolizing an action-oriented approach to finding answers and solutions.

Yin Associations with Justice	Yang Associations with Justice
Scales	Sword
Woman	Focused
Passionate	Direct
Fair	Assertive
Equitable	Honor
Inner strength	Realist

Look again at the Major Arcana card you chose to represent yourself. What characteristics come to mind that describe your reactions and responses to the card's imagery? Make your own list of *yin* and *yang* words. You can look back to the table at the beginning of this chapter if you want some prompting.

Yin Associations with:	Yang Associations with:
________________	________________
________________	________________
________________	________________
________________	________________
________________	________________

You might find that different cards represent you depending on which family relationships you're exploring. Trying to understand sibling rivalry? You might feel like the Tower with your older sister whose actions and comments seem to be always blasting you off base ... or like the Hanged Man with your younger brother who can't decide whether you're friend or foe. If you are a single parent or the family arbiter, you might feel more like the Magician!

Tarot's Seven-Card Spread Takes You Below the Surface of Yin and Yang

Yin and *yang*, of course, are just the surface of family dynamics. Although these polarities establish the foundation of family relationships, they don't come close to defining the infinite complexities of how family members get along (or don't) with each other. Tarot's Seven-Card Spread offers a way for you to dig a little deeper into the energies beneath the *yin* and the *yang* of your family's interactions. This deceptively simple spread can reveal epiphanous insights.

The Seven-Card Spread is what it sounds like—seven cards laid out in a row. The first two cards represent the past, the middle three cards represent the present, and the final two cards represent the future. It helps you to understand issues, resolve concerns, and find answers to questions about family relationships. When Kristin wanted to know whether the timing was right for her and her husband Mark to have a second child, Arlene chose this spread to explore the family's circumstances surrounding this question.

Kristin became pregnant soon after the couple made the decision to start a family early in their marriage. She received a major promotion the month before son Eli was born, and returned to work full-time two months after his birth. Kristin and Mark had decided three months ago that it was time to have a second child, but Kristin wasn't pregnant yet. So she had a twofold question for Arlene: Is it really the right time to have a second child, and if so why isn't she pregnant yet?

Kristin shuffles the Tarot cards while thinking about her question. When she's ready, she cuts the deck and Arlene deals the cards.

Kristin's Seven-Card Spread addresses her question, "Is it time for us to have another baby?"

The Past. The first two cards, the 2 of Swords R and the King of Wands, represent the past. Arlene interprets that these cards represent the happy and proud time for Kristin and Mark when Eli was born. Their decision to have a child was a good one, and they remain happy about it.

The Present. The next three cards—the Star R, the Magician R, and the 6 of Pentacles—represent the present. Right now, it seems that Kristin is conflicted about having another child. The reversed Star and Magician cards indicate that she's not at ease with this decision, and perhaps is confused about whether to have another child. There is a lot going on right now for Kristin in terms of her abilities and her work. She is not focused and has not tapped into her potential and her hidden abilities. Although she feels a lack of enthusiasm about this, she needs to focus on developing these abilities and balancing her life. There are also some new circumstances unfolding at work that have positive potential for Kristin now, either financially or in terms of career advancement.

The Future. The final two cards in this spread, the 7 of Pentacles and the 5 of Swords R, represent the future. The 7 of Pentacles indicates that Kristin will reap the rewards of some hard work—perhaps the work she puts in on discovering her true potential—but in terms of her question about pregnancy, she may be facing a situation with emotional difficulty. She may not be ready to have another child right now, and as she has fears about this—she worries that she will be too old when she feels ready—this could be a difficult and conflicted time for her. Arlene also suggested that Kristin needs to work on her issues about money. She should ask herself these questions: Is there enough coming in for another child? Are we ready to have our lifestyle change with a new addition now? Arlene suggested that it would be fine for Kristin to wait and not put pressure on herself or her husband at this time.

It seems that Kristin is as worried about *having* a baby as she is about *not* having a baby. She doesn't seem to have physical difficulties preventing her pregnancy, but she might not be prepared in other ways to be pregnant right now. Kristin may also want to work on her personal *yin* and *yang* balance before another baby joins their family.

What Do the Cards Show for Your Family?

The Tarot's Seven-Card Spread can help you understand your concerns and worries about questions you have regarding your own family. You can ask any question you like. Do you have a question in mind? Write it here:

____

Next, think about your question and shuffle your Tarot cards. When you're ready, you can cut the deck if you like, and then lay out seven cards in a row.

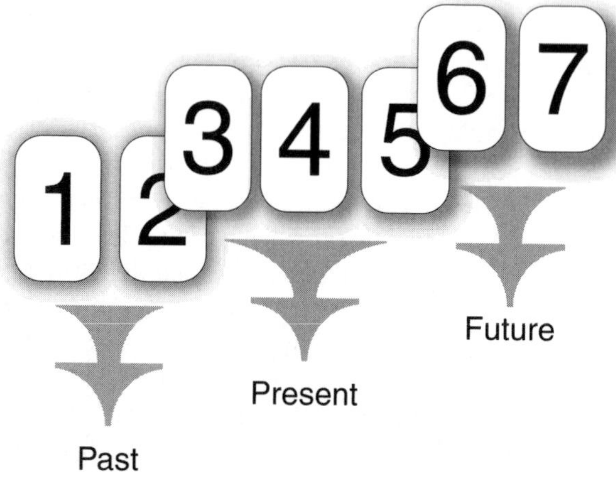

In the Seven-Card Spread, cards 1 and 2 are the past; cards 3, 4, and 5 are the present; and cards 6 and 7 are the future.

Look at the cards as a group to get a sense of the story that they tell about the question you asked. Are there messages that jump out at you right away? Do certain cards represent people, events, or situations? Do the cards seem predominantly *yin, yang,* or balanced in their energies? The Tarot's imagery is symbolic and metaphoric, and often cards will immediately make connections for you. If they don't, let your Psychic Intuition wander through the images. As you begin to explore the individual cards, the connections will become clear. The story of your Seven-Card Spread might explain what's been going on between you and a family member in ways you hadn't considered before, or cause pieces of confusion to fall away as the entire picture unfolds to make perfect sense to you in this visual, intuitive presentation.

Write your initial perceptions of this Seven-Card Spread:

____

Now, explore each card one at a time. Remember, the first two cards represent the past, the next three cards the present, and the final two cards the future. Write the cards of your Seven-Card Spread and your initial perceptions about them here:

Cards 1 and 2 (the past): ______________________

Perceptions: ______________________

Cards 3, 4, and 5 (the present): ______________________

Perceptions: ______________________

Cards 6 and 7 (the future): ______________________

Perceptions: ______________________

Reversing Polarity with Psychic Intuition

You know now whether your approach to life is primarily *yin* or *yang*. You've explored your polarity through your astrological birth chart and through the Tarot. Now how do you put these insights to work to improve your family relationships? We're glad you asked!

Most of the time, polarity is polarity—what is *yin* stays *yin*, what is *yang* remains *yang*. But with the Intuitive Art of Psychic Intuition, you can create an experience of reversed polarity to help you better understand how others perceive the *yin* and *yang* of family relationships. You've heard the expression "put yourself in my shoes." Well, you're going to let your Psychic Intuition put you in another family member's polarity. You're going to trade your *yin* for *yang* or *yang* for *yin*, whichever fits your situation.

This is a meditative exercise, so find a quiet place where you can relax and focus without interruptions or distractions. Using your Psychic Intuition, envision a family member with whom your relationship is challenging or even downright difficult. Consider the push and pull, the *yin* and *yang*, of your interactions with this person. Are you the *yin* or the *yang* of this relationship, or of its area of struggle? Are you the assertive one, raising the issues of conflict or getting in the first jabs? Or are you on the receiving end?

Visualize a recent interaction you've had with this family member. Replay the situation on the "big screen" of your inner vision. Where were the two of you? Who spoke first? What was said? With what words, or at what point, did the exchange become confrontational or quarrelsome? Feel now the feelings you felt then.

Now, hit the pause button. If you're the *yin* energy in this encounter, become the *yang*—and if you're the *yang*, become the *yin*. Take a few moments to settle into this new energy. It might feel a bit stiff and uncomfortable at first. Move around in it a little. Let your Psychic Intuition shrug and twist and shuffle. Now hit the replay button. Re-experience the exchange, only this time you are the opposite polarity. You're not becoming the other person, just stepping into his or her *yin* or *yang* energy. How does the exchange unfold any differently? Do you speak the same words but with different intonation? Do you choose different words entirely? Does the clash even happen? Let yourself return to your natural polarity and the present moment. When you are restored, write down your perceptions of your polarity reversal in your Intuitive Arts notebook.

Did you feel awkward pulling from the opposite energy to interact with this family member in this exercise? Although you might use predominantly *yin* or *yang* energy as your "default" mode when you interact with family members, you have both *yin* and *yang* energy to draw from. Sometimes improving a relationship means learning to activate your nondominant energy.

The point of this exercise is to see where the energies are in this family relationship, and where the tension of push and pull lies. Once you figure this out, you can adjust to use your respective energies to bring balance to the relationship. This isn't always easy, of course. Family dynamics become routine and comfortable. We evolve into patterns of behavior that might've been appropriate at some point but are now just habit. With awareness and intent, you can change patterns—even patterns of energy. You can't change the *yin* and the *yang* of your energies. But you can learn how to use your personal energy balances to interact acceptingly and productively with your family.

chapter 3

Family Bonds Are Elemental

From *yin* and *yang* to the four Elements
Elemental combinations
Tarot explores the Elements
Using your birth chart to find your Elemental Family Signature
Making a mandala for your model family
Unraveling your family's Elemental combinations

Your family represents many combinations of characteristics that shape and explain beliefs, thoughts, and actions. You don't have to look so far to find the essence of these combinations; they are the very Elements of existence. Fire, Earth, Air, and Water are the foundation of nature—and the foundation of your family. Each family member has an Elemental Family Signature that defines his or her Elemental influences. These signatures can reveal quite a lot about how you interact and get along. In this chapter, we show you how to use your astrological birth chart to identify your Elemental Family Signature. We let the Tarot tell the stories of how you and your family members identify and meet each other's needs. And we use Psychic Intuition to explore the meanings and potential of your Elemental combinations. Through these Intuitive Arts, you'll begin to discover why your family exists in its current state of harmony, conflict, or somewhere in between.

The Elemental Foundations of Family Relationships

As *yin* and *yang* are the "couple" of balance between opposing forces, the four Elements—Fire, Earth, Air, and Water—are the "family." They exist in multiple combinations, accounting for the palette of characteristics we collectively might call personality. Just as each sign is *yin* or *yang*, it also has an Element affiliation. *Yang* signs are Fire or Air, and *yin* signs are Earth or Water.

Fire (Yang)	**Earth (Yin)**	**Air (Yang)**	**Water (Yin)**
Aries ♈	Taurus ♉	Gemini ♊	Cancer ♋
Leo ♌	Virgo ♍	Libra ♎	Scorpio ♏
Sagittarius ♐	Capricorn ♑	Aquarius ♒	Pisces ♓

We can ascribe certain key traits to each of the Elements. Your Psychic Intuition can probably identify some of them right off; we allude to them all the time when we speak of people as "fiery" or "grounded," for example—these are key characteristics of Fire and Earth, respectively. Here is a table of key characteristics we can relate to each of the Elements.

Fire	**Earth**	**Air**	**Water**
Enthusiastic	Productive	Inventive	Creative
Adventurous	Practical	Idealistic	Emotional
Competitive	Hardworking	Thoughtful	Empathetic
Passionate	Content	Social	Romantic
Physical	Tangible	Intellectual	Intuitive
Direct	Nurturing	Detached	Sensitive

Each suit of the Tarot's Minor Arcana also corresponds to an Element.

Fire	**Earth**	**Air**	**Water**
Wands	Pentacles	Swords	Cups

The Elements, as they coexist within the configuration of your astrological birth chart, help to shape and define who you are and explain why you act—and interact with others—in the ways that you do. Some Elements support and complement each other, providing a steady balance between their energies. Other Elements challenge each other, presenting strain and struggle either to blend or to remain distinct from one another. Still other Elemental combinations are conditional, capable of fostering harmony or instigating dissonance depending on the circumstances.

When you look at the following table, you can see that far more combinations are conditional than either supportive or challenging.

Elemental Combinations	Supportive	Challenging	Conditional
	Fire + Air	Fire + Earth	Fire + Fire
	Earth + Water	Air + Water	Earth + Earth
		Air + Air	
		Water + Water	
		Fire + Water	
		Earth + Air	

In family relationships, Elemental combinations tend to shift depending on which family members are involved in particular circumstances. The more family members, the more combinations are possible. This is where knowing each person's Elemental Family Signature can be a great help in understanding and anticipating actions, reactions, and behaviors from each other.

Exploring Your Elemental Family Signature

Let's look to the Tarot for insights about how the Elements shape the structure of your family relationships. For this exercise, you need to know your Sun ☉ signs and their Elemental associations, and you need your deck of Tarot cards. Oh—and wake up your Psychic Intuition … you need that, too. First we show you what Cathy and her mom learned about each other and their relationship through this exercise as an example, and then you can try the exercise on your own.

To start, Cathy and her mom identified their Sun ☉ signs and looked at the table earlier in this chapter to identify their Elemental associations. Cathy's Sun is in the Water sign Pisces ♓, and her mom's is in the Air sign Gemini ♊. Although Cathy and her mom feel that they get along pretty well, they know they have their differences, so this challenging Elemental combination is not a surprise.

Cathy then separated her Tarot deck into the Major Arcana cards, which she set aside, and into the four suits: Wands, Pentacles, Swords, Cups. From the suit that corresponds with the Element of their respective Sun signs, Cathy and her mom each selected a card to represent themselves. The Tarot suit that corresponds to Pisces, a Water Element, is Cups. Cathy chose the 10 of Cups to represent herself. The Tarot suit that corresponds to Gemini, an Air Element, is Swords. Cathy's mom selected the 3 of Swords to represent herself. Then Cathy and her mom selected cards from their respective suits that they felt represented each other. From the suit of Swords, her mom's Air Element, Cathy chose the 10 of Swords. From the suit of Cups, Cathy's Water Element, Cathy's mom picked the 4 of Cups.

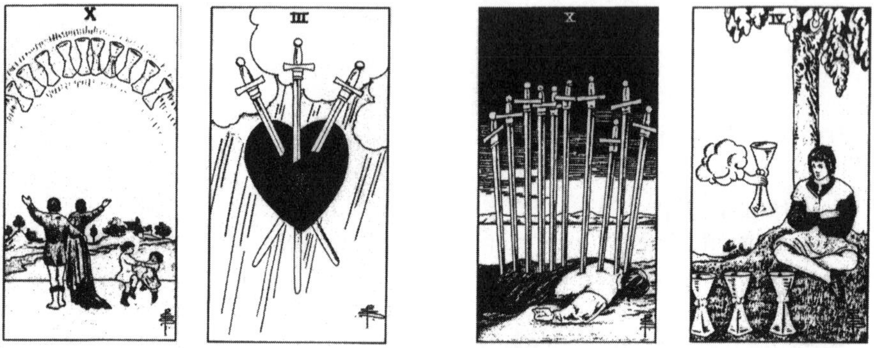

The cards Cathy and her mom chose to represent themselves (left) and each other (right).

Cathy noticed right away that she and her mom both chose challenging-looking cards to represent her mom: the 3 of Swords and the 10 of Swords. "My mom said she picked the 3 of Swords because of the big red heart—she loves red," Cathy said. "Ignoring, I suppose, those three swords piercing the heart!" And what about those storm clouds gathering in the background? Cathy mused. Did her mom not notice those? "I'm really not a count-your-blessings kind of person," Cathy's mom said. "I enjoy the good things life provides, but I worry about what could go wrong next. There are struggles in life, and things are not easy. Who knows what loss might be around the next bend?"

Cathy realized her mom *did* notice the clouds and the piercing swords, and that was precisely why her mom chose this card. "Within our family, we sometimes call Mom the NVM, or Negative Vibe Merchant," Cathy said. "She has a way of always seeing the half-empty glass, the rain clouds on the horizon. I can say this because she's my mom and we've talked about it. The 3 of Swords that my mom chose to represent herself is a card of heartache and disappointment. This is not to say that my mom has had more than her fair share of these, whatever a fair share might be, but that's how she tends to view things. She has a tendency to dwell on the struggle and the loss, rather than the bounty. We work to get her to enjoy life more and recognize the good things."

The card Cathy chose for herself, the joyous 10 of Cups, is the Tarot's happily-ever-after card. It represents happiness and fulfillment—how Cathy feels about her life. There is an abundance of Water energy, the Element of Cathy's Pisces ♓ Sun ☉. "The card I selected for myself looks like a fairy tale, doesn't it?" Cathy said. "A rainbow of cups in the sky, dancing children, the happy parents surveying the beauty and bounty before them. What can I say? I have a good life. *Very good.* I picked this card because it shows a happy family, and that's a big part of my life. I have a wonderful family life, a great husband, a terrific daughter, and when I can see past the areas of my life that are chaos, I feel like this card, overjoyed with my bounty."

To represent her daughter, Cathy's mom picked the 4 of Cups. "It reminds me of Cathy sitting quietly in nature," Cathy's mom said. "And those crossed arms make the person look somewhat stubborn, like Cathy can be sometimes." When Cathy let her Psychic Intuition explore the card her mom chose, she experienced distance and detachment. Here was this beautiful tree, and a hand coming from nowhere to offer yet another cup. Yet the character on the card just sits, contemplating the three cups on the grass and seeming not to even see the fourth one. This person appears so lost in personal issues that the outside world doesn't even exist!

"I'd like to think my mom chose this card because of the tree, but I suspect it's more because of the detachment she sees in me," Cathy said. "My family is very undemonstrative and I am sometimes reserved, which can be seen as withholding, I know. It may also be true that I don't spend enough energy on the emotional needs of others, and I am pretty introverted. So, especially in terms of my relationship with my mom, she picked a telling card for me. If nothing else, it makes me see that I should think about her feelings more often, and not think that my detached observations (*'you're always so negative'*) are really helpful or even considerate."

To represent her mom, Cathy chose the 10 of Swords. Although the imagery of the swords piercing the body lying so still on the ground is intense, this is a card that represents the end of a cycle and the completion of grief. It's dark and cloudy, yet the horizon shines bright in the distance. "The swords made me think of how everything negative seems to be bombarding my mom all the time—or at least that's how it seems to her," Cathy said. "I know this looks like a frightening card, with the desolate background and the person immobilized by the swords, but I didn't choose it because I wish my mom would have 10 swords through her body! Perhaps this is more about how I see my mom and her role in our relationship than my mom herself. We have to complete our cycle, work through our grief and loss, so a new cycle can begin."

Now try this exercise for your family. Like Cathy and her mom did, first identify your Sun ☉ signs (from your astrological charts or birth dates) and their Elemental associations. Then select Tarot cards from the related suit (use the table earlier in this chapter)—pick a card to represent yourself and cards to represent each other family member. Write your selections here, or record them in your Intuitive Arts notebook.

Person	Astro Sign	Element	Tarot Suit	Card for Self	Cards for Others
________	________	________	________	________	________
________	________	________	________	________	________
________	________	________	________	________	________
________	________	________	________	________	________

You can do this exercise for any part of your family. Better yet, have other family members participate, as well. You don't need to know the meanings of the cards for this exercise—it's strictly intuitive. Choose a card within your suit that appeals to you, with imagery that you find meaningful or representative. Don't think too much about your card choices—put your Psychic Intuition in charge. If you analyze the cards too much, you may find it difficult to make a choice.

Once you've selected your cards, make some notes in your Intuitive Arts notebook about *why* you selected the cards you did. If you're doing the exercise alone, make notes on why you chose particular cards to represent each family member. If family members are doing this exercise with you, let them explain, in turn, why they chose the cards they did—for themselves and for others.

It's often insightful to see how others perceive us. Because this exercise is intuitive, the selection of a card for its imagery can surface hidden knowledge, feelings, or beliefs about ourselves and our family members. It can be very interesting to see the cards your children or your spouse or your siblings select for you. What might your sister be trying to say about you when she selects the 8 of Swords for you, your father when he chooses the 4 of Pentacles, or your brother when he picks the 10 of Wands?

What might these cards reveal when family members choose them to represent each other?

You can then put the cards together in various ways to form pictures of your family (all the different cards chosen for each person, for example, or the entire family in cards each person selected to represent himself or herself). What story do the cards tell? It's useful to repeat this exercise over time, and to keep track of the cards family members choose. You might find that at times of family crisis or discord, the cards people select are particularly unbalanced or have potentially negative connotations. You can use the discussion of imagery and representation to open up a positive dialogue about perceptions and assumptions.

Your Elemental Family Signature: Read the Signs

Finding your Sun ☉ sign's Element, as you did in the preceding Tarot exercise, is a good place to start when it comes to understanding how the fundamentals of Astrology affect your family's relationships. Your birth chart tells you more about the Elemental you … and how you relate with other family members. From this you can determine your overall Elemental balance—your Elemental Family Signature.

Let's look at the birth charts of a famous mother/daughter pair—the effervescent and beautiful actress Goldie Hawn whose daughter, Kate Hudson, is following her mother's footsteps. We'll start with mom Goldie.

To begin, let's find Goldie's Elemental Family Signature signs: the placements of her Sun ☉, Moon ☽, Mercury ☿, Venus ♀, and Mars ♂, and her ascendant. The five personal planets indicate how we truly are to our loved ones and the close associates in our lives. The ascendant reflects how we appear to those outside our inner circle of relationships. Here are the signs that give us Goldie's Elemental Family Signature:

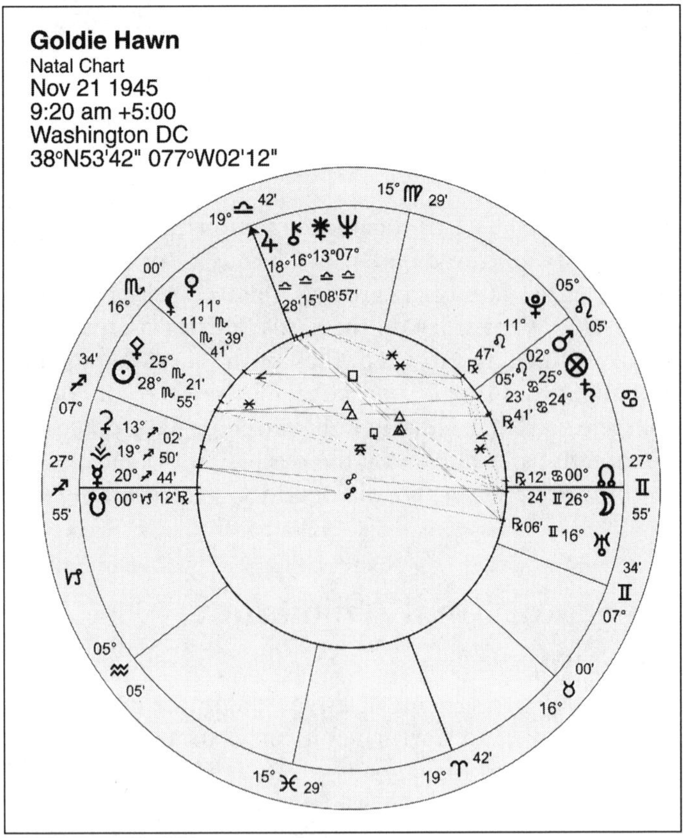

Actress Goldie Hawn's birth chart.

Astro Planet	Astro Sign	Astro Element
Sun ☉	Scorpio ♏	Water
Moon ☽	Gemini ♊	Air
Mercury ☿	Sagittarius ♐	Fire
Venus ♀	Scorpio ♏	Water
Mars ♂	Leo ♌	Fire
Ascendant	Sagittarius ♐	Fire

Next, we tallied how many signs Goldie has in each Element:

Element	Number of Signs
Fire	3
Earth	0
Air	1
Water	2

Goldie has an intriguing Elemental blend. With her Sun ☉ in intense Water sign Scorpio ♏ and her Moon ☽ in perky, talkative Air sign Gemini ♊, we know this is a progressive, transformational individual. Sun in Scorpio meditates and contemplates conditions that are unseen by the human eye, while Moon in Gemini asks the questions "Why?" and "How did you come to that conclusion?" Goldie is always digging beneath the surface of situations, in her personal life and in her work, with the intent to create a better life for herself and her family.

When we look at the tally of Elements, we see that the predominant Element is Fire. This gives Goldie an Elemental Family Signature of Fire, suggesting a person whose adventurous spirit supports and applauds new and innovative ways of working around problems. Such a person takes the "just do it" approach to any and all experiences. The Elemental Family Signature of Fire needs to experience, at least once, every condition in life. This signature wants to grow, create, and produce, and tries not to waste too much time on the details! When it comes to movers and shakers, the Zodiac turns to the Fire signs.

Now let's take a look at the birth chart for Goldie's daughter, the charming and talented Kate Hudson. Arlene cast a noon chart for Kate, so Kate could have different ascendant and Moon ☽ signs than what the noon chart indicates depending on how far from noon she was born.

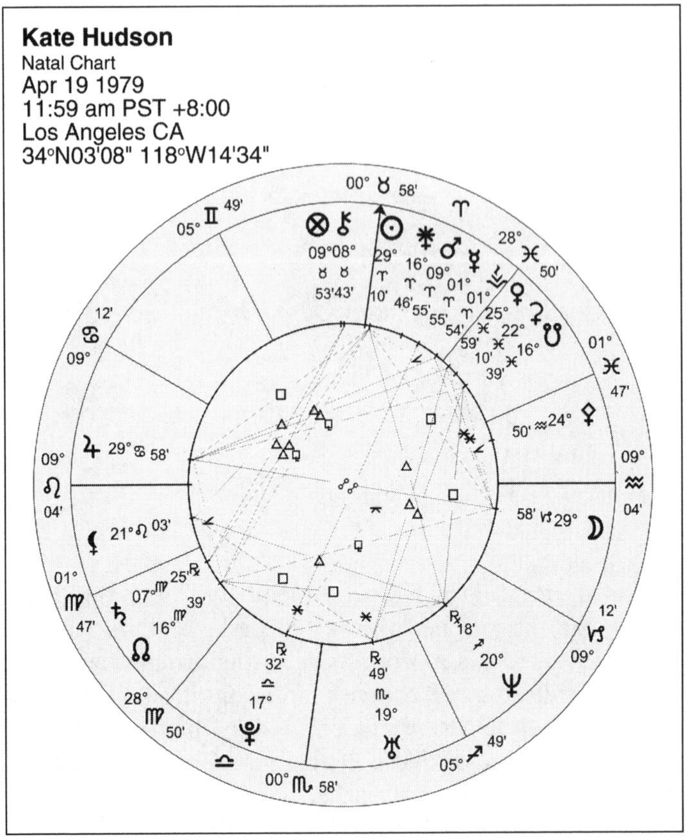

Actress Kate Hudson's birth chart.

As we did for mom Goldie, let's look at Kate's birth chart to determine her Elemental Family Signature. First, we note the sign for each of Kate's personal planets and for her ascendant. Then we identify the Element for each sign.

Astro Planet	Astro Sign	Astro Element
Sun ☉	Aries ♈	Fire
Moon ☽	Capricorn ♑	Earth
Mercury ☿	Aries ♈	Fire
Venus ♀	Pisces ♓	Water
Mars ♂	Aries ♈	Fire
Ascendant	Leo ♌	Fire

Next, we total the signs Kate has in each Element:

Element	**Number of Signs**
Fire	4
Earth	1
Air	0
Water	1

Like mother like daughter, and then some—Goldie Hawn and Kate Hudson both have Fire as their Elemental Family Signatures! Fire harmonizes with Fire in that there is a mutual understanding of how each uses her power, drive, and ambition. This mother/daughter team likely interacts in a very enthusiastic way, cheering each other on. The Fire signs (Aries ♈, Leo ♌, and Sagittarius ♐) have in common an optimistic attitude and belief that anything can be accomplished—they share an outgoing, positive, and sometimes overly enthusiastic approach to life.

With her fiery, freedom-loving Sun ☉ in adventurous Aries ♈, Kate will try new things in life just to experience the experience. She's a hands-on person who learns by trying something new. Kate likes to experiment with new ideas and new avenues for work, and she loves trying out new concepts. She *needs* to experience every experience or emotion that humans are. She is funny and witty like her mom—they share a great sense of humor as well as a "don't sweat the small stuff, everything is small stuff!" attitude.

Kate's Moon ☽ is in the Earth sign Capricorn ♑, which pushes her to work diligently toward any goal. She focuses on career and service to the public, and has the ability to use the difficult parts of her own life to see (and help us see) that we are all in this life experience together.

How does their shared Elemental Family Signature affect the way Goldie Hawn and Kate Hudson combine as Mother and Daughter? As the table earlier in this chapter shows, a Fire + Fire combination is conditional. With nearly the same balance of Fire signs (Goldie has three and Kate has four), these two are equally fiery. They could feed each other's passions ... or become intensely competitive. Each has her Venus ♀, the planet of love, in a Water sign, though, establishing a harmonious flow between them to support a loving relationship. However explosive things might become, this flow helps to soothe wounded feelings.

What's your Elemental Family Signature? Let's look at your birth chart. Find each of your personal planets, and write down each planet's sign. Also find your ascendant (the sign on the cusp of your 1st house), and write its sign, too. Then identify the Element for each of those signs (refer to the table earlier in this chapter if you need to) and write it in the table.

Astro Planet	**Astro Sign**	**Astro Element**
Sun ☉	____________	____________
Moon ☽	____________	____________
Mercury ☿	____________	____________
Venus ♀	____________	____________
Mars ♂	____________	____________
Ascendant	____________	____________

Now, total up how many signs you've got in each Element.

Element	**Number of Signs**
Fire	____________
Earth	____________
Air	____________
Water	____________

Which Element appears most? This is your Elemental Family Signature. Write it here: ________________________________

There's more to you than your Elemental Family Signature, of course, just as there's more to you than your Sun ☉ sign. The other Elements in which you have planets also influence your beliefs, thoughts, desires, and actions, and we talk more about this in later chapters. From your Elemental Family Signature, however, you can learn how you and other family members relate to one another and try to meet each other's needs.

A Mandala for a Model Family

A *mandala* is a geometrically patterned, circular diagram, often symmetrical, made of symbolic images. The word is Sanskrit and means "circle of healing." Many people use mandalas to guide their meditations. A mandala that you create yourself can have incredible meaning for you, serving as a powerful tool of Psychic Intuition to help you manifest your vision of the family you'd like for yours to be.

There are many ways to create a mandala, from simple drawings on paper to elaborate computer-generated images. Tibetan monks have become famous for their mandalas, made painstakingly with colored rice or sand, which take months or years to complete. The power of a mandala is in the intent with which you make it and the symbolism it has for you. Once completed, the mandala is like a portal that gives your Psychic Intuition access to the energy of the universe. It is both a means of projection and of regeneration. Using your mandala to meditate opens you to the wisdom, love, and strength the energy of the universe offers.

For your family mandala, we want you to create a geometric pattern that symbolizes, for you, the family that you desire. Because your family is a structure that you construct with care and over time, we're going to have you create a mandala with similar care and loving attention. It might take you some time to decide what to use and how to design your mandala, and this is fine. The process of crafting your mandala is just as important as the mandala itself.

Here's what you need:

- A piece of heavy paper or light cardboard, cut into a circle with at least a 12-inch diameter
- A pencil
- Magazines, newspapers, old family photos—all that you can rip up
- A glue stick
- Colored markers, paints, or crayons

Think of a geometric design that to you represents the concept of family. You can practice sketching your ideas on paper until you're certain of the design you want. Draw the design onto your circle. The only "rule" is that your design should have a clear center that aligns with the center of the circle. We suggest you do this in pencil first; you can come back to it later and go over it with colored markers, paints, crayons, or whatever you want to do to enhance it.

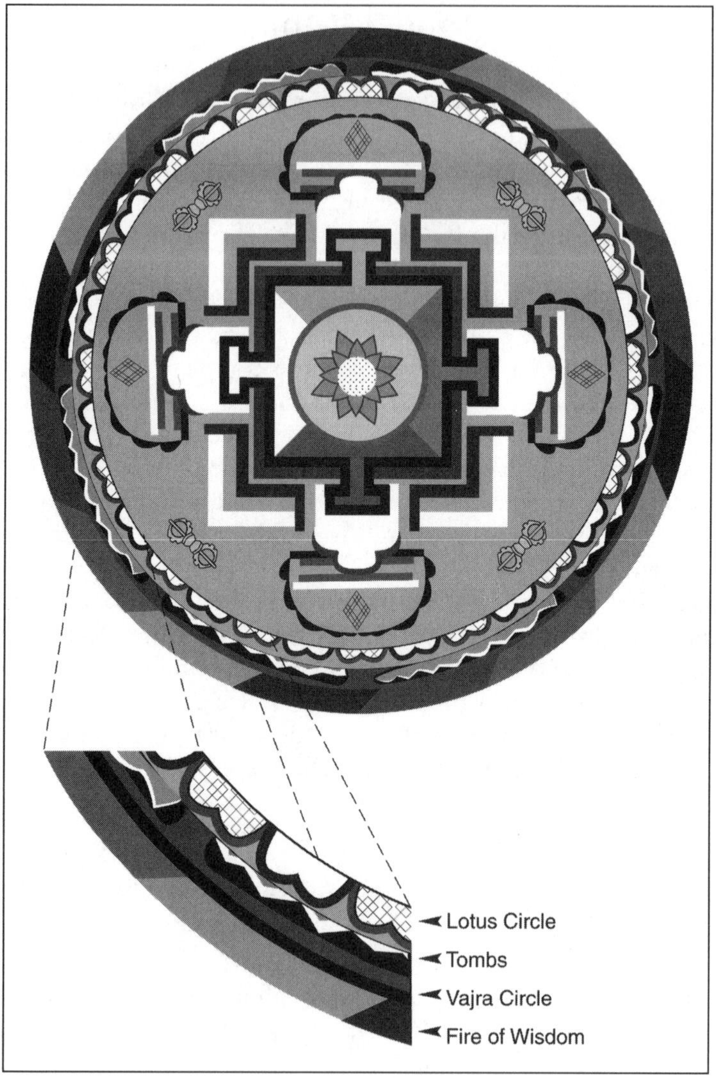

Create your own mandala.

Choose items from magazines and newspapers, and items such as old family photos and other memorabilia, that represent family to you. Make sure the family items are ones you can destroy. Once you've gathered a good supply, tear each item into small pieces—you're going to place them like tiles to execute the design of your mandala. You can keep the pieces of each item separate or mix them together. They can be of varying sizes, but none should be larger than a dime. What you want to see in your finished mandala is the symbolic representation of your design—*not,* as you would with a collage, the elements that go into making it. Consider the colors and textures of the pieces.

Begin gluing the pieces into the pattern you drew on your circle. Take your time; remember, this is as much about the process as the finished product. Place each piece with purpose and intent, and focus on the representation of family that you're creating. When you have all the pieces glued in place, you can go back now to color or otherwise enhance the lines of your pattern if you choose.

Use your mandala to meditate. Sit in a comfortable position, in a quiet location where you can be free of interruptions for 10 to 20 minutes. The mandala can induce a deep meditative state. Hold the mandala in both hands and take three deep, cleansing breaths. Look at your mandala, and let the inner vision of your Psychic Intuition see and explore the pattern. Feel the intent with which you crafted the mandala, the purpose you had in mind, the model family you desire to have.

When you feel ready to end your meditation, slowly allow your vision to return to the control of your eyesight. Continue looking at the mandala until you are again fully aware of your surroundings. Take three deep, restorative breaths. When you're not using it to meditate, you can put your mandala on the wall where you can see it, so it can be a continual reminder of what you envision as your model family.

Your Elemental Family

Within your family, you might have just a few Elemental combinations—or too many to count. When there are just two of you, the combination is pretty straightforward. When there are four or five or six of you, the possibilities can make your head spin! Each family member adds a different texture and balance to the mix.

When Lawrence and Carole sat down with daughters Sara and Sasha to do their Elemental Family Signatures, they found that they were a Fire (Lawrence), an Earth (Carole), and two Airs (Sara and Sasha). To figure out what this Elemental combination said about how they relate to, and interact with, one another, they first wrote it out:

Fire + Earth + Air + Air

Going back to the table earlier in this chapter, they next identified the possible pairings and determined whether they were supportive, challenging, or conditional:

Fire + Earth = Challenging
Fire + Air = Supportive
Earth + Air = Conditional
Air + Air = Conditional

Right away, they could see the reasons for some of their family cohesiveness as well as challenges. As a *yang* Fire and a *yin* Earth, Lawrence and Carole balance each other's energies at the core level of their relationship. This helps to offset the challenging combination of Fire + Earth in their Elemental Family Signatures. It's this Fire + Earth combination, however, that accounts for some of the tension between them. We can use our Elemental key characteristics, listed at the start of this chapter, to describe how this plays out.

Practical and **hardworking,** Carole likes to keep the home fires burning. She's **content** to stay at home, **nurturing** her family and providing for their needs. **Adventurous** and **passionate,** Lawrence dives into everything he does with great **enthusiasm.** He loves nothing more than being involved in **physical** activities, especially those that are **competitive,** and is constantly on the go.

When it comes to interactions with their daughters, Lawrence generally gets their cooperation while Carole often finds things turning confrontational. Lawrence and Carole have joked about this as a representation of the relationships between Fathers and Daughters and Mothers and Daughters. In looking at the Elemental Family Signatures, however, both Lawrence and Carole realize there's more to it.

Fire + Air, Lawrence's Elemental combination with each of his daughters, is supportive. Father and Daughters fuel each other—their **inventiveness** sparks his **passion** and **competitive** nature. His **adventurous** spirit encourages their **idealism** and desire for **social** interaction. Carole's Earth + Air Elemental combination with her daughters is conditional. Depending on the situation or circumstances, these energies either support or challenge each other. Although Carole's **intuitive** nature connects with the **thoughtful** side of her daughters, her need to be **emotional** in expressing her affection and feelings collides with their more **detached** demeanors.

The girls, too, can see that their Elemental combination of Air + Air sometimes supports and sometimes challenges their relationship with each other. Three years apart in age, each daughter has a clear sense of who she is and how she fits in her world. Each is **idealistic** and **intellectual**, giving a perception of self-centeredness, and doesn't always tune in when the other is feeling down or irritated.

Looking at the balance of Elements in their family, they could see that although they might not always see things eye to eye—what with the practical Earth, the passionate Fire, and the lofty, verbal Air—Lawrence and Carole will bring enthusiasm and groundedness to their daughters, who in turn will induce their parents to become more verbal in how they express themselves.

To gain further insight into their family dynamics, Lawrence brought out the Tarot deck. In Tarot, the court cards—King, Queen, Knight, and Page—represent people. Archetypally, the King represents the Father figure, the Queen the Mother figure, and the Knight and Page the older and younger child. For himself, Lawrence pulled out the King of Wands—Wands is the Tarot suit affiliated with the Element of Fire, and Lawrence is the Father figure in his family. Carole took the Queen of Pentacles. As the older Daughter, Sara got the Knight of Swords, and as the younger Daughter, Sasha was the Page of Swords.

The Tarot cards representing Lawrence, Carole, Sara, and Sasha.

Lawrence feels that the King of Wands card suits him. All the orange and gold in the card feels prosperous and generous, characteristics that Carole and the girls agree fit him. The lions and lizards on the king's robe and behind him on the throne represent growth and new beginnings—Lawrence's sense of adventure that takes him into new areas of personal exploration. The king holds his wand—the torch of light and life—with confidence and passion. This king, like Lawrence, is a good mentor and Father.

Sara observes that the Queen of Pentacles is the quintessential Earth Mother, and her mother agrees. The colors of generosity—orange, yellow, red, and green—fill this card. This queen looks as though she's finally sitting down to rest and enjoy the abundance of her efforts. She gazes at the golden coin she holds in her lap, surrounded by a bounty of greenery, flowers, and fruit. This queen is the picture of abundance—a creative, generous, and nurturing mother, just like Carole.

Lawrence and Carole place their two cards next to each other. Despite the challenging nature of their Fire + Earth Elemental combination, these two cards seem to fit together. Nonetheless, no matter how these cards are placed, one always has the back to the other. Lawrence and Carole read this as a message that they need to take care, in their relationship with each other, to be mindful of the other's needs.

Sara is less than enthusiastic about her card, the Knight of Swords. He looks like he's rushing in without regard for where he's going or why he's there, she says. (Carole smiles; to her this card suits her older daughter to a T!) This knight's horse doesn't appear to have even one foot on the ground, and the knight's head is clearly in the clouds. The knight appears intense and focused on his mission, whatever it is. Lawrence points out that Sara is just like this—she commits herself fully to whatever she's doing, and can manage multiple "missions" simultaneously. Sara agrees with her dad that she does sometimes rush into things, and doesn't always care what other people might think about what she's doing.

Also an Air Element, the Page of Swords looks more innocent than the Knight of Swords and, well, a little flighty. The page stands at the ready to take action, but isn't doing anything yet. He appears to be waiting—for a signal, for the right circumstances, for the rest of the information? The page seems intent on thinking things through first. He's vigilant but won't do anything rash, yet stands with just one foot on the ground and his head in the clouds. Sasha agrees that this card is a good representation of her. Although she can be flighty, she generally thinks before acting. Even too much so, her mom observes, sometimes inhibiting her or causing her to miss opportunities.

When the girls put the two Swords together, they intuitively place the page as though he is following the knight. It's the only way the combination makes sense, they feel. Sara sees a message in the cards that she needs to slow down sometimes, to listen to what others (including her sister) have to say. Sasha wishes she could be more like the knight sometimes.

You can try this exercise with your family. First, use your astrological birth charts to identify the signs of your personal planets and your ascendant and their Elements. Then tally the Elements to determine your Elemental Family Signature. Write your Elemental combination like an equation, as we did for Lawrence, Carole, Sara, and Sasha. Then break it down into all possible pairings to see how the Elements support or challenge each other. Finally, choose the Tarot cards that represent each family member's Element and family position or role.

If yours is a family with a Mother and three children, the King might better represent your role in the family. If you can't decide, or feel that you are Mother and Father in equal parts, take both the King and the Queen in the suit of your Element to represent yourself! Are there more children than remaining court cards? Select other cards from the Element's suit that seem to represent them. Grandparents might be represented by cards from the Major Arcana—perhaps the Emperor to represent a Grandfather and the Empress a Grandmother. Let your Psychic Intuition choose!

Building Your Understanding

Whether it's enthusiastic Fire, productive Earth, inventive Air, or sensitive Water, an understanding of how each Element's energy influences behaviors and interactions can add a new dimension to your family dynamic. Now that you've read this chapter, you can add your new understanding of the Elements to your intuitive sense of these four essentials in your family, and begin to create the family harmony you want in your life.

chapter 4

Attracting the Love and Acceptance You Want

Signs and timing: The Tarot's Horoscope Spread
Elemental foundations
How does your family relate?
Aspects and the house of family
Psychic Intuition and your family wheel of energy

In this chapter, we use family Astrology, Tarot, and Psychic Intuition exercises to help you discover what it is you need from family members, what you want for your family, and how to get it. We do a Horoscope Tarot Spread, to look at the year ahead for your family, we do another Elemental Family Signature exercise, and we look at how planetary aspects in your astrological birth chart affect your family relationships. Finally, we practice meditating on your family goals: Learn to separate fantasy from reality and nurture real, loving family bonds.

Your House of Cards

What is an issue you feel will be important to your family in the coming year? Is there a question you have concerning your family for the same period? Or an energy you would like to manifest? The Tarot's Horoscope Spread gives some insights into what might be in store and how events might unfold over the course of the year. It follows the astrological wheel of houses, with one card placed for each house. This wheel is the foundation of your birth chart, and each house represents an area of your life.

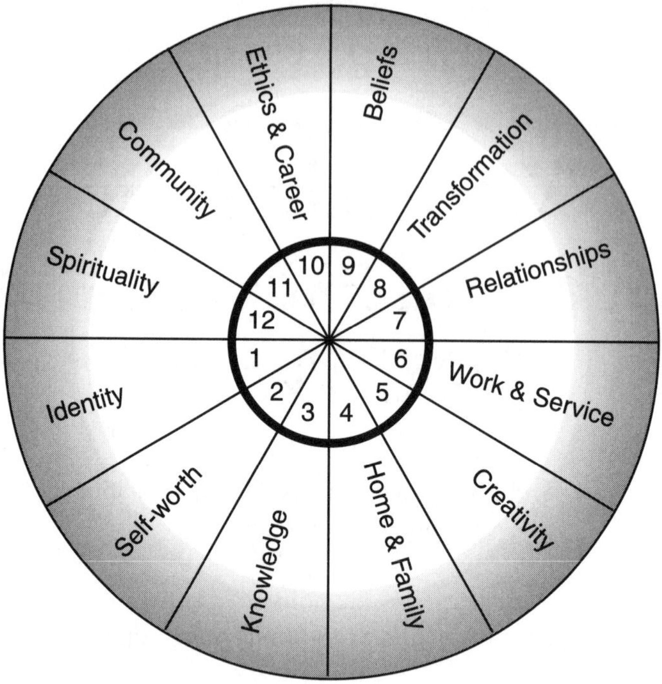

The 12 houses of Astrology.

The cards of the Horoscope Spread relate to the calendar, too: 12 houses … 12 months in the year. Each card that you place tells you two things: what to expect within the area of your life that the house represents, and about when in the year to expect it. For instance, the 1st house is all about your physical self and your personality. The Tarot card here shows you what is happening with you in these areas. It also tells you that these are events, issues, or circumstances to expect within the first of the next 12 months.

Let's do a Tarot Horoscope Spread now so you can see how this unfolds. Arlene did this Tarot reading for Sergio, who wanted to know if his relationship with his mother (his only parent) would become more harmonious in the coming year. Arlene shuffled the cards while she and Sergio focused on thoughts of Sergio's question and the year ahead. Then Arlene laid out the 12 cards. Like the houses in a birth chart, the cards are spread in a circle starting in the 1st house and moving counterclockwise through the rest of the houses. Each card represents a house and a month.

Let's look at each of the cards in Sergio's Horoscope Spread, and see what they have to say regarding his question.

Month 1: 5 of Swords. The 1st house relates to the physical self. The 5 of Swords signals a warning to Sergio. It could indicate destructive behavior in the coming month, or deceit or manipulation. There is also a possibility, with this card, that Sergio feels at a loss about how to communicate with his mother. The 5 of Swords may indicate a fear of intimacy or fear of being rejected. Sergio, his mother, or both of them might feel this fear. Sergio also needs to be aware of the stressful emotions he feels and to calm himself before he does speak with his mother.

Month 2: Page of Swords. The 2nd house deals with self-esteem and possessions. The Page of Swords is a messenger urging vigilance—this card asks that Sergio have the courage to take a close look at these areas of his life and brave possible setbacks. Sergio should use good common sense in dealing with his personal possessions and finances and try not to let himself become negative regarding his self-esteem during this time. Instead, he should study his situation closely and realize that a studious, resourceful, logical approach would better suit his present situation. This card also sounds a note of caution about signing any contracts at this time that could obligate Sergio financially.

Month 3: 2 of Pentacles. Siblings, knowledge, and environment are described in the 3rd house, and the juggler in the 2 of Pentacles indicates Sergio's ability to maintain balance in these areas. A project he wants to start may be difficult to get off the ground (mending his relationship with his mother?), but he should work hard to maintain balance and not let the slow start upset him. He must accept that it takes time to heal old wounds, and with this awareness he can communicate accordingly with his mother. He needs to be willing to let her make suggestions about how to proceed with their relationship, as well as making his own. Sergio should take things slowly, because this card indicates the need to balance and maintain focus. Patience is a virtue!

Month 4: Ace of Pentacles R. The 4th house deals with home and family, and the Ace of Pentacles in a reversed position here may indicate that Sergio needs to look at the situation he is trying to work on with his mother, to be sure he is prepared for the next step before making any decisions. The first meeting or condition may be a little slow to get off the ground, and Sergio may also have different values than his mother about family or family of origin issues; he and his mother may not see eye to eye on past issues in their family. Both could be preoccupied with guilt, or be defensive and wary of getting hurt.

Sergio's Horoscope Spread.

Month 5: 9 of Pentacles R. The 5th house represents creativity, as well as children and romance. The 9 of Pentacles in a reversed position indicates that Sergio is not satisfied with the state of his home life; he's anxious, and he may fear losing what he's worked for. He has had some setbacks financially and may be afraid of losing something of value or his security. This card may also indicate that what he has been doing in life could be risky or speculative. This could relate to his love life or a family relationship or to decisions about having his own family.

Month 6: 2 of Wands. The 6th house represents personal responsibilities and health, particularly as relates to daily routine. The 2 of Wands is a card of delays and waiting. Events are in motion, but results are slow to manifest. Sergio can anticipate positive outcomes, perhaps in regard to his day-to-day relationship with his mother, but may have to be patient when they don't happen on his timetable. Because Sergio is waiting and watching for new opportunities, however, he won't miss them. Despite delays, his vigilance will pay off.

Month 7: Queen of Swords. The 7th house relates to primary relationships, and the appearance of the Queen of Swords here could represent Sergio's desire to connect with his mother. Like the Queen of Swords, Sergio's mother is intelligent, thoughtful, and logical. She, like Sergio, has known sorrow and loss, and desires to work through the grief that separates her son from her. The Queen of Swords is upright in this spread, indicating that Sergio's mother will be open to him and supportive of what he would like to know. This card also can relate in a more general way to Sergio's self-esteem when it comes to women, suggesting that once Sergio works through his issues with his mother, he will be better able to form relationships with other women.

Month 8: 3 of Pentacles. Joint resources and transformation are the realm of the 8th house. The 3 of Pentacles here indicates that some recognition will come for hard work, perhaps in the form of a bonus or a promotion in the near future. This house's connection with regeneration suggests that Sergio might finally heal old wounds and transform his life through meeting and relating with his mother, because this is the focus of his concerns—Mother and family issues.

Month 9: Knight of Cups. The 9th house represents travel, education, beliefs, and other social areas. Sergio may find himself traveling during the ninth month following this Horoscope Spread reading. However, Sergio could find himself on a journey of the heart as he does some soul searching about his relationship with his mother. If he can open his heart and his mind, his beliefs about relationships will change and he will be able to accept new relationships in his life.

Month 10: The Hierophant R. The 10th house relates to career and public reputation, and the Hierophant in a reversed position may signify some unconventional ideas and behavior, or perhaps a new direction, in Sergio's career. Old conditions in the workplace or career environment will certainly change. Sergio may accept a new offer in his career arena or he may find himself embarking on a very different career path—one he didn't plan on. This change may appear unconventional when it first arrives, but Sergio will be open to accepting it, and as a result, he may see his career—and his life—from a new perspective. Will his mother approve of these changes? Sergio would like for that to be the case, and might be pleasantly surprised!

Month 11: Justice R. The 11th house is the house of goals, and Justice reversed here indicates the possibility of unwise decisions. Sergio should beware of making any questionable agreements or arrangements with friends or groups in the eleventh month of this reading's year and should try to be aware of biased views or delays in attaining the truth he seeks. What Sergio desires and wishes for (perhaps a renewal of his relationship with his mother) is coming, but this card reversed would indicate a twist in direction, or a turn of events that seems unfair. This may slow Sergio's progress, but he should remember that the block may be a stepping-stone in disguise!

Month 12: Ace of Swords. The 12th house relates to the subconscious and to past karma. The Ace of Swords signifies the beginning of a project that will prove successful, provided it is acted upon swiftly and decisively. This card indicates that Sergio has made it through a difficult period, and now, at the end of the year, he is focused and strong enough to work out the project successfully. He may finally be in a place to resolve things with his mother. New courage and perseverance will bring victory, and past feelings and karmic lessons will be learned and accepted. This card indicates that conclusion will come in a satisfactory way!

Now try a Horoscope Spread for yourself. You can ask a question about a specific family member, or something more general about the situation of your family in the next year. Will you resolve things with your brother? Will you and your sister settle your differences? Will your family finally find abundance this year? Focus on your concern or question while you shuffle your Tarot cards, and then lay out 12 cards to follow the wheel of the astrological houses. Make your notes here or in your Intuitive Arts notebook about what this spread says in relation to your question for your family in the coming year.

Your family question for the coming 12 months: ________________

____

1st house (physical self) card: ________________________

Month 1 Message: ______________________________

2nd house (self-esteem and possessions) card: ________________

____

Month 2 Message: ________________________________

3rd house (siblings, knowledge/communication, and environment) card: ________________________________

Month 3 Message: ________________________________

4th house (home and family) card: ________________________

Month 4 Message: ________________________________

5th house (creativity, children, and romance) card: ____________

____

Month 5 Message: ________________________________

6th house (daily routine, personal responsibilities and health) card:

____

Month 6 Message: ________________________________

7th house (primary relationships) card: ____________________

Month 7 Message: ________________________________

8th house (joint resources and transformation) card: ___________

____

Month 8 Message: ________________________________

9th house (travel, education, and beliefs) card: _______________

____

Month 9 Message: ________________________________

10th house (career and public reputation) card: ______________

____

Month 10 Message: ______________________________

11th house (life goals) card: ______________________

Month 11 Message: ______________________________

12th house (subconscious) card: ____________________

Month 12 Message: ______________________________

Tell Me What You Want, and I'll Give You What You Need

To look at how we get what we want in our family relationships, let's return to Astrology's four Elements—Fire, Earth, Air, and Water. We explored the Elemental Family Signature in Chapter 3, to see how compatible family members were. (Remember the charts for Goldie Hawn and Kate Hudson?) Now we'll find the Elemental Family Signature for two more people, Mel Gibson and Jennifer Lopez, and use the signature to look deeper into their astrological birth charts to see what the charts say about how Mel and Jennifer create and nurture family relationships in their lives. Here's a refresher on the astrological signs and their Elements.

Fire	Earth	Air	Water
Aries ♈	Taurus ♉	Gemini ♊	Cancer ♋
Leo ♌	Virgo ♍	Libra ♎	Scorpio ♏
Sagittarius ♐	Capricorn ♑	Aquarius ♒	Pisces ♓

We start with Mel Gibson, that independent Aussie superstar who also happens to be the Father of seven! Here's Mel's birth chart.

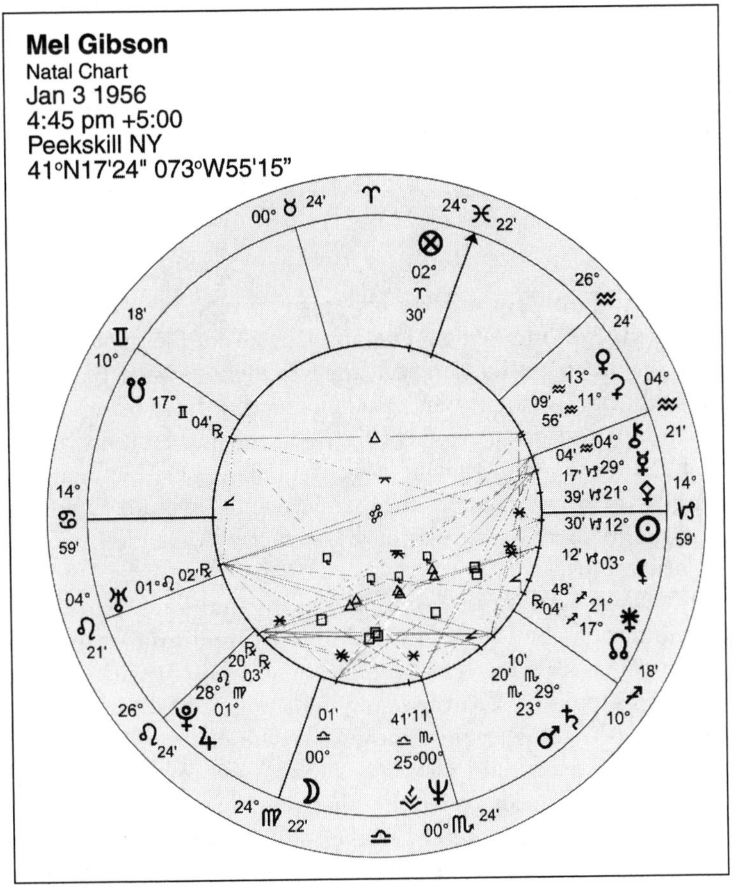

Mel Gibson's birth chart.

First we look for Mel's rising sign and his personal planets—the Sun ☉, the Moon ☽, Mercury ☿, Venus ♀, and Mars ♂. The signs these planets are in determine their Elements.

Astro Planet	**Astro Sign**	**Astro Element**
Ascendant	Cancer ♋	Water
Sun ☉	Capricorn ♑	Earth
Moon ☽	Libra ♎	Air
Mercury ☿	Capricorn ♑	Earth
Venus ♀	Aquarius ♒	Air
Mars ♂	Scorpio ♏	Water

From this, we can see how many signs Mel has in each Element:

Element	**Number of Signs**
Fire	0
Earth	2
Air	2
Water	2

Mel has no Fire signs among his personal planets, and he has two each of Earth, Air, and Water. The absence of the Element Fire in his signature means that Mel will seek that Element outside of himself. The equal distribution of the other signs tells us that he is both emotional and grounded, and quite sensitive to the needs and responsibility of family. The Fire Element that he needs to balance his Elemental Family Signature will likely be found in other Fire signs around him: He will integrate the Element he is missing by attracting that Element in his close relationships.

That Mel's ascendant is Cancer ♋ means that he is learning about family foundations and home life—family is important to the Cancer rising. He is also learning how to nurture and prepare his children for their lives and families. Cancer rising is the sign of family and learning how to parent—Mel is learning how to create his own "tribe," so to speak. A Cancer ascendant also needs the family unit for its own sense of rootedness. Mel needs to feel like he is participating in everyone's growth and well-being, whether in the family group or the work team.

Let's look now at a few houses in his chart in particular. The 4th house relates to home and family, and Mel's Moon ☽, the sign of his emotional self, appears here. This is significant because it stresses the importance for Mel of family and his sincere devotion to his loved ones. He is very nurturing with his family, and he relates well to children of all ages. With his Moon in the 4th house, Mel identifies emotionally with family and home—the center and the heart of his life!

The 5th house represents fun, romance, and children. Mel has Mars ♂ in this house, which makes him very good with children. (His other calling may have been to coach a school sport.) Mars in this house also indicates a strong sex drive, which could account for those seven children! And in the 6th house, which relates to work, we find Mel's Sun ☉. Mel has a strong sense of purpose about his work and about serving others, and when he feels called, he will give himself 100 percent to his work. When he is working, and also when he is creating a work environment, he needs to be completely focused.

The 7th house describes primary relationships, including marriage. With the personal planet Mercury ☿ in his 7th house, Mel's connections with his life and business partners are deep and communicative. He needs to have a partner who is intelligent, communicates in all areas of life, and is intellectually and mentally stimulating. Both in marriage and business partnerships, Mel needs his partners to be on the same page with him—it is important that they understand his mindset and the importance of family life for him.

Mercury in the 7th house indicates that for Mel's marriage with his wife to be successful, his wife would not mind that he becomes focused on his work when he is working. She would support his creative drive and understand that he cannot have interference when he is involved with a work or career project. She could take over the family duties without feeling left out or overburdened. When he's not involved in work, Mel's attention and focus returns completely to his family, and with a good partnership, neither area suffers from a lack of his attention!

Now let's look at the birth chart of another celebrity, pop icon Jennifer Lopez. Will Jennifer find success in creating a nurturing family? We say yes!

As we did for Mel Gibson, let's first look for Jennifer's ascendant and personal planets, their signs and Elements.

Astro Planet	**Astro Sign**	**Astro Element**
Ascendant	Virgo ♍	Earth
Sun ☉	Leo ♌	Fire
Moon ☽	Aries ♈	Fire
Mercury ☿	Leo ♌	Fire
Venus ♀	Virgo ♍	Earth
Mars ♂	Leo ♌	Fire

Now let's note how many signs Jennifer has in each Element:

Element	**Number of Signs**
Fire	4
Earth	2
Air	0
Water	0

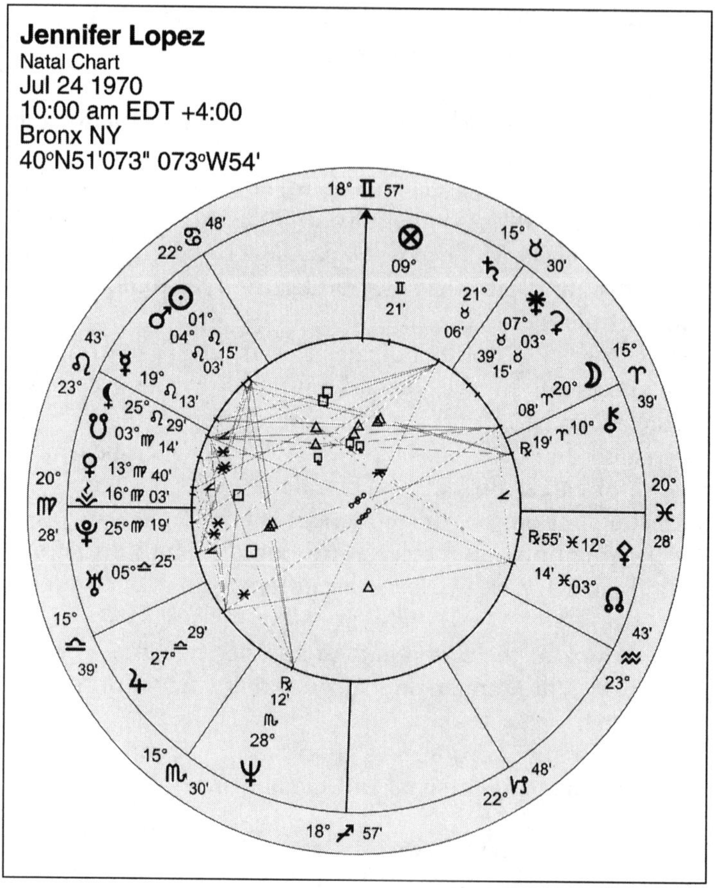

Jennifer Lopez's birth chart.

Jennifer has a lot of Fire among her personal planets, and a little Earth mixed in for balance, with no Water or Air signs. She is, well, *fiery*—passionate, creative, energetic. She is amazingly talented and focused on her passion. Jennifer has a need to follow her bliss. Her zeal and intensity are grounded in physical, sensual, earthy qualities. She can make her audience feel the physicality of her music, allowing them to feel the rhythm and dance of life through her.

Jennifer's Earth signs make her dig down deep into the realism of life, perhaps helping her to harness some of her fiery energy. Her ascendant is earthy Virgo ♍, making her work very important to her. Her planets of self, communication, and action—Sun ☉, Mercury ☿, and

Mars ♂—are all in strong, creative, and expressive Leo ♌ in the 11th house, which relates to goals as well as friendships. Yet her Moon ☽ in passionate Aries ♈ makes Jennifer independent and self-confident in love. Its placement in her 8th house makes her very charismatic, sensual, and appealing to both sexes. Her music also has a universal appeal: Many cultures and walks of life can identify with her.

The Elements Jennifer lacks in her Elemental Family Signature she would need to fulfill through others. She meets some of her emotional needs through her work, especially through the response of her audience and the public. This response keeps her thirsting for more—she wants to create emotional responses through all of her connections, including within her own family. She needs to balance her passion and her need for success from the outside world with her home and family life.

Now let's look at some of those family-related houses in Jennifer's chart. You'll notice right away that the 4th house, which relates to home and family, the 5th house, which represents romance and children, and the 7th house, which relates to marriage, have no planets in them. To find out about matters related to those houses, we need to look to the planets that rule the signs on the cusps of the houses.

Jupiter ♃ rules Sagittarius ♐ in her 4th house, indicating that Jennifer highly values family. The 4th house brings Jennifer toward her family as a support and keeps her working even stronger. She knows that there is that tribe of people cheering them on to her success. And Jupiter is in Libra ♎ in Jennifer's 2nd house of personal values, finances, and earning capacity, indicating that her family was able to get her into higher education and cultural pursuits early in her life. Jennifer would value the pursuit of the arts and relate it back to her family of origin. She truly believes in the strength of family.

Jennifer has her natal Saturn ♄ in Taurus ♉, but Saturn rules the sign in the 5th house, which is Capricorn ♑. Capricorn is a sign of serious thought and responsibility. With Saturn ruling her 5th house, which pertains to how one relates to children, Jennifer would naturally be focused on children's well-being, children's rights, and responsibility toward children. Jennifer, like Mel, loves kids and has given her support to many causes on behalf of children, the arts for children, and the well-being of children.

Jennifer has Pisces ♓ as the sign on her 7th house, so she is very idealistic about marriage and partnerships. She is *in love* with *love!* She has a great emotional attachment to love and romance, and could be married more than just once or twice. This is because she may continue searching for the very best love she can find. Jennifer always will be devoted to whomever she does love.

From her birth chart, it seems that Jennifer might find it difficult not to be constantly "out there" with the public feeding her emotions and her passion for music. She may need to look back at her parents and relate their ideals to her life to help her find the balance she seeks. She will be able to create this balance, and will be the type of mother who brings her kids to her rehearsals, concerts, or movie sets.

Now try this exercise for yourself. Look at your birth chart, and once again note the signs and Elements for each of the personal planets, and your ascendant, in the chart below. Look back to Chapter 3 and record your Elemental Family Signature.

My Elemental Family Signature is: ______________________.

Astro Planet	Astro Sign	Astro Element
Ascendant	____________	____________
Sun ☉	____________	____________
Moon ☽	____________	____________
Mercury ☿	____________	____________
Venus ♀	____________	____________
Mars ♂	____________	____________

How does your Elemental Family Signature relate to the placement of your personal planets and ascendant in your birth chart? Identify what you want in your family life, and see how it is represented in your chart. Look particularly in the houses we considered for Mel Gibson and Jennifer Lopez: the 4th, 5th, and 7th houses.

Your House	Your Planet(s)	Your Ruler(s)
4th house of home and family	____________	____________
5th house of creativity, home, and romance	____________	____________
7th house of primary relationships	____________	____________

If you don't find what you are looking for, think about what you might need to do to achieve the family life you want. What would be the best combination for your family? What you don't have in your own Elemental Family Signature, you will likely attract to create your own family. And you may also find that the members of your family with whom you relate to the best are also compatible with your Elemental family Signature. Think of a relative you're very simpatico with—the aunt you really, really love—and compare your Elemental Family Signature with hers. You could be surprised with what your birth charts show!

How Does Your Family Relate?

Let's do a quick Tarot spread to answer this question, or to ask how you would like your family to relate. This is a 4-card spread, and we'll use only the Major Arcana cards. As you spread out all 22 Major Arcana cards face down before you, focus on either how your family relates or how you would like your family to relate. Then from among the Major Arcana cards face down in front of you, choose four cards and lay them out face up in a diamond shape, like this:

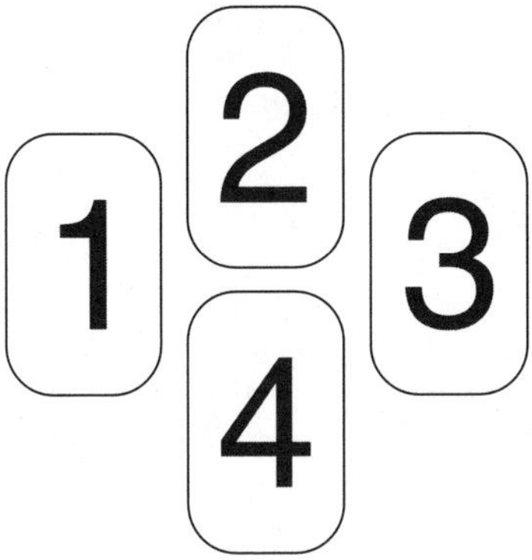

These cards represent the family dynamics you have today in your family, and also the lessons your family is learning now. You could do this reading once a year, or even more often, to see how your family is growing and evolving, or possibly even regressing. Here is a sample reading Arlene did for herself, asking herself how she and her family relate as we're writing this book.

Arlene's 4-card family relationship Tarot spread.

Here's Arlene's interpretation of the cards and her family dynamic: "We relate pretty well now; my parents are getting older, so my siblings and I are watching out for their health. There have also been some problems with them and another brother, so I think the Hanged Man describes the sacrifices we have made and will continue to make. My parents cannot visit or travel any longer, so we have to go to them. We are all relaxed with one another, and understand that we have different lives, and tend to realize more that life has its difficulties and strife, and this makes us appreciate one another more. I think my mother is the Empress, though this card might also be a collective representation of both my parents. Both Mom and Dad were always concerned about the family basics and made sure we were secure in home, shelter, food, and education.

"The Lovers are my brothers to me. We always had fun play-acting and loved to play together. We were quite creative, doing photography, being mimics and actors—my parents always thought it was great that we all connected strongly to the arts, and we got along very well. We lived in Los Angeles, and the movies and theater provided great ways for us to bond: We would act out movies and television shows, and also made home movies of our own adventures. The Lovers can be the artistic, creative urge we shared as siblings. We accepted one another's choices for work or lifestyle as we became adults. Judgement in this spread means to me that I have to get ready to handle things when my parents can't any more. The Hanged Man relates to this as well: We will all make necessary lifestyle changes as the elders need more of us."

Aspects: The House of Family

As we noted earlier, the 4th house is the house of family and home. We looked at this house in Jennifer Lopez's and Mel Gibson's birth charts. Let's look at Mel's chart again, and this time we'll be looking at the *aspects* in his chart. Aspects are simply the relationships between the planets in your birth chart. (To be exact, aspects are the angles the planets create.) We go through aspects in greater detail in Chapter 5, but for now we're going to look at what your aspects say about your house of family, the 4th house.

There are six major aspects, which can range the spectrum from favorable to challenging. We've listed these six aspects here.

Astro Aspect	**Symbol**	**Keywords**
Conjunction	☌	Neutral, energies intensify each other, unpredictable
Sextile	⚹	Favorable, opportunity or ability, attraction
Square	□	Challenging, needs action
Trine	△	Favorable, flowing, smooth, easy
Opposition	☍	Challenging, out of balance, competitive
Quincunx	⚻	Need for adjustment, change of attitude/behavior

If you look inside the center circle of Mel's chart, you will see lines as well as the symbols that appear in this table. These indicate the aspects in Mel's birth chart. You can also look at aspects using an *aspect grid.* The triangular aspect grid shows the aspects for all of the planets in your birth chart. Although the aspect grid looks complicated, it's really an easy way to look at aspects. Simply find the junction between two planets and note the symbol that appears in the grid box. In Mel's chart, for example, go down the left column to the symbol for Saturn ♄ and across the diagonal to the symbol for Mercury ☿. The symbol in the grid box at this intersection is a sextile ⚹, telling us that Mel enjoys a favorable aspect between these two planets.

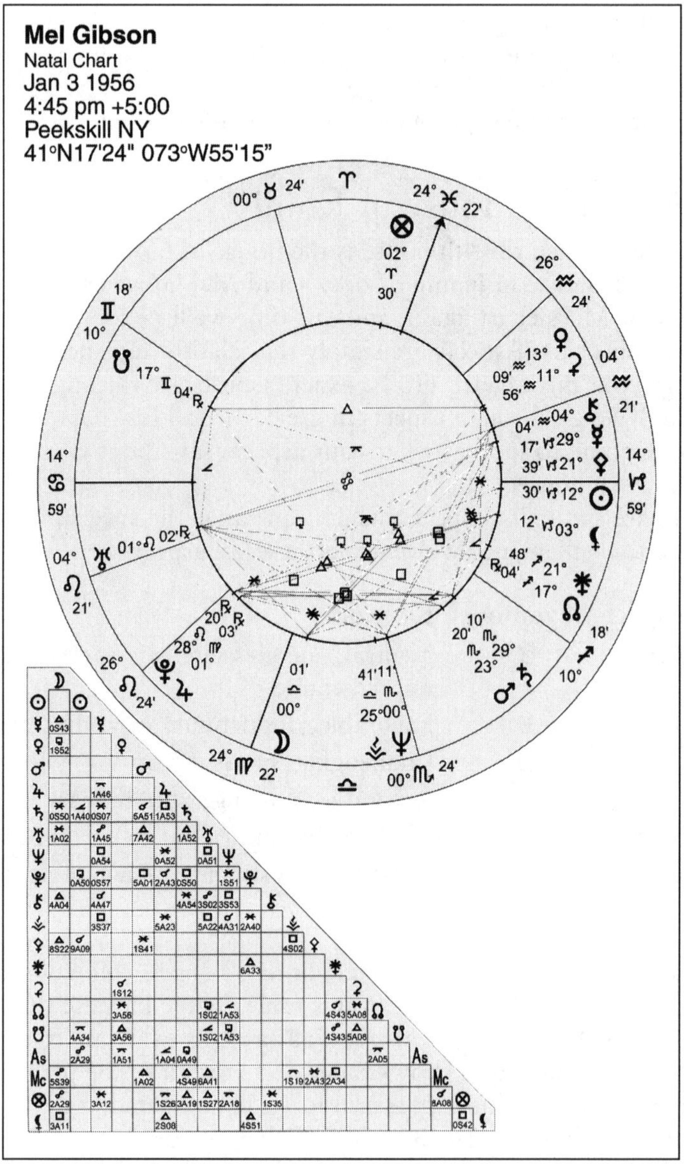

Mel Gibson's birth chart and aspect grid.

Aspects give you a way to find the flows of energy in your birth chart. Each kind of aspect has a particular energy ranging from challenging to favorable. So the energy of trines △ and sextiles △ flows smoothly, and the energy of squares □, oppositions ☍, and quincunxes ⚻ is tumultuous. The energy of a conjunction ☌ can be smooth or tumultuous, depending on the planets.

Let's look at Mel's birth chart and aspect grid, particularly in terms of his 4th house, to see what aspects he has in his house of family. Mel's Moon ☽ is in Libra ♎ in his 4th house, and Neptune ♆ in Scorpio ♏ is also in this house. Mel has trines △ and sextiles ⚹ with his Moon ☽, but Neptune ♆, on the other hand, has a number of squares □. We've completed a chart indicating Mel's aspects for his 4th house of family and whether they are supportive or challenging.

Planet	Astro Aspect	Planet	Supportive or Challenging?
Moon ☽ in Libra ♎	Trine △	Mercury ☿ (7th house)	Supports family communication
Moon ☽ in Libra ♎	Sextile ⚹	Saturn ♄ (5th house)	Supports discipline and mutual respect
Moon ☽ in Libra ♎	Sextile ⚹	Uranus ♅ (1st house)	Supportive; his personality is accepted by family; he needs this acceptance
Neptune ♆ in Scorpio ♏	Square □	Mercury ☿ (7th house)	Challenging; Mel's creative drive can overpower his need to stay home; frustration may be felt by his partner
Neptune ♆ in Scorpio ♏	Square □	Uranus ♅ (1st house)	Challenging; Mel would need to make a few sacrifices in career or family life
Neptune ♆ in Scorpio ♏	Square □	Chiron ⚷ (7th house)	Challenging to his spouse/partners; biggest challenge to his family is his need to be in the public
Neptune ♆ in Scorpio ♏	Sextile ⚹	Jupiter ♃ (3rd house)	Supports Mel's ability to get into his characters!

As you can see, we can discover a lot about Mel and his family by looking at his planetary aspects. Now take a look at your own birth chart—if you have an aspect grid as well, you can also use it. See what planets you have in your 4th house and also look at the aspects for those planets. Note your findings in the following chart, and also note whether these are challenging or supportive aspects.

Planet	**Astro Aspect**	**Planet**	**Supportive or Challenging?**
___________	___________	___________	___________
___________	___________	___________	___________
___________	___________	___________	___________
___________	___________	___________	___________

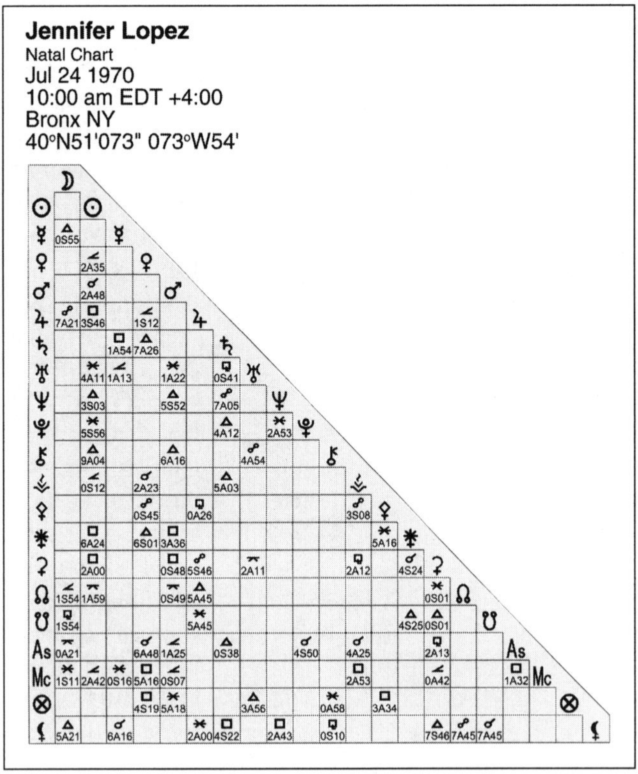

Aspect grid for Jennifer Lopez.

Do you have mostly challenging or supportive aspects in your 4th house? If there are no planets in your 4th house (remember, this was the case for Jennifer Lopez), then look to the ruler of that house, Jupiter ♃, for insight. If no other planets appear in your 4th house, the aspects between Jupiter and the other planets would tell you the support or challenges you have in this house.

In Jennifer Lopez's aspect grid, we can see that Jupiter ♃, the 4th house's natural ruler, is in opposition ☍ to Jennifer's Moon ☽ and square □ her Sun ☉, two rather challenging aspects. Jennifer will have to focus her efforts to achieve and maintain balance in family relationships.

Aspects are not something you can change, but an awareness of your aspects is like a secret view into yourself; knowing that a certain aspect in your astrological birth chart challenges you can help you work with that difficulty, and choose to channel this tumultuous energy in a productive way. You can look at the aspects for all of your planets in this same way, and you can also compare your aspects with another family member's. We do this in Chapter 5.

Your Family Wheel of Energy

What do you want most for your family right now? Think about this for a minute or two—it could be something general, such as harmony, love, abundance, honor, support, or peace; and it might also be something specific, such as a renewed relationship with a sibling, a more harmonious marriage, or a better understanding of your teen-ager. Now, what would it take to make this dream become a reality?

The family wheel of energy is a Psychic Intuition exercise to help you focus on what matters to you so you can begin to manifest your desires as your reality. This exercise is most effective when you can do it together with the members who are part of the relationship you desire to manifest. If you cannot or prefer not to involve others, you can do it by yourself as a meditation.

Wheel of Energy Meditation with the Whole Family: Start by gathering family members together in a location that is comfortable and relaxed for everyone. Sit in a circle—you can sit around a table, in chairs, or on the floor. Just sit close enough together that you can all put your hands together in the center of your circle, to form the "hub" of your family energy wheel. As your hands touch, feel the energy reach out from you to the others and from the others to you. Watch and feel the energy swirl and wrap around your arms and your body, encircling you in a protective "force field" of love and security. Watch and feel as it envelops each family member, drawing all of you together.

Keep your hands together in the center of your wheel of energy. Ask the question, "Where are we as a family *right now*, and where do we want to be?" Give each family member the opportunity to say what he or she sees as a *family* goal. Discuss—without judgment or bias—what each family member offers. When the discussion feels complete, go back around the circle to have each family member summarize his or her goal in a single word. Have the family member say the word out loud, and then have the entire family, as a group, repeat the word. Go around the circle until everyone who has a goal has offered it.

To bring your wheel of energy to a close, have each family member choose a goal word that someone else offered and say one thing the family could do to help manifest that goal. Slowly disengage your hands from your wheel's hub, releasing the wheel's energy back to each person. Welcome your energy as it returns to you.

Solitary Wheel of Energy Meditation: If you can't do the family wheel of energy exercise with other family members, you can do the wheel of energy meditation by yourself. Sit in a quiet, comfortable place. Close your eyes, if that helps you to focus, and concentrate on a single goal you'd like to see your family accomplish. Envision the goal—how would your family act or look if this goal were reality?

As you focus on the goal, narrow it to a single word. Say the word out loud, like a meditation mantra. Use your Psychic Intuition to *experience* what the word embodies. See and feel the word's energy reaching out from you to the other members of your family. Experience what it's like for the word to become the reality. Feel the energy that comes back to you, through your Psychic Intuition, from other family members. Spend at least 10 minutes in this meditative state.

You may find it exciting and synergistic, both individually and as a family, to give form and substance to the energy surrounding your family's purpose and goals!

chapter 5

Home: When You Have to Go There ...

Angles, aspects, and relationships
Exploring your family compatibility through synastry
My sign, your house ... fulfilling each other's needs
Which family is your model?
Tarot's Mission Spread: Looking at your family's past, present, and future
Let your Psychic Intuition take you on a journey through time

We show you how to make the best of the family you've got by exploring your family connections through Astrology, Tarot, and Psychic Intuition. You'll discover strategies and techniques for understanding and improving family relationships, determining family goals and priorities, and forging stronger family bonds. What is your family model? Characterize your family patterns and explore four archetypal family models to discover the kind of family you want. Synastry, the Astrology of relationships, can show you how your family relationships work. The Tarot's Mission Spread can help you see generational issues in your family. And Psychic Intuition can link your family's past to its present and future. Learn how to love your family as it is right now, while still striving to make it the supportive and harmonious haven you all deserve.

Planetary Relationships, Family Relationships

Synastry—the Astrology of relationships and compatibility—lets us look at the deeper connections and challenges that exist in families. Synastry compares the energies of the planets in one person's astrological birth chart to the energies of the planets in another person's birth chart by looking at the aspects that form between aligned planets to provide comprehensive insights into how two people get along. Aspects are angles that denote planetary relationships, and you first examined them in Chapter 4. Two planets directly opposite each other in your birth chart are 180 degrees apart—an astrological aspect called, not surprisingly, an opposition ☍. Astrologers like Arlene consider numerous aspects when doing synastry analysis. Let's look more deeply at the six major aspects.

Major Astro Aspect	**Degree of Separation**	**Effect on Planets' Energies**
Conjunction ☌	Within 10° each other	Harmonious or challenging, focuses and intensifies the energies of the aspected planets
Sextile ✶	60° from each other	Favorable in supporting your interests in what the energy of the planets represents or supports
Square □	90° from each other	Challenging and even harsh, but presents the greatest opportunities for growth and progress
Trine △	120° from each other	Fortuitous, allowing things to happen seemingly without effort
Quincunx ⚻	150° from each other	Generally challenging as there is no connection between the planets, although you can focus your efforts to create synergy between energies
Opposition ☍	180° from each other	Confrontational, but presents great opportunities if you can first work through the challenges

Favorable aspects between birth charts—trines △, sextiles ✶, and often conjunctions ☌—help relationships to proceed smoothly. When the aspects are more challenging, on the other hand—squares □, oppositions ☍, and quincunxes ⚻—you may often find yourself in conflict with the other person. Although we all know a little conflict can be a useful thing in a relationship, challenging aspects can make it seem that you can't even agree to disagree! Synastry helps you to identify the energies you have in common with other family members and to understand the energies that conflict so you can learn to work with (or at least around!) them and each other.

Synastry offers two methods for exploring these energies. The **synastry grid** presents planetary energies from each person's birth chart in a grid format similar to the aspect grid that accompanies your birth chart. You need an astrologer to create a synastry grid for you; it requires that you have the birth charts (or full birth information) for the two people whose astrological aspects and family relationship you want to analyze.

The other method, a **relationship analysis,** is something you can do yourself—and we show you how. Relationship analysis looks at the placement of your respective planets in each other's birth charts, showing where and how their energies complement or challenge one another. This provides insight and understanding into why you each think and act the way you do, and how and why you respond and react to each other.

Aspects of Family Compatibility

Do your family relationships come easily, or do you have to work at them? We chose a famous family pair to examine: presidential father and son George H. W. Bush and George W. Bush. Here is the synastry grid Arlene cast for these two.

The first aspect we notice in the Bush Father and Son synastry grid is their conjunct Moons ☽ ☌ ☽. A conjunction intensifies and focuses the energies of the aspects planets, enhancing the natural tendencies of those energies. The Moon's energy is flowing, emotional, and intuitive. This conjunction is a favorable aspect for this Father and Son, giving them the ability to know and understand each other's deepest emotions and to share those emotions with each other.

We also see that George H. W.'s Moon squares George W.'s Sun ☽ □ ☉, an aspect that establishes some challenges relating to ego. George W. would want the approval of George H. W. and would strive to be accepted by his father. Conflicts could come between the two, as the Son seeks the Father's approval while the Father tries to convince the Son that he has already been approved of!

Two points in the birth chart that are significant in relationships, although they're not planets, are the North Node ☊ and South Node ☋. We discuss the Nodes in detail in Chapter 8, but we want to comment about their aspects here. The Nodes, which denote points in the Moon's orbit, represent karmic lessons and duties. The North Node symbolizes the lessons to be learned in this lifetime, and the South Node symbolizes lessons already learned that have become a foundation of understanding for this lifetime.

Across
George H. W. Bush
Natal Chart
Jun 12 1924
11:48 am EDT +4:00
Milton MA
42°N15'071" 071°W05'

Down
George W. Bush
Natal Chart
Jul 6 1946
7:26 am EST +5:00
New Haven CT
41°N18' 072°W55'

	☽	☉	☿	♀	♂	♃	♄	♅	♆	♇	⚷	⚶	⚴	⚵	⚳	☊	☋	As	Mc	⊗	⚸
☽	☌ 0A45	△ 4A09		□ 0A14	△ 8A15	⚹ 3S02	☌ 8A37	⚻ 4A13	⚹ 0A55	□ 5S52	☍ 6A34	⚼ 0A36	⚻ 1A40		☍ 6A36		△ 8A01		△ 8S52		△ 8S06
☉	□ 4A09		∠ 0A36	☌ 3A38		⚻ 0A22		△ 7A37		☌ 2S28			△ 5A04					⚹ 2S05		☍ 5S29	
☿						△ 4A20			☌ 8A16										⚹ 1S31		⚹ 0S45
♀	⚹ 3S35	⚹ 0S11			☍ 3A56	△ 7S21	⚹ 4A18	⚻ 0S06	☌ 3S25		△ 2A14				△ 2A17	☌ 3A42	☍ 3A42			⚼ 1A48	
♂						□ 4A52	∠ 1A30			⚹ 2A01	⚼ 0S33				⚼ 0S30			☌ 2A25	□ 0S59	△ 1S00	□ 0S13
♃	☌ 0S11	△ 3A13		□ 0S42	△ 7A19		☌ 7A41		⚹ 0S01		☍ 5A38	⚼ 0S19	⚻ 0A44		☍ 5A41		△ 7A06				
♄			⚹ 2A54		⚻ 1S02		□ 0S40	△ 5S04			□ 2S44		△ 7S38		□ 2S41		⚻ 1S16	∠ 0A14			
♅	△ 1S12	☌ 2A13			△ 6A19	☍ 4S58	△ 6A41	□ 2A17	⚹ 1S01		⚹ 4A38		□ 0S16		⚹ 4A40		△ 6A05				
♆			△ 6S32							□ 5A25				☌ 2S57					△ 2A25	□ 2A24	△ 3A11
♇						△ 3A37			☌ 7A33										⚹ 2S13		⚹ 1S27
⚷	☌ 2A32	△ 5A56	⚼ 1S01	□ 2A01		⚹ 1S14			⚹ 2A42	□ 4S04		⚼ 2A24							△ 7S04		△ 6S18
⚶									⚼ 0S32					☍ 0S41					⚹ 4A42	□ 4A41	⚹ 5A28
⚴									⚼ 1A49			⚹ 2A08		□ 1A58				△ 6S47		☌ 3S23	
⚵	☌ 1A14	△ 4A38		□ 0A43		⚹ 2S32			⚹ 1A24		☍ 7A03	⚼ 1A05	⚻ 2A09		☍ 7A06						△ 7S37
⚳	△ 7S10									⚻ 0S34				△ 7A49				⚻ 0S57	△ 2A26		△ 1A41
☊	△ 2S38	☌ 0A47			△ 4A53		△ 5A15	□ 0A51	⚹ 2S27		⚹ 3A12		□ 1S42		⚹ 3A14	⚹ 4A39	△ 4A39				
☋	⚹ 2S38	☍ 0A47			⚹ 4A53	☌ 6S24	⚹ 5A15	□ 0A51	△ 2S27		△ 3A12		□ 1S42		△ 3A14	△ 4A39	⚹ 4A39				
As	⚹ 0A52	⚹ 2A32			☍ 6A38	△ 4A39			☌ 0A42		△ 4A57		⚻ 0A03	∠ 0A51	△ 4A59	☌ 6A24	☍ 6A24				
Mc										⚹ 1A29								△ 1A52		△ 1A32	
⊗		⚻ 0A52	☍ 7A11	△ 4A47	□ 3A14			△ 0A48	□ 4A06		⚻ 1A33		△ 3A21		⚻ 1A36	□ 3A00	□ 3A00			∠ 1A06	
⚸						☌ 7A17					⚼ 1A52	□ 4S05			⚼ 1A55			□ 4A50	☍ 1A27		☍ 2A13

Across: George H. W. Bush; down: George W. Bush.

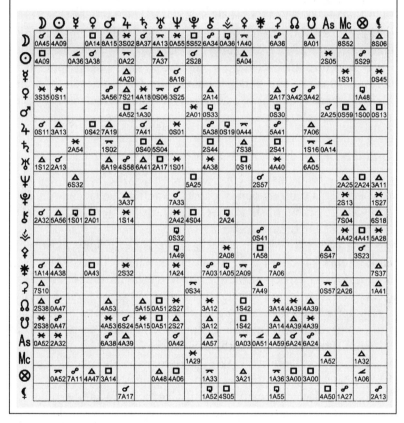

In the Bush Father-Son synastry grid, we see that George H. W.'s Moon is sextile George W.'s South Node ☽ ✶ ☋—and trine his North Node ☽ △ ☊. And George W.'s Moon is trine George H. W.'s South Node ☽ △ ☋. These are positive aspects that tell us these two are clearly fulfilling the karmic duties between them. They feel a strong sense of duty, especially when it comes to family expectations and responsibilities.

The North Node ☊ represents what the pair would want to encourage as growth and new dynamics; the South Node ☋ represents that which is already familiar territory or lessons that have a pattern to them. It's interesting that George H. W. is aspecting both of his son's Nodes; this reveals that the father has a responsibility to teach his son. George W.'s Nodes do not have the same intensity or energy to teach George H. W.

Mars, the *yang* planet of energy, challenges and pushes forward the ideals. George H. W.'s Mars trines both George W.'s Moon and Jupiter ♂ △ ☽ ♃. This is another positive aspect, affirming the values they share. They are generous with each other's ideas and share in past experiences. These aspects are beneficial to this Father-Son pair, as they challenge and force growth in their relationship, supporting an enduring, long-term relationship.

We also see several aspects with Saturn ♄ that further speak to endurability and longevity in this Father-Son relationship. Saturn represents the wisdom of the ages, and this planet in George H. W.'s chart is conjunct his son's Moon and Jupiter ♄ ☌ ☽ ♃. George H. W. will pass on to George W. his knowledge and discipline. George H. W. can also help George W. to cooperate with large groups or organizations: George W. receives from his father the benefit of George H. W.'s career experiences. Saturn is the planetary teacher, and so George H. W. is the elder who can and will help his son. This pair's relationship regarding serious issues of life will endure. They will have a good give and take, and listen to each other. After all, it is ideal that Fathers can help their sons mature and grow. These two will always be asking for advice from each other.

How Do You Relate?

A relationship analysis takes synastry a few steps further. It lets us look not only at the aspects the planets form between the birth charts of two people, but how the signs and placements of the planets influence the relationship those two people have with one another. We continue to explore the relationship of famous Father and Son George H. W. Bush and George W. Bush, this time looking at their individual birth charts.

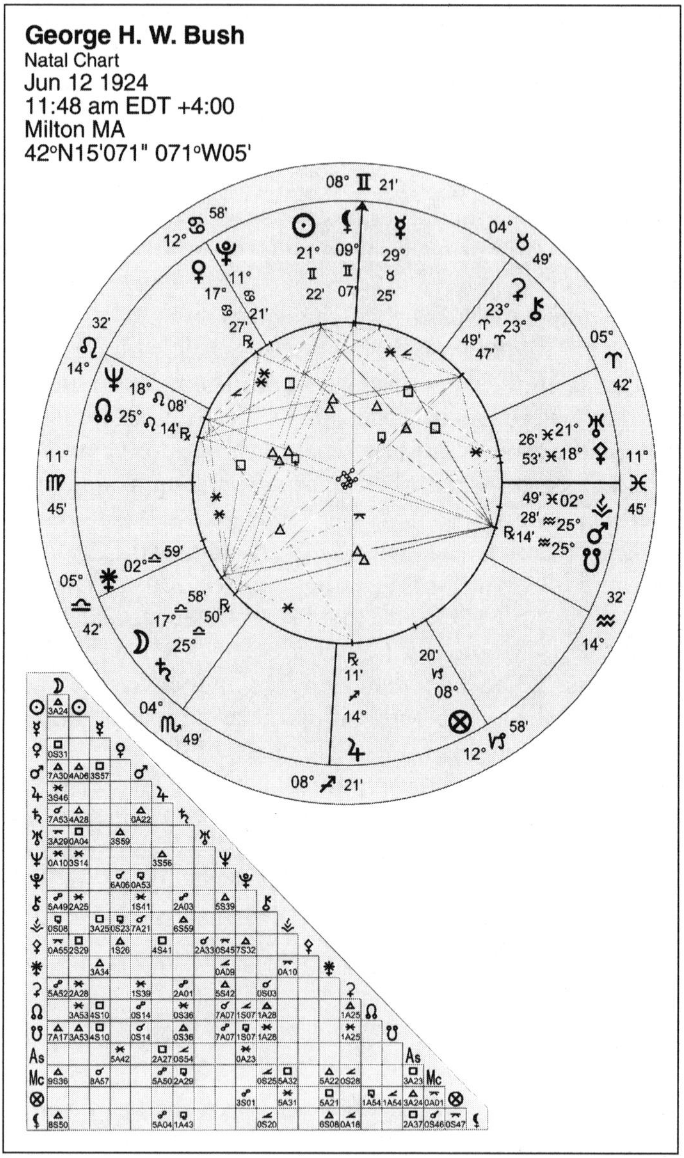

Birth chart for George H. W. Bush.

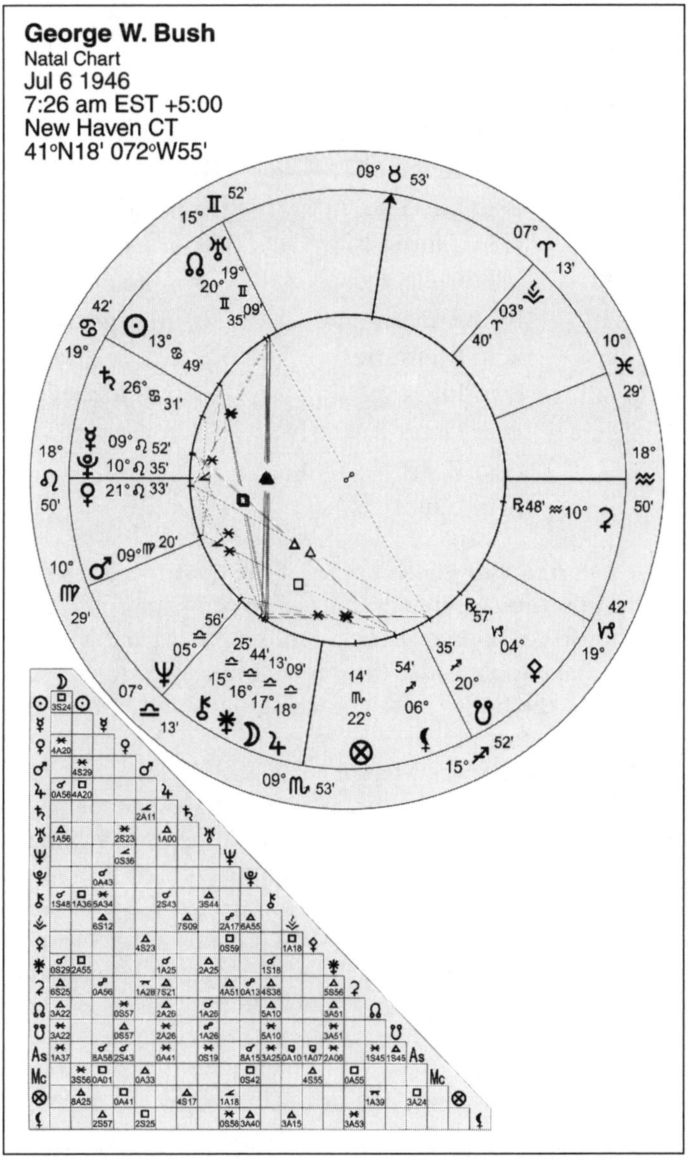

Birth chart for George W. Bush.

We start a relationship analysis by listing each planet's sign for each person:

Planet	George H. W.'s Astro Sign	George W.'s Astro Sign
Sun ☉	is in Gemini ♊	is in Cancer ♋
Moon ☽	is in Libra ♎	is in Libra ♎
Mercury ☿	is in Taurus ♉	is in Leo ♌
Venus ♀	is in Cancer ♋	is in Leo ♌
Mars ♂	is in Aquarius ♒	is in Virgo ♍
Jupiter ♃	is in Sagittarius ♐	is in Libra ♎
Saturn ♄	is in Libra ♎	is in Cancer ♋
Uranus ♅	is in Pisces ♓	is in Gemini ♊
Neptune ♆	is in Leo ♌	is in Libra ♎
Pluto ♇	is in Cancer ♋	is in Leo ♌

Next, we determine in which house of the other person's chart that planet falls. To do this, we match the sign of the planet in one person's chart to the house containing that sign in the other person's chart. This means we also have to consider the *degree* of the sign for the planet in the one chart and the house in the other, as signs and houses don't always start in the same places.

For example, George W.'s Mercury ☿ is at 9 degrees and 52 minutes Leo ♌ (look in his 12th house). When we go to George H. W.'s birth chart, we find Leo ♌ on the cusp of his 12th house and see that the 12th house starts at 14 degrees and 32 minutes of Leo. George W.'s Mercury ☿ in Leo ♌ is *earlier* than that, so George W.'s Mercury falls in the part of Leo that's in George H. W.'s 11th house.

As we add this dimension to our relationship analysis for the Bush Father and Son, in the next table, we include the degrees of the signs so you can see how we made our determinations.

Planet	H. W.'s Sign	W.'s House	W.'s Sign	H. W.'s House
Sun ☉	Gemini ♊ 21° ♊ 22'	11th	Cancer ♋ 13° ♋ 49'	11th
Moon ☽	Libra ♎ 17° ♎ 58'	3rd	Libra ♎ 17° ♎ 13'	2nd
Mercury ☿	Taurus ♉ 29° ♉ 25'	10th	Leo ♌ 09° ♌ 52'	11th

Planet	H. W.'s Sign	W.'s House	W.'s Sign	H. W.'s House
Venus ♀	Cancer ♋ 17° ♋ 27'	11th	Leo ♌ 21° ♌ 33'	12th
Mars ♂	Aquarius ♒ 25° ♒ 28'	7th	Virgo ♍ 09° ♍ 20'	12th
Jupiter ♃	Sagittarius ♐ 14° ♐ 11'	4th	Libra ♎ 18° ♎ 09'	2nd
Saturn ♄	Libra ♎ 25° ♎ 50'	3rd	Cancer ♋ 26° ♋ 31'	11th
Uranus ♅	Pisces ♓ 21° ♓ 26'	8th	Gemini ♊ 19° ♊ 09'	10th
Neptune ♆	Leo ♌ 18° ♌ 08'	12th	Libra ♎ 05° ♎ 56'	2nd
Pluto ♇	Cancer♋ 11° ♋ 21'	11th	Leo ♌ 10° ♌ 36'	11th

To help us explore what this tells us about how this Father and Son perceive and relate to each other, we use the keywords we developed in Chapter 1. We assign each sign, planet, and house a keyword that captures its essential characteristic.

Sign	Keyword	Sign	Keyword
Aries ♈	Energy	Libra ♎	Balance
Taurus ♉	Grounding	Scorpio ♏	Power
Gemini ♊	Communication	Sagittarius ♐	Enthusiasm
Cancer ♋	Emotion	Capricorn ♑	Responsibility
Leo ♌	Confidence	Aquarius ♒	Idealism
Virgo ♍	Resourcefulness	Pisces ♓	Spirituality

Planet	Keyword	Planet	Keyword
Sun ☉	Explores	Jupiter ♃	Benefits
Moon ☽	Senses	Saturn ♄	Cooperates
Mercury ☿	Communicates	Uranus ♅	Innovates
Venus ♀	Enjoys	Neptune ♆	Dreams
Mars ♂	Engages	Pluto ♇	Transforms

House	Keyword	House	Keyword
1st	Identity	7th	Relationships
2nd	Self-worth	8th	Transformation
3rd	Knowledge	9th	Beliefs
4th	Family	10th	Ethics and career
5th	Creativity	11th	Community
6th	Work	12th	Spirituality

Now we can use these keywords to interpret the placement of signs in the houses of George H. W. and George W., and begin to understand how these energies influence their relationship. It's a template that, when you do this same exercise for yourself and another family member, you can use to interpret and understand your own family relationships. Here's how it works.

George W.'s planet of action, Mars ♂ is in Virgo ♍, corresponding to father George H. W.'s 12th house. So we replace the sign, planet, and house with their respective keywords:

Mars ♂ = Engages
Virgo ♍ = Resourcefulness
7th house = Spirituality

Then we put this into context: In his relationship with his father, George W. **engages** his **resourcefulness** through his father's **spirituality.**

George H. W.'s Mars ♂ in Aquarius ♒ corresponds to son George W.'s 7th house. We replace the sign, planet, and house with their respective keywords:

Mars ♂ = Engages
Aquarius ♒ = Idealism
7th house = Relationships

We then put this into context: In his relationship with his son, George H. W. **engages** his **idealism** through his son's **relationships.**

When we look at the correlations of signs and houses for their most personal of signs, Sun ☉ and Moon ☽, we find an interesting and revealing symbiosis. Their Suns in different signs are in the same house in each other's birth charts; their Moons are in the same sign but in different houses in each other's charts. Here's how we can use our keywords to understand what this means.

George H. W.'s Sun ☉ in Gemini ♊ is in George W.'s 11th house: Through his relationship with son George W., George H. W. **explores** his **communication** skills through his son's authority in the **community.** George W.'s Sun ☉ in Cancer ♋ is in George H. W.'s 11th house: Through his relationship with his father, George W. **explores** his **emotions** through his father's leadership in the **community.** Each uses the other's role in the community to develop and grow.

Both Bushes have Libra ♎ Moons ☽—George H. W.'s is in his son George W.'s 3rd house, and George W.'s is in his father George H. W.'s 2nd house. George H. W. **senses balance** through the **knowledge** his son George W. provides. George W. **senses balance** through the **self-worth** that George H. W. provides.

We're going to sidestep the arena of politics and let you apply your own interpretations and insights to these summaries! But as you can see, synastry gives a good look at how one person in the family fulfills the needs of the other through their relationship. Do a few more of these for the Bush Father and Son if you like, to hone your new relationship analysis skills. You can write them here:

____

____

____

One final factor that we consider in relationship analysis is whether either person's birth chart contains retrograde ℞ planets. We talked about retrogrades in Chapter 1. A retrograde planet is one that appears to be moving *backward* in its orbit. Of course, it's not really—the planets always move in the same direction along their orbits. It's just the position of Earth, which is itself always in motion, causes planets to appear, at times, that they've shifted into reverse.

It feels like the planet's energy is in reverse, too. Instead of being focused and directed, the planet's energy becomes scattered and indistinct. Astrologers like to think of retrogrades as opportunities for "re" actions—rethinking, redoing, reconsidering, reforming. A planet that is retrograde at the time of your birth symbolizes karmic lessons for you to relearn. You can find retrograde planets in your birth chart by looking for the ℞ symbol.

When we look at the birth charts for George H. W. and George W., we see that George H. W. has two retrograde planets: Venus ♀ ℞, the planet of love and money; and Jupiter ♃ ℞, the planet of good fortune. When we look at George W.'s birth chart, we see that he has *no* retrograde planets!

This can indicate that George W. has more free will in making decisions and when he makes a decision, he's clear and resolute about it—he doesn't waffle. George W. may not have a lot of karmic duties, but rather can choose his path more easily than his father could. The retrograde planets tend to bring about introspection, sometimes even hesitation to follow through immediately. George H. W. would tend to watch, wait, and analyze more than George W. might. The benefit of the retrograde pattern for this pair could be that the one who has the retrogrades (Dad) can teach the one who has none (Son).

Now try your own relationship analysis. Choose another family member, and get your birth charts. Go through the same steps we followed for Father and Son Bush; here are the tables for you to complete. Take your time, and refer back to what we did to compare the birth charts of George H. W. and George W.

List each planet's astrological sign and keywords for you and for your other family member. We included the keywords for the planets; refer back to the tables of keywords to write in those that apply to your astrological signs.

Planet	**Your Astro Sign and Keyword**	**Your Family Member's Astro Sign and Keyword**
Sun ☉ *Explores*	____________	____________
Moon ☽ *Senses*	____________	____________
Mercury ☿ *Communicates*	____________	____________
Venus ♀ *Enjoys*	____________	____________
Mars ♂ *Engages*	____________	____________
Jupiter ♃ *Benefits*	____________	____________
Saturn ♄ *Cooperates*	____________	____________
Uranus ♅ *Innovates*	____________	____________
Neptune ♆ *Dreams*	____________	____________
Pluto ♇ *Transforms*	____________	____________

Now, put both birth charts out in front of you. One planet at a time, identify the planet's sign in your chart and the corresponding house containing that sign in your family member's birth chart.

Remember to look at the sign's degree, so you get it in the right house. Fill in the information in this table. When you're finished doing this with your birth chart, do the same with your family member's birth chart.

Planet	Your Astro Sign and Keyword	House and Keyword for This Sign in Your Family Member's Chart
Sun ☉ *Explores*	______________	______________
Moon ☽ *Senses*	______________	______________
Mercury ☿ *Communicates*	______________	______________
Venus ♀ *Enjoys*	______________	______________
Mars ♂ *Engages*	______________	______________
Jupiter ♃ *Benefits*	______________	______________
Saturn ♄ *Cooperates*	______________	______________
Uranus ♅ *Innovates*	______________	______________
Neptune ♆ *Dreams*	______________	______________
Pluto ♇ *Transforms*	______________	______________

Planet	Your Family Member's Astro Sign and Keyword	House and Keyword for This Sign in Your Birth Chart
Sun ☉ *Explores*	______________	______________
Moon ☽ *Senses*	______________	______________
Mercury ☿ *Communicates*	______________	______________
Venus ♀ *Enjoys*	______________	______________
Mars ♂ *Engages*	______________	______________
Jupiter ♃ *Benefits*	______________	______________
Saturn ♄ *Cooperates*	______________	______________
Uranus ♅ *Innovates*	______________	______________
Neptune ♆ *Dreams*	______________	______________
Pluto ♇ *Transforms*	______________	______________

When you're done filling in the tables, you have what you need to begin your analysis. As we did for George H. W. and George W., choose a planet and write its keyword. Identify this planet's sign in your list, and write the sign's keyword. Then identify this planet's corresponding placement in your family member's birth chart, and write this keyword. Last, put the keywords together in a sentence that describes how you and your family member fulfill each other's needs.

____

____

____

What does this relationship analysis reveal about how you and your family member get along? Are there any surprises? Light bulbs of enlightenment? You might have had an intuitive sense about how the two of you complement one another that this analysis affirms, or might see why it is that the two of you continually butt heads over certain issues.

Family Models

American poet Robert Frost wrote famously of home as the place where you are guaranteed a welcome, for better or worse. Your family, after all, is your family. What is the ideal family? Is there one "model" we all want to have, one that would make every one of us happy? We bet not! Even within your own family, it's likely that family members disagree on what would be the ideal family structure. Let's turn to pop culture to explore different family configurations and patterns—to television, specifically. Regardless of what you think about how closely—or remotely—television represents real life, certain television families have weathered the Nielsen ratings to become ensconced as contemporary archetypes. We've selected four of them, and matched them with representative Tarot cards to help us explore their dynamics.

As you read each of these archetypal examples, is there one that you identify with more than the others? Perhaps not in its entirety—few of us lead archetypal lives! But as simplified representations either of what our families are or what we might want our families to be like—and, sometimes, what we're glad our families are *not* like—these model families resonate with us in enduring ways. Millions of Americans welcomed these television families into their living rooms for years and sometimes long enough for their own children to grow up.

The traditional American family, represented by the Hierophant and the 10 of Cups R.

Ozzie and Harriet: Real Life Family, the Ideal: Ozzie and Harriet Nelson and their sons David and Ricky were the perfect 1950s family: Dad, Mom, two great kids, and a family dog. What could be more traditional? Happy, secure, and on the surface, at least, they appeared to have it all. This is the family with a perfect exterior—from the outside you can't tell what's really going on. If you look closely enough, however, you might see a crack in that veneer.

Though no one else is supposed to see it, this family has its flaws like any other. Family members gloss them over, sweep them under the rug, and continue on their orderly way. Not a lot of open communication going on in this kind of family, and perhaps some serious trouble brewing underneath, though it would be difficult to get anyone to admit it. Of course, they are accepted by society as the perfect family model, and they are likely a loyal and harmonious bunch.

The chaotic family, with the unpredictability and psychic attachment represented by the Moon and the emotional attachment of the 5 of Cups R.

Ozzy and Sharon: Real-Life Family, the Reality: This family appears to be the exact opposite of Ozzie and Harriet, and in many ways, it is. One thing you *can't* say about the Osbournes is that they present a smooth veneer for outsiders—they definitely let their reality show. This is not the traditional model, and there is a lot of volatility and unpredictability in their behavior and communication. This family appears chaotic and argumentative. But when you look beneath the surface of this volatile family, you'll notice that Ozzy and Sharon have been married for more than 20 years and are raising 3 kids.

There is a very strong sense of loyalty in this family model. Family members give each other hope through difficulties, support through crises, and always will be there for each other. Chaos may actually be the way they end up bonding even deeper with each other. And as much as they appear to be antagonistic, there is the underlying commitment of pulling together through adversity. It's a chaotic mix that stands the concept of traditional family on end, but it works for many.

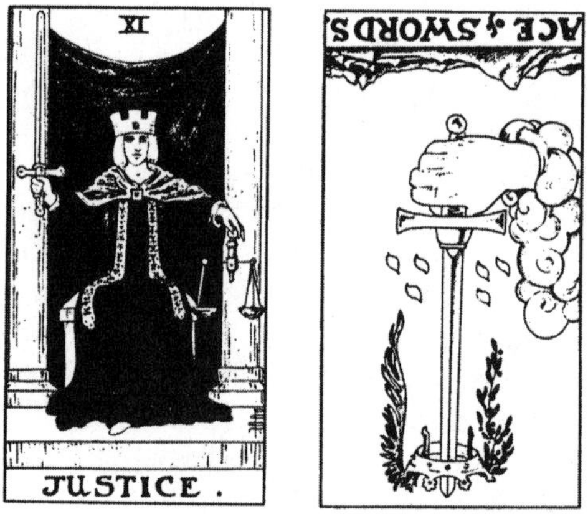

The controlling family model, represented by Justice and the Ace of Swords R. This family believes in justice and feel justified in their opinions. Their communication style is seen in the Ace of Swords R—what might this mean?

Archie and Edith: All in the Family: This television family seems to submit, however uncomfortably, to the domineering dysfunction of its patriarch, Archie Bunker. The family's primary mode of communication is confrontation—one-sidedly favoring yelling—with Archie riding rail as jury and judge. His "Aw, gee whiz!" becomes the closing comment and final judgment for the family's arguments. Do these people not understand each other *at all?* There's little listening going on, with each family member feeling very much justified in his or her strong opinions and not hesitating to shout them out—with mother Edith quietly asserting the bond that holds them all together.

Yet beneath all the yelling and name-calling is a deep and connecting love—although Archie would say, "That's just a pigment of your imagination!" Mike, Gloria, and Archie seem not to get along, but they actually understand each other all too well. Opinionated, argumentative, and forceful, these family members yell their thoughts and feelings to make sure they're heard. But in times of crisis they're always there for each other—Edith makes sure of it. This group kept their world turning all in the family, as did the millions of us who tuned in each week to watch.

The balanced family model represented by the World R and the 6 of Cups. This family will work to become a family unit (that's the World R), and children, the home, and family security are very important (6 of Cups).

The Brady Bunch's Blending Balance: This "ready-made" family combines two previous marriages—but that's a device to advance the story line. For the most part, this blended family gets along remarkably well, with all family members free to be themselves. They love each other and try hard to get along because, well, they're a family. It's not perfect, and at times it's downright hectic, but everyone is at least in there trying. The understanding, sympathetic parents work at being partners, and they work things out with the kids: They communicate.

As a family model, this is an optimistic group with all family members working toward the goal of harmony and sharing in the activities of the household. These folks not only have feelings, they talk about their feelings and what they need from each other. The members of this family are strongly bonded as a family despite being "thrown" together through the marriage of the two adults, and as a bonus they actually like each other!

The kids are important in this model, and the family dynamic is to help each other attain family goals as well as individual goals. Family members support each other's opinions, goals, aspirations, and security needs. The size of the family makes for entertaining television, but it isn't the driving force. This family—despite occasional bickering and disagreement—is welcoming and adaptive, and they work hard to make their family relationships work.

Your Family Model

Each of these family models reveals a different type of family dynamics. Whether you prefer the even keel or the chaotic whirlwind or something else altogether, knowing what kind of family you have, and how you fit into it, can help you work your way toward the family you want to become.

These families each represent a general relationship dynamic:

- **The Nelsons** represent a *traditional* family dynamic.
- **The Osbournes** represent a *chaotic* family dynamic.
- **The Bunkers** represent a *controlling* family dynamic.
- **The Bradys** represent a *balanced* family dynamic.

In the following table, we distill each model's defining characteristics into keywords that help decode the unique nature of each type of family relationship. Do any of these keywords sound like your family?

Relationship	Communication	Sharing	Decision-Making	Values
Traditional	Cautious	Give and take	Unilateral	Imposed
Chaotic	Confrontational	Give and take	Mutual	Similar
Controlling	As necessary	Separate but equal	Unilateral	Imposed
Balanced	Open, honest	Give and take	Mutual	Accepted

These dynamics have commonalities and differences. Communication style leads the dynamic, shaping how the family shares, makes decisions, and establishes values. Sometimes the similarities are not very obvious. The chaotic family's communication style is confrontational, yet its dynamics for sharing, decision-making, and values give each family member equal importance.

How your family *appears* is not always how it really is, and of course there's far more to most families than just keywords. None of these family examples is inherently good or bad, positive or negative. Different styles work for different people. What's important is to know what you have and what you want, and see if the two can meet in the middle. Some of the happiest families we know seem to thrive on chaos, yet others relish the predictability of order.

Tarot's Mission Spread: Exploring Your Family's Past, Present, and Future

The Tarot's Mission Spread takes you deep into the story of your family—where you've been, where you are now, and where you're headed. Its 21 cards lay out your past, present, and future in 3 rows of 7 cards. Arlene did this Family Mission Spread reading for William, who felt that his family was encountering more than their fair share of troubles and wondered why this was happening. First Arlene gave a general interpretation of the cards, and then William used the information to explore and better understand his family experiences. Here are the cards Arlene drew for William's Family Mission Spread, and her interpretations and comments about William's cards.

Row 1: Family's Past Mission and Experiences

Knight of Pentacles: The beginning of prosperity and focus on home and money: a good start!

Queen of Pentacles: Fertility and abundance is available within this family; they share and can prosper financially or with children.

6 of Wands R: There may be some delays getting energies together between all members, and compromises need to be made.

The Lovers: A good combination of love and the desire to agree on decisions within the family relationship. This family would consider each other's choices.

2 of Wands R: The family watches for opportunities to develop their ideas, and some goals have to be put on hold.

The Fool R: There may be faulty choices or impulsive actions. The family should be cautious about leaping before they know where they are going as a family.

8 of Wands: The love and generosity that is inherent in this family can win the day! They have been able to focus their energy and go for what is important.

Row 2: Family's Present Mission and Experiences

The Chariot: This card indicates the ability to overcome difficulties or health problems: The family can focus and survive some critical areas of difficulty in their lives. The Chariot starts this row, telling us the family will face some type of hardship, but the family is strong and can survive because of its responsible nature. This tempers the potential harshness of the cards that follow, which caution about spending extra money or a health problem that may cost more than expected. In the end, if this family is careful in its financial decisions, all will turn out well.

10 of Wands: They can carry the heavy burdens and work with each other through rocky times.

3 of Swords: There will be a crisis or some loss in the family, or a disappointment.

The Tower R: This indicates sudden surprises or slowdowns that might relate to a crisis or delay that was unexpected.

4 of Pentacles: It may be difficult for the family to hold on to the financial security they have built; they may have to spend more than they thought on a home or goods or health care.

7 of Cups: There are many choices this family can make, and they need to be cautious about making choices that might be more of a fantasy than reality. They should study all choices and decisions in depth!

5 of Swords: Caution is advised on dealing with all legal documents or commitments.

Row 3: Family's Future Mission and Experiences

The Devil R: This family has a lot of connectedness. The Devil reversed reflects their ability to let go of the ego and not let material issues distract them.

Justice: The family will be on a mission in the future to be fair and honorable, to give each other fair treatment, and to judge together what decisions are best for the whole family.

Judgement: The family that works together … stays together! This family will work out problems by making sure everyone is heard. They will respect each other's goals and spiritual philosophies.

The King of Cups: The Father of this family will be a benevolent leader, helping his "tribe" assimilate in the world. Hope and inspiration come with this King of Cups!

The Star: The Father of this family is connected to the Star card. He is benevolent and wants the best for this family and home. He is hopeful and optimistic!

4 of Wands: This family will enjoy the work they do together and will share in the joys of working through life's challenges.

10 of Cups: A happy family with children, and pleasure in taking care of each other.

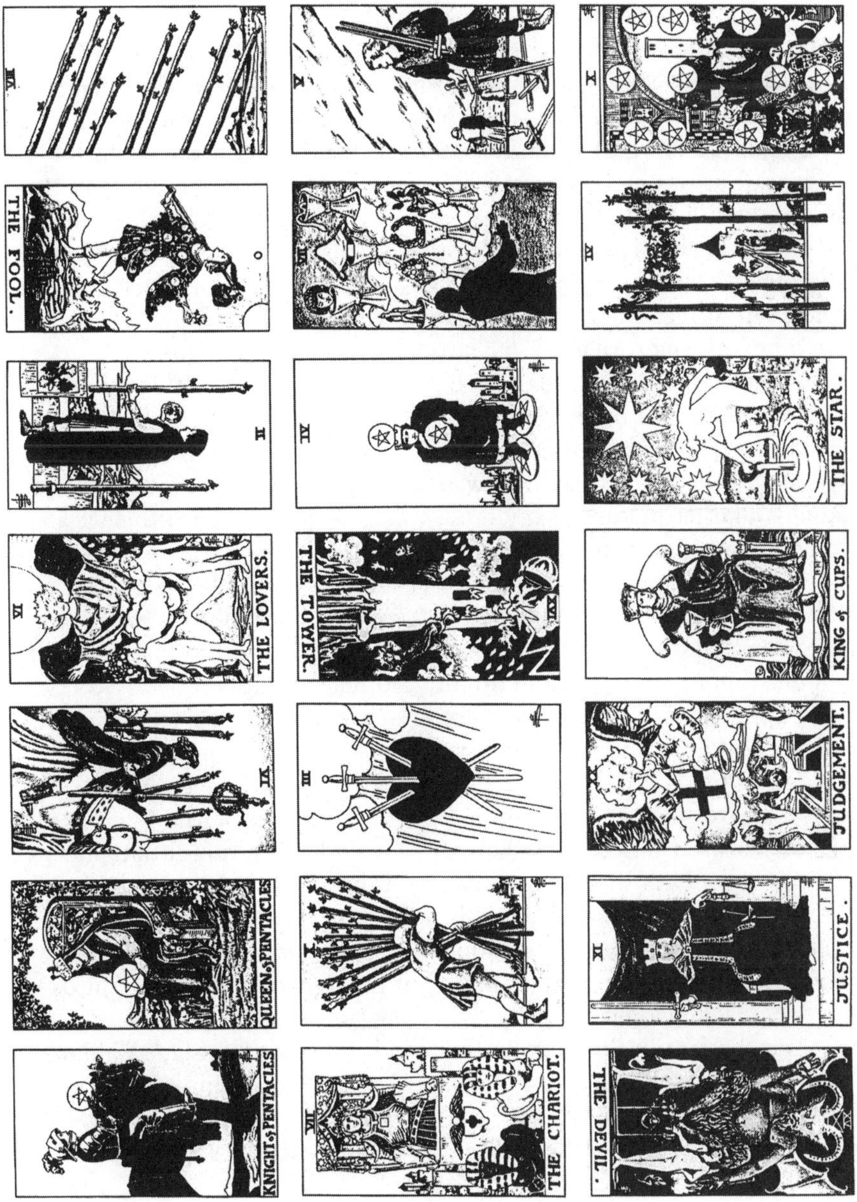

William's Family Mission Spread.

The first three cards in William's family's future mission are karmic cards, indicating that this family is learning together to work with law and order and material issues, and to become aware of each other's individual missions. There seems to be a mutual respect for one another's goals and yet the family is bonded for their collective good. No one is jealous or envious here! The remaining cards in this row say that this family will raise its members to be responsive to their community and environment. This family's mission seems to be one of setting an example in its own community, either by intent or by happenstance. Others will notice the family's strong devotion and also their desire to help others through sharing and caring, and will follow the lead.

"When Arlene first started reading the Tarot cards," William says, "I was a bit lost—I expected this to be about me, so I thought row one would be my parents, row two would be me, and row three would be my kids. But it didn't look that way, and then I realized that this was actually a larger picture of my family, as generations. With this view, my grandparents are row one, my parents and family are row two, and the family I've created is row three. This made perfect sense to me, because my maternal grandfather was well off but then lost everything in the depression and died relatively young. My maternal grandmother died when my mother was an infant, and her grandparents raised my mother, in poverty. They were close-knit, and my mother feels she had a happy childhood.

"The family I grew up in struggled a great deal financially, as well, mainly due to poor choices and lack of education about money. One of my older brothers died when he was 21, and had an infant daughter; this, his only child, died of lung cancer at age 23. These are the kinds of things that have made my family suffer but also stick together. More recently, my father died after a long illness that was an emotional and financial strain on the entire family. But this struggle also brought us all very close together.

"And the family I'm making for myself now is amazing," William says. "We're very happy, and work hard to keep our family going in the direction we want. We have our difficulties, of course, but my wife and I are very much on the same page about what we want for our family, and we will sacrifice to get there."

Your Multigenerational Family

Are you ready to try a Mission Spread of your own? Begin by shuffling your Tarot deck until you feel it is ready, thinking about your family and its place in the world. When you're ready, lay out three rows of cards with seven cards in each row as Arlene did for William.

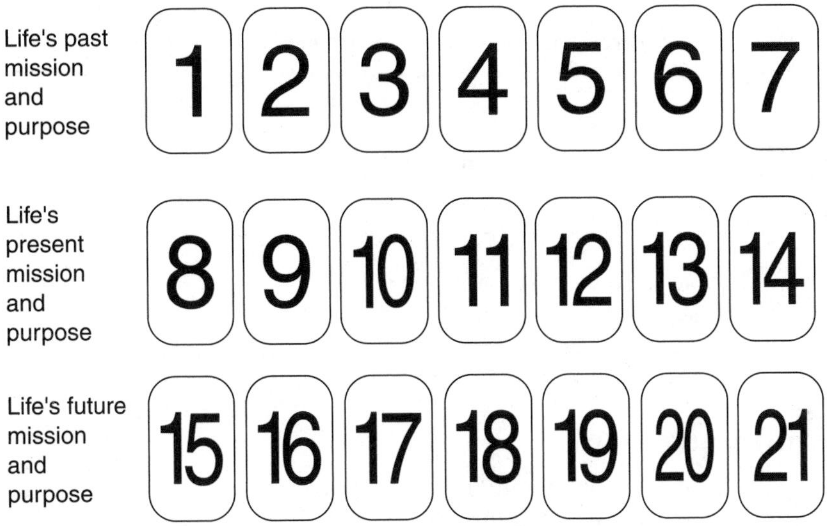

Tarot's Mission Spread.

First, use the inner vision of your Psychic Intuition to look at the cards collectively. Do you sense any patterns or themes? Do the rows seem to have similar or different themes? Next, look at each row. How are the cards grouped? Are there Major Arcana cards—which represent karmic messages or lessons—in any of the rows? Are many of the cards in reversed positions? Do you get any immediate "ahas!" when you look at the images on the cards? Write your initial overall reaction to the cards here:

Overall perceptions of the cards in your family's Mission Spread:

Then, let your Psychic Intuition explore each card, row by row. Remember, the first row represents the past, the second row the present, and the third row the future. These representations might be in the context of generations, as with William's reading, or could relate specifically to your present family depending on your situation and the issues or questions that concern you. Write your impressions here:

Perceptions of the cards in row one (past): ____________________

____

Perceptions of the cards in row two (present): ________________

____

Perceptions of the cards in row three (future): _______________

____

Cards that seem to have particular significance: ______________

____

Family Treasures

Is there anyone in your family history, someone long passed on, who you feel a connection with? Or perhaps there's someone you've heard stories about or seen pictures of that you'd like to know about. How would you like to communicate with this person from your family's past? This Psychic Intuition exercise can help you to make a connection through time to a family member. And no, we're not having a séance or pulling out the Ouija board! Your Psychic Intuition represents your ability to use your inner senses to hear, see, feel, touch, and taste experiences that are beyond the reach of your physical senses. So we're going to resonate to that psychic sense that connects you to your family.

To get started, you need to find an item or object that relates to the person you want to know more about. Perhaps you want to connect to your great-grandmother, and you know that a pin your mother now wears once belonged to her—ask to borrow it. Or go to your grandmother and ask if she has anything that belonged to her mother. It doesn't have to be any one thing in particular—it can be a photo, a letter, a watch, or any artifact of his or her earthly life.

Next, find a place where you can relax and focus, without distractions or interruptions, and make yourself comfortable. Hold the artifact in your hands. How does it feel and look? Experience through your Psychic Intuition its textures, colors, flavors, and smells. Let this item transport you to the existence it once had with the family member you desire to connect with. Is this a letter? Feel the hand writing the words, pausing in search of the right phrases and then continuing. Is your artifact a piece of jewelry? When did this person wear it? What special meaning does the jewelry have?

Open yourself to the messages the artifact can convey to you. Be patient, and keep your analytical brain out of the way. This is an intuitive connection, and it isn't likely to unfold in the kind of rational, linear, logical manner you might expect of an intellectual connection. Allow sensory fragments to emerge, even if they seem out of context or unorthodox. Let your Psychic Intuition shape their messages. Can you begin to sense images, fragrances, gestures? What made this person laugh and cry? What do you want to know from this family member? Does this person have a message for you? Feel free to remain in this psychic meditation for as long as you like.

When you're finished, spend a few minutes contemplating the images that came to you. Write your perceptions here:

____

____

____

Follow up on this exercise by tracking down real information about this family member. Ask other family members about this person. Describe your experience of the exercise, and the perceptions that came to you. Show or explain the artifact that you used to establish your connection to this family member. At the least, you have an opportunity to connect with other family members who are part of your present life experience, perhaps letting them recall long-forgotten events and circumstances involving an important person in your family's history.

We Are Family!

As you've discovered in this chapter, there are many model families, but no single family relationship is ideal for everyone. Through our relationships with others in our families, we grow and evolve as individuals—and help them to do the same. As we learn more about ourselves and how we relate to others in our families, we also grow and evolve as families. Your experience of family, in the end, is what you make it. To get to where you want to be, you have to know where you are now and how you got here. Then, your family's future is in your hands!

chapter 6

They Just Don't Understand, and Other Family Challenges

When family troubles get you down
Moon moods
M.C. and I.C.: Your descendant and your nadir
Planetary returns and transits: Saturn and Pluto
Unlocking stubborn problems in family relationships
Is your cup half-full or half-empty?

Family relationships are not always easy. Use family Astrology, Tarot, and Psychic Intuition to get to the root of family problems, understand the causes, and effect positive change in yourself and your family to achieve a more loving bond. In this chapter, you learn how to deal with difficult family relationships. We discuss Moon signs and the effect the Moon has on each of us, and you learn how to find the descendant and the nadir on an astrological birth chart, and how to use this information to know yourself—and your family members—better. We look at planetary transits, and see how Saturn returns and Pluto transits effect our growth and change, in all relationships. Finally, we try to unlock some of the more stubborn problems in family relationships with a Psychic Intuition exercise.

When Family Troubles Get You Down

No matter what kind of family you have, it's likely there are times when not everyone gets along—there may be lots of personalities in your family mix, and you won't always see eye to eye with all of them. This is just part of the normal ebb and flow of family relationships. What we want you to do is learn to go with, understand, and use the flow for your and your family's benefit. You'll be able to relate all your family members more responsively, using what you've learned about them from their birth charts and using other Intuitive Arts resources. We show you how to use the Moon's cycles and planetary returns and transits to figure out when trouble might be brewing with a family member—and prepare yourself accordingly. When the Moon is coming full, we should be more compassionate toward family members. When the Moon is in its new phase, family members might need space to evaluate issues on their own. Let's start developing some of the tools we need to get through the difficult times with our family relationships intact.

The Man in the Moon

Sometimes you feel fine, other times you're wild with emotion—that's the Moon! The Moon ☽ has a powerful effect on us all, even if we aren't aware of it. The Moon controls everything from the ocean's tides to human emotions. This is because the Moon has a gravitational pull on the Earth, and this affects all the water on our planet (and what are humans made of? ... lots of water!). So though you may not associate your emotional ups and downs with the Moon, if you consider the Moon's cycles, you might be surprised to find a correlation. The Moon is so powerful that it's one of the most important facets of Astrology—along with the Sun ☉ and the rising sign, or ascendant—and you can learn a lot about yourself, and others, from the Moon.

Your emotional and bodily changes can be related to the Moon's full monthly cycle, and they may also be related to the path the Moon travels in a full year. Your Moon sign has a lot to do with this—if your Moon is in Pisces ♓, you might have a difficult time when the Moon is in Libra ♎ (which is a *yang* Air sign, as compared to the Pisces *yin* Water sign—water doesn't mix well with air!). The energy is inconsistent and may even be challenging, causing frustration to mount on that day. You can use Moon signs to help understand your own emotional reactions, as well as those of your family—the Moon is all about how we deal with our emotions, which is a very important part of any family relationship. We discuss this important part of your (and your family's) birth chart next.

Tarot's Moon: Are you wild or tame, or both?

Moon ☽ Signs

Figure out what your Moon ☽ sign is by looking at your astrological birth chart. All you need to do is find the Moon symbol on your birth chart and see what sign it's in. Then find that section in the following text and see how well it describes you. Do this for each of your family members, and consider how you all fit together, emotionally.

Moon in Aries: This king is a passionate Father or Grandfather who is able to get others in the family motivated toward their personal goals.

Moon ☽ in Aries ♈. There's nothing shy about you! Energetic and independent, you feel with your head, and will jump into all relationships with great self-confidence—you like to relate to others. You aren't the most patient person—you don't get what everyone else is so *emotional* about!

Moon in Taurus: This king is a Father or an Uncle who is a rock of Gibraltar in the family. He's practical and reliable, and can be counted on to follow through on what he says he will do.

Moon ☽ in Taurus ♉. You're warm and affectionate, and you feel with all of your senses. Romantic and loyal, you like to feel stable—once you've decided how you feel, you can be pretty stubborn about it. You are calming for others and your family feels secure and stable in your loyalty.

Moon in Gemini: A Brother or an Uncle to whom you might communicate your deepest ideas or apprehensions, he's a relative you can really talk with and relate to.

Moon ☽ in Gemini ♊. You're emotionally erratic, but also analytical. You might jump around emotionally, but you think about your feelings and verbalize them well, because you feel with your lively mind. You are certainly the communicator! You keep others *thinking* about their own emotional needs.

Moon in Cancer: Here is a benevolent Father or Grandfather able to understand and sympathize with your needs. He has a keen observational sense and is a good listener. Compassion is his byline!

Moon ☽ in Cancer ♋. This is the sign the Moon naturally rules, so the Moon is very much at home in Cancer. The Cancer Moon is creative and may also be moody and easily hurt—though they try not to show this vulnerable side of themselves. If you're a Cancer Moon, you feel with your feelings, and try hard to protect all of your heart attachments.

Moon in Leo: This queen is a good Sister or Mother figure who will tell you the way it is. She is direct and wants you to get to your truth without delay. Time should not be wasted—move on with your life, she says!

Moon ☽ in Leo ♌. You're very affectionate and perhaps a bit dramatic. You can be hurt when your emotional needs are not met with the same joy you try to share with others. You may feel a protective urge toward children and feel strongly about their need for education. You feel with your big heart, and have a great enthusiasm for life and a desire for family unity.

Moon in Virgo: This Mother, Aunt, or Grandmother is nurturing, and you come to her with your questions and anxieties about life. She relates well with children and grandchildren, and shares her wisdom with her family. History is something she knows can repeat itself!

Moon ☽ in Virgo ♍. This is the logical sign, and that's how you feel if your Moon is in Virgo. You're practical, and like to make sense of what you—and others—are feeling. Others may think you're actually not very emotional because of this, and you could have a difficult time understanding your more emotionally spontaneous family members. Underneath this cool exterior is a devoted and thoughtful individual.

Moon in Libra: This king is a great spokesperson for the family, a wise Grandfather and tribal elder. He is honest and wants the family to understand that truth and justice is the only way to go. He is a wise counselor and mentor to his family.

Moon ☽ in Libra ♎. This Moon sign likes harmony, and tries to create it—for themselves and others. If your Moon is in Libra, chances are you're a social person, and you feel through others. You have a difficult time being happy when others aren't. You need to have fairness and balance in life, and are the peacemaker and negotiator in your family.

Moon in Scorpio: This queen is an excellent Mother, Grandmother, and Great-Grandmother. She understands that we are all human and make mistakes. She is emotionally attached to all that she believes and loves in family, and holds the memory of family in her heart.

Moon ☽ in Scorpio ♏. If your Moon is in Scorpio, you're an emotionally intense person, and you feel with those powerful emotions. You might be a little suspicious and even tend to hold grudges, but you also are very intuitive. You tend to be cautious about whom you trust and are able to sense who is devoted and trustworthy within your family.

Moon in Sagittarius: This young Brother, Son, or Nephew is out to create a wonderful life full of adventure. He wants an environment of uplifting energy for his family. Go for what you want in life, he says—create your own reality and enjoy the adventures that come your way!

Moon ☽ in Sagittarius ♐. The Moon in Sagittarius is very adaptable and extremely adventurous. You like to experience life, and don't have time to brood or be moody, which may make you insensitive to your more emotional family members. You feel through your experiences. You are enthusiastic about life's adventures and encourage others to be adventurous as well.

Moon in Capricorn: This young man is a good Brother, Cousin, or child in the family who is forever responsible for what he does. He remembers who has helped him and never forgets a favor. Resourceful and patient with others, he will always follow through on family responsibilities.

Moon ☽ in Capricorn ♑. You feel through control, and may seem to be remote and emotionally reserved—you have a lot of self-control and discipline, and you exercise it well. You don't have patience for what you see as overly emotional people, and are likely very successful, though success could cost you in your emotional life. You work hard to express your emotions and you tend to observe emotional situations. You try to problem-solve family issues with logic.

Moon in Aquarius: This queen represents a Grandmother, Sister, or Aunt who has the wisdom of personal experience. Life is a struggle at times, and this lady can teach the family how to protect themselves against adversity and loss. She also has great intelligence and wisdom to pass down through the family generations. Mind over matter, she says!

Moon ☽ in Aquarius ♒. This is a very independent Moon, and if this is your Moon sign, you feel through your individuality. You might be a bit unconventional, and you definitely have your own way of doing things. You tend to be aloof emotionally, but you're also very intuitive. You communicate your emotions through your idealism, which can sometimes be confusing for others.

Moon in Pisces: This young man is your Brother or your Uncle. He wishes people well and takes a spiritual approach to life's problems. He is a peacemaker and wants all members of the family to live in harmony and peace. Peace be with you, he says!

Moon ☽ in Pisces ♓. If this is your Moon sign, you may need to remind yourself of the difference between reality and dreams. You're dreamy, and may see the world through rose-colored glasses a lot of the time—which is not a bad thing! You're very sensitive (maybe overly so—you get hurt easily) and intuitive, creative, and forgiving. This Moon sign feels with the imagination. You see the highest potential in others. You *believe* in the dream.

What Sign Is the Moon In? How Do You Feel?

If you want to know where the Moon ☽ is today, you can look at an astrological calendar, which will tell you the Moon's transits for the entire year ahead. We've listed each Moon sign along with the beneficial and challenging aspects the Moon brings with it in each sign. You can use this chart to remind yourself what each Moon sign is like, and also to make note of what the Moon may have in store for you and your loved ones in any given sign. If you find yourself or a family member behaving unusually moodily, perhaps the Moon in Cancer ♋ will help explain it—don't take it personally. And if you're feeling more energetic than you have in months, perhaps the Moon is in Aries ♈—take advantage of this while you can!

Moon In	Moon Sign Advantages	Moon Sign Challenges
Aries ♈	Energy, self-confident	Impatient, irritable
Taurus ♉	Affectionate, calm	Stubborn, rigid
Gemini ♊	Analytical, communicative	Erratic, irrational
Cancer ♋	Creative, sensitive	Moody, insecure

Moon In	Moon Sign Advantages	Moon Sign Challenges
Leo ♌	Outgoing, warm	Arrogant, melodramatic
Virgo ♍	Logical, practical	Reserved, rigid
Libra ♎	Social, cooperative	Hesitant, superficial
Scorpio ♏	Powerful, intense	Unforgiving, suspicious
Sagittarius ♐	Adaptable, adventurous	Irresponsible, insensitive
Capricorn ♑	Determined, disciplined	Remote, inflexible
Aquarius ♒	Independent, unconventional	Aloof, unpredictable
Pisces ♓	Compassionate, forgiving	Self-pitying, helpless

Moon Phases

You can also look at Moon phases to see how the monthly cycle of the Moon can affect human—and family—behavior. The New Moon is a time of initiation and starting new things, the Waxing Moon is a time of growth and action and movement toward a goal or purpose, the Full Moon is a time of completion and, well, fullness (many babies are delivered during Full Moons!), and the Waning Moon is a time of harvesting as you prepare to begin the cycle all over again. The period of total darkness between the Waning Moon and the New Moon is called the Balsamic Moon, a time of introspection and inner work that prepares you to once again harness the energy of initiation with the coming New Moon. Observe how your family resonates unconsciously to Moon phases and begin to learn how you can use the Moon's energy to understand people's moods and actions and how to apply your efforts in harmony with lunar cycles.

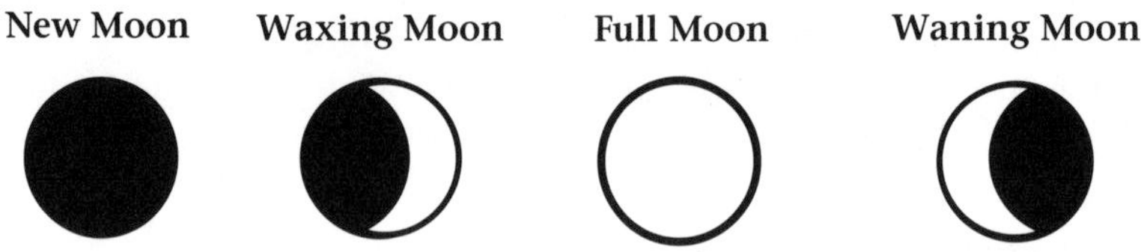

M.C. and I.C.: Your Descendant and Your Nadir

So far in this book, we've spent a lot of time looking at birth charts, noting planets, signs, and houses, and trying to gain some insight into ourselves and our families. Now we're going to continue with this quest, but this time we'll be looking at something different: the nadir and descendant. Here is a birth chart for Oscar-winning actress Nicole Kidman. Note that Nicole's is a noon chart. Depending on how far from noon Nicole's precise birth time is, her ascendant, descendant, nadir, and midheaven could be different from the ones in the chart we've cast. However, we feel these placements are intuitively strong for Nicole.

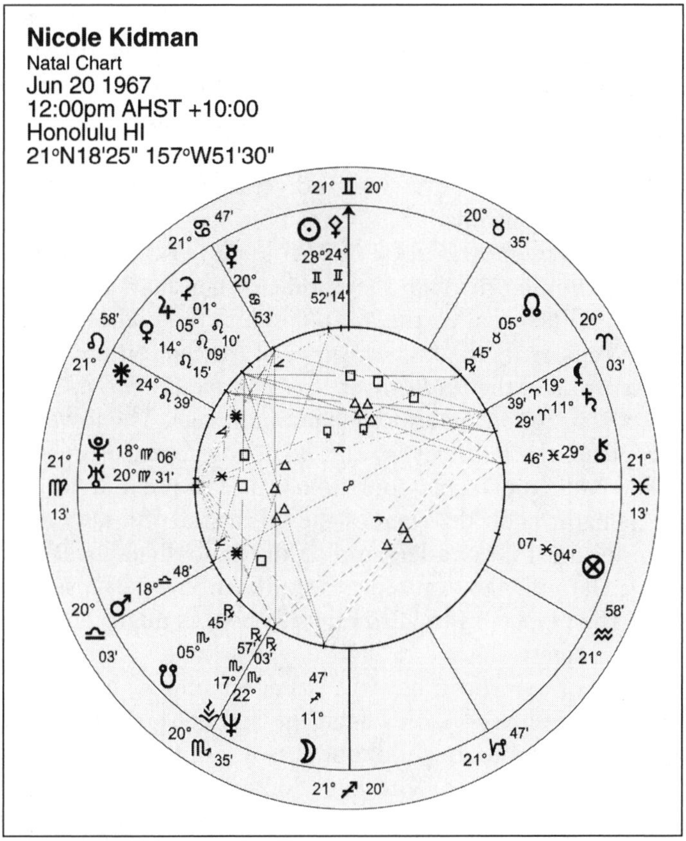

Nicole Kidman's birth chart.

The horizontal line running through the middle of Nicole's chart is called the *horizon;* the sign rising in the east at her birth is called the *ascendant.* Unlike on a map, the east on an astrological birth chart is to the left. (If you were looking down from atop the world, east would be left, as it is here.) On Nicole's chart, the left horizon line leads to the sign of Virgo ♍, which is her rising sign. The line on the right half of the horizon leads to the *descendant.* For Nicole, the descendant is Pisces ♓. The descendant is important when looking at family relationships, because it indicates how you deal with family and friends in relationships, and how you bond with others. The descendant borders, or is on the cusp of, the 7th house of primary relationships, including spouses and other partners. This house speaks about whom you attract and how you connect with partners—all partners, in business and love.

What does this mean for Nicole? With her Pisces ♓ descendant, Nicole attracts idealistic partners, creative partners, and family who see *her* potentials. She would be very supportive of her partners' or family's talents and abilities. Saturn ♄ in her 7th house makes it difficult for Nicole to find her ideal partner—or to find a partner who is her equal. Nicole needs a spiritual, creative, and yet logical and mature partner in all personal relationships.

Now let's take another look at Nicole's birth chart. Do you see the vertical line running through the middle of her chart, with an arrow at the top? This line is called the *meridian,* and the highest portion, with the arrow, represents the highest point of the Sun on the day she was born, and is called the *midheaven,* or *Medium Coeli* (M.C.). This line represents your ambition and your public image. The lowest end of this line is opposite the midheaven, and is called the *nadir* or *Imum Coeli* (I.C.). The nadir represents your foundation in life and your family roots. The nadir is on the cusp of the 4th house of family and home, and is important to an understanding of family dynamics. How do you create your family? Do you repeat family patterns? The sign at your nadir and the planets in the 3rd and 4th houses might help you to answer these questions.

In Nicole's birth chart, her M.C. is at Gemini ♊, her nadir is at Sagittarius ♐, and her Moon ☽ is in the 3rd house, also in Sagittarius ♐. This is the house of early childhood lessons and siblings, as well the environment of early life. With her Moon ☽ in this house, Nicole is emotionally connected to her family, particularly to her childhood. She likely is very attached to her parents, especially to her mother. There could have been upheaval in the family early in her life or perhaps her family traveled or moved often. The natal Moon ☽ in Sagittarius ♐ and in her solar 3rd house can account for all that movement and travel, which could set up a cycle in her life of feeling detached or not rooted in a home. Free will can change that—Nicole can choose a different way of life. Because Nicole is a Gemini Sun ♊ ☉, she could more readily adapt to changing residences or traveling as a youth.

Nicole's mother is likely the biggest influence in her life. Family is important to Nicole, and her family probably gave her the support she needed to be independent. Nicole's nadir is in the sign of Sagittarius ♐, the mutable Fire sign of freedom and exploration. Encouraged by her family to explore her potential and her talents, by age 6 she already performed at school. Her mother and father introduced their children to the arts and culture very early, and from them, Nicole received much support to be herself. Her early exposure to the arts developed her interest in them and gave her confidence in her abilities.

Knowing what we know about how Nicole is in relationships, we can say that with relationship difficulties, including marriage and family, she would want to know what is truly bothering the partner or family member. She might analyze or ask for help from either a professional or a spiritual counselor to get some sense of why the situation is out of control. Nicole is philosophical in her approach to problem-solving in family matters. Nicole respects and appreciates independent thinking and admires people who stand up for their rights. She would be a negotiator in talks between family members. With the Moon ☽ in her 3rd house, she would communicate well with her mother and understand her mother's way of negotiating in the family. Nicole can handle much adversity within a person or personality and can probably handle volatile personalities in family. She would try to understand the reasons a person gets upset without taking it personally. She is adaptable and yet at the same time intelligent, with a desire to get to the bottom of a difficult family issue.

In your own astrological birth chart, the meridian line indicating the midheaven may not run perfectly at the apex of your chart wheel, but you will recognize it because it is a heavier line, with an arrow at the top. The nadir is opposite the midheaven on the cusp of the 4th house. The descendant is on the cusp of the 7th house, and is the sign at the far right along the horizontal line through the center of your birth chart. Take a look at your birth chart and note your descendant and nadir below, or in your Intuitive Arts notebook.

Descendant: ______________________________

Nadir: ______________________________

Think about what the descendant and nadir might mean in terms of how you connect with others in relationships (the descendant), as well as how you work within your family (the nadir). The 7th house cusp is the descendant and the 4th house cusp is the beginning of the nadir. Both of these areas of your birth chart reflect personal development from partners and family. We include our keywords for each sign again in the following table, to help you remember what they mean. You might want to check back in Chapter 5, where we also listed keywords for each planet and for each house. These will help you interpret your nadir and descendant, as you'll also look at the planets in your 7th house and 4th house on your birth chart. You can use the information you get from this exercise to guide you and help you adjust your own thinking about family, as well as when dealing with family members. What's your dad's nadir? Your sister's descendant? Just like the other elements in a birth chart (including your Moon ☽ sign, as discussed earlier), the nadir and descendant are two more pieces to the puzzle of who you and your family members are, and how you fit together.

Astro Sign	Keyword	Astro Sign	Keyword
Aries ♈	Energy	Libra ♎	Balance
Taurus ♉	Grounding	Scorpio ♏	Power
Gemini ♊	Communication	Sagittarius ♐	Enthusiasm
Cancer ♋	Emotion	Capricorn ♑	Responsibility
Leo ♌	Confidence	Aquarius ♒	Idealism
Virgo ♍	Resourcefulness	Pisces ♓	Spirituality

Planetary Returns and Transits: Saturn ♄ and Pluto ♇

We've seen how important the Moon is in our daily lives, and now we're going to look at some other planets, and how their cycles, or transits, can affect us. Just as the Moon does, each planet travels through the 12 houses and signs during its cycle; some planets simply have very long or short cycles. The Moon takes 29½ days, for example, and Saturn takes 28 to 30 years to make the same journey through the Zodiac. The following table indicates the time each planet takes to transit, as well as the astrological sign the planet rules and some keywords for each planet.

Planet	Rules the Astro Sign(s)	Keywords	Transits Each Astro Sign
Sun ☉	Leo ♌	Self, creativity, will	Every year
Moon ☽	Cancer ♋	Emotions, instincts, unconscious	Every month
Mercury ☿	Gemini ♊ and Virgo ♍	Intelligence, logic, communication	Every year
Venus ♀	Taurus ♉ and Libra ♎	Love, money, possessions	Every year
Mars ♂	Aries ♈ and Scorpio ♏	Energy, courage, ego	Every 2 years
Jupiter ♃	Sagittarius ♐ and Pisces ♓	Fortune, wisdom, philosophy	Every 12 years
Saturn ♄	Capricorn ♑ and Aquarius ♒	Responsibility, structure, discipline	Every 28 to 30 years
Uranus ♅	Aquarius ♒	Originality, intuition, liberation	Every 84 years
Neptune ♆	Pisces ♓	Idealism, spirituality, intuition	Every 165 years
Pluto ♇	Scorpio ♏	Power, destruction, transformation	Every 248 years

While the transits of each of these planets will have interesting effects on you and your family, we'll be taking a closer look at two planets, Saturn ♄ and Pluto ♇.

When Will Saturn ♄ Return?

Saturn ♄, the planet of structure and responsibility, visits each sign/house every 28 to 30 years, and when it comes for a visit, it settles in for about 2½ years. With a visit this long, you're not likely to overlook its effects on you. If you look at a Saturn return chart, it can show you when Saturn will be coming to call. As the teacher of the planets, Saturn will have some lessons for you in terms of responsibility, self-discipline, and perseverance. During a Saturn return, you'll feel challenged to evaluate your present career, your family, or your partnerships. Saturn's return allows us to look back on the areas of our lives we have not yet accomplished. We review our lives and become aware of our successes or failures up to that time—of course, success and failure is all a matter of perception!

The Devil: materialism; the World: success.

People make lots of changes during their Saturn returns; they get married and divorced, change careers, move to new places. During Arlene's Saturn return, she started a new career, teaching the Tarot, and left an old career in the restaurant industry behind. Arlene also reviewed her own family dynamics and focused on her desire to get married. Let's look again at Nicole Kidman's birth chart, this time showing her Saturn return. The inner wheel is her birth chart; Nicole's Saturn return is the outer wheel.

If you look in the 7th house of Nicole's chart, you will find Saturn ♄ in both the inner wheel and the outer wheel—Saturn has returned to the house and sign of her birth. A lot was going on during Nicole's Saturn return. Her Saturn return began in 1996. Just after this, Nicole had lots of changes going on in her life—both personal and family-related—and a whole new lifestyle unfolded for her after 1999. (Her divorce from Tom Cruise became final in 2000.) By the time the Saturn return was prominent in 1996 to 1998, she was likely experiencing difficulties in either her marriage or business partnerships. Astrology can help us "know" ahead of time when these planetary alignments will occur—and we believe that saying "Knowledge is power!" If you are aware that something might be brewing for you—in the planets—you can use your free will to prepare yourself, make changes in advance, and perhaps even remedy the situation.

Because Saturn returns occur every 28 to 30 years, most of us will see at least 2 in our lifetimes—maybe 3!—so you'll have a few chances to work on this one, and should be prepared to learn new lessons from Saturn during each return. The first Saturn return generally happens near age 28 to 30; the second between ages 58 and 60; and the third from age 88 to 91.

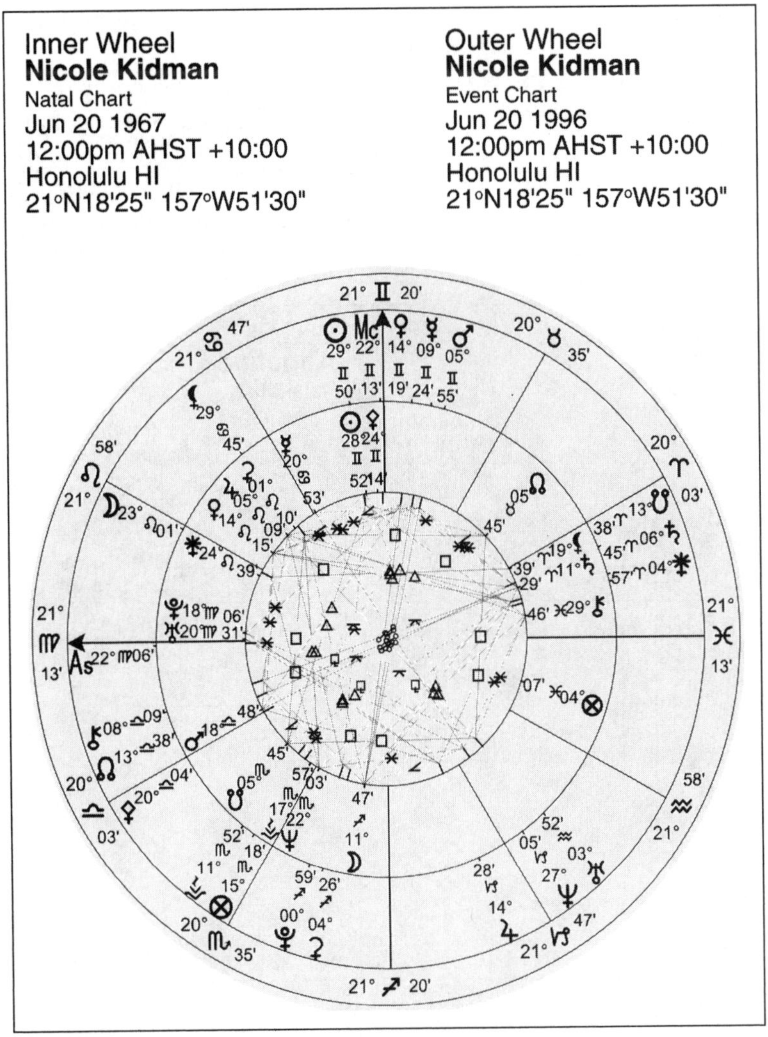

Nicole Kidman's noon birth chart, with Saturn ♄ return.

Pluto ♇, the Planet with a Soul

Pluto ♇ takes 248 years to complete its transformational orbit. Obviously, Pluto moves very slowly; it's what we call a generational planet. This is because it generally stays from 11 to 32 years in each sign, and so a whole generation of people will share Pluto in the same sign of their birth chart. Did you ever wonder why grandparents and grandchildren get along so well, while they both might conflict with the parents? We think this is Pluto at work, and you'd have to compare your own chart with, say, your mother's and your grandmother's, but it's likely there's a positive aspect between your Pluto and your grandmother's that's just not there between you and your mom. We looked at Arlene's chart, along with her grandmother's, to see this link in action. They share some very positive aspects. A synastry grid for them follows.

Across
Arlene
Natal Chart

Down
Angelina
Natal Chart

	☽	☉	☿	♀	♂	♃	♄	♅	♆	♇	⚷	⚳	⚴	⚵	⚶	☊	☋	As	Mc	⊗	Vx
☽				⚼ 2A08					⚹ 0S58	☌ 2S10	⚼ 1A05		☍ 3A25		⚻ 3A21	☍ 8A04	☌ 8A04		△ 1A01	∠ 2A50	
☉	△ 4S50	△ 4A05	△ 8S09	□ 0S57		☍ 0A19	☌ 4A09	□ 0S04			□ 1S59		⚼ 0A20							□ 0S15	
☿	⚼ 1A02	△ 7A06					☌ 7A03		☌ 0A15	⚹ 1A27			△ 4S09	□ 2A50					⚹ 1S44		□ 2S14
♀	⚻ 2A07		□ 1S12		☌ 3A01			△ 6A53			⚹ 4A58		△ 7S42			△ 3S04		⚼ 0A38		△ 6A42	
♂		△ 9S03							△ 2S11				△ 2A12		□ 2A08	△ 6A51		□ 4S28	☍ 0S12		
♃	□ 4A54		⚻ 1A34		⚹ 5A47		∠ 1S08				△ 7A44		☍ 4S56			☍ 0S18	☌ 0S18		△ 7S21		
♄		□ 2S14						△ 6S23		□ 3A25				⚹ 2A03				△ 2A21		△ 6S34	△ 7A06
♅										□ 1S45	∠ 1A30		□ 3A50		△ 3A46			△ 2S50			△ 1A55
♆		△ 5A28					△ 5A24		△ 1S24	⚹ 0S12			△ 5S47	⚻ 1A11				□ 0A53	☍ 3S23		
♇	☌ 7A46	△ 1S09				⚹ 2A38	△ 1S12					□ 0A52									
⚷			□ 3A02		☌ 7A15								△ 3S28			△ 1A10	⚹ 1A10				
⚳				☍ 4A24	△ 1A24	□ 5A39		☌ 5A17		∠ 0A06	☍ 3A21					△ 4S40				☌ 5A06	
⚴	△ 9A59	☌ 1A04				⚹ 4A51	△ 1A01		△ 5S47	☍ 4S35											
⚵									△ 5S07				△ 0S43		□ 0S48	△ 3A55	⚹ 3A55		☍ 3S08		
⚶															☌ 1A04			☌ 7A40	□ 3A25		△ 2A55
☊				∠ 1A09		∠ 2A24		⚼ 2A01	△ 1S58	☍ 3S10	∠ 0A06		☌ 2A26			☌ 7A04	☍ 7A04		⚹ 0A01	⚼ 1A50	⚻ 0A30
☋				⚼ 1A09		⚼ 2A24		∠ 2A01	⚹ 1S58	☌ 3S10	⚼ 0A06		☍ 2A26		⚻ 2A21	☍ 7A04	☌ 7A04		△ 0A01	∠ 1A50	
As	☍ 6A33	⚹ 2A23				△ 1A24	⚹ 2A26	⚻ 1A47				□ 0A22								⚻ 1A58	
Mc	△ 1A06	△ 7A49	△ 4A26	□ 2A47		☍ 4A02	☌ 7A52	□ 3A40		∠ 1A32	□ 1A44									□ 3A29	
⊗		△ 9A32							☌ 2A41	⚹ 3A53			△ 1A43	□ 5A16	⚻ 1A38	△ 6A21			⚹ 0A42		□ 0A12
Vx	∠ 1S26								☍ 0S39	△ 1S51			⚹ 3A44	□ 3S14					△ 1A20		□ 1A49

Synastry grid for Arlene and her grandmother.

Arlene's Moon is trine her grandmother's Sun ☽ △ ☉, and their Suns are also trine ☉ △ ☉. Arlene always felt comfortable talking with her grandmother about anything. Says Arlene, "Grandma would tell me her pearls of wisdom without making me feel insecure or embarrassed." Arlene felt happy to help her grandmother with chores around the house and farm, and her grandmother would explain to Arlene how to fix things or do things in the orchard, garden, and with the farm animals. Arlene's ego would be received well by her grandmother's Sun ☉. They would harmonize in regard to mutual respect for each other's opinions and feelings. Each of them might also sense the other's need to be recognized and appreciated.

Arlene's grandmother's Pluto ♇ is in Gemini ♊, making great aspects to Arlene's Moon ☽, Sun ☉, and Jupiter ♃. As the synastry grid shows, her grandmother's Pluto is conjunct Arlene's Moon ♇ ☌ ☽, trine Arlene's Sun ♇ △ ☉, and sextile Arlene's Jupiter ♇ ⚹ ♃. And Arlene's Pluto is conjunct her grandmother's Moon in Leo ♇ ☌ ☽ ♌, and sextile her grandmother's Mercury in Libra ♇ ⚹ ☿ ♎. These are positive aspects of relationships and for forming a strong bond, which Arlene says remains alive to this day. The communication between the two charts, with Pluto ♇ acting as the conduit of transformation, bridges any generation gap. What Arlene and her grandmother receive through these Pluto ♇ aspects is a mutual growth cycle. Wisdom is passed down from the elder to the younger and remembered. Her grandmother helps Arlene to become more introspective and aware of her strengths, whereas Arlene helps her grandmother focus on the future. Arlene can also show her grandmother that life can go on after any type of loss.

Now let's look at how Pluto ♇ transits affect each of us. A transit is a particular moment in time during which a planet will go through a Zodiac sign in the sky. A transit chart shows your birth chart with the present position of the planets in an outer wheel. As it transits through our houses, transiting Pluto creates aspects to our natal Pluto: These aspects create the beginning of transformations in one's life. Major evolutionary cycles take place when transiting Pluto aspects your natal planets. Transits can be thought of as triggers, as quick movements that force you into action. Pluto is associated with destruction and transformation, and a Pluto transit will force you to change your life in some way, particularly in an area in which you aren't being true to yourself. The area of change will relate to the area ruled by the planet Pluto contacts in the transit. Let's look at Goldie Hawn's birth chart and Pluto ♇ transit.

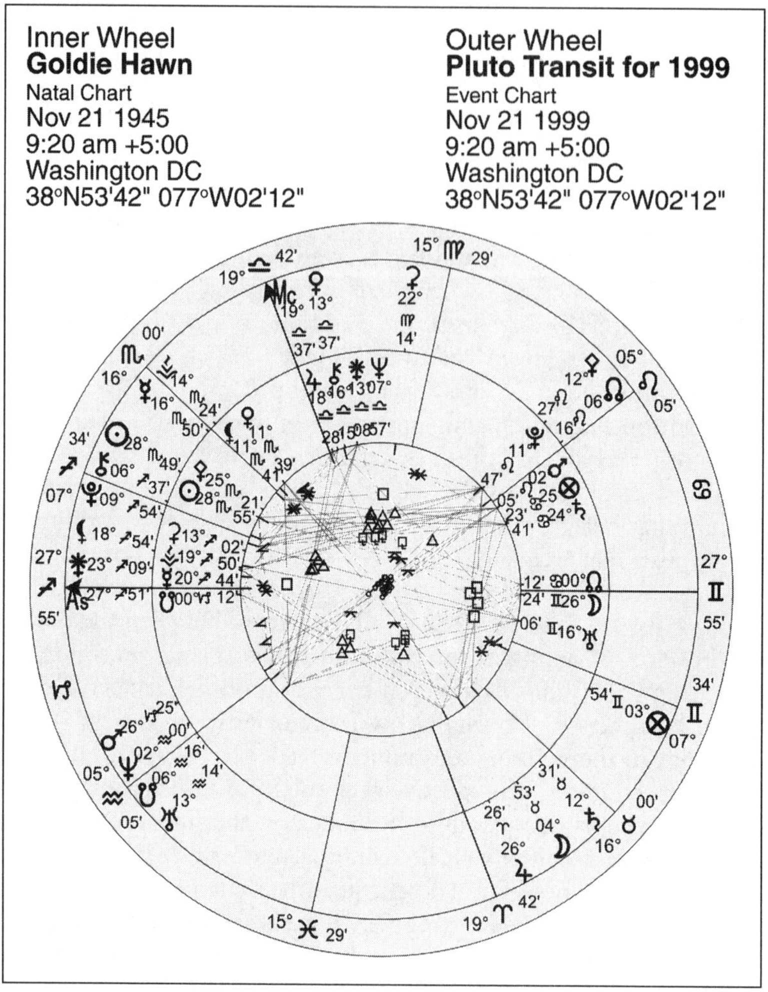

Goldie Hawn's Pluto ♇ transit.

Goldie Hawn had transiting Pluto in Sagittarius trine her natal Pluto in Leo ♇ △ ♇ from the latter half of 1999 through 2000. This positive, harmonious trine sent a lucky flow toward a rebirthing of herself, bringing ♇ a great opportunity into her life for personal examination. Goldie took advantage of this energy by using this time to explore her spiritual nature and write a book, *A Lotus Grows in Mud: Footprints of a Spiritual Life,* sharing her insights with the public on walking the spiritual path. Her evolution may take her in Goldie's new direction will be welcomed by the public, even though it is different from what has been known about her before this transit occurred in her life.

Remember that life can be very difficult for you when you try to resist the Pluto transit's urge to transform. And you can't sit still and hope the Pluto transit passes you by—Pluto will push you to transform if you don't take the initiative yourself. Look at your family's charts, and have a transit chart done—if your brother has been acting a little, well, not like himself, if he seems to be going through many changes and you don't know how to help him, take a look at his chart and see if that pesky Pluto is doing something to explain this change. Your brother could be experiencing his Pluto transit—otherwise known as the midlife crisis!

Death and Judgement: death and rebirth through Pluto ♇.

The Pluto transit will force you to take a good long look at yourself (Pluto will stay a minimum of 7 to 10 years in each house) and get rid of old behaviors and ways of thinking that are no longer relevant to who you are—it's an evolutionary process. You may find that goals you once had are no longer important, and you may have a new set of priorities. You'll have to do a lot of thinking about who you really are to make it through this process, but a whole new perspective on your life and lifestyle comes with a Pluto transit over your 1st, 4th, 7th, or 10th house. (No one gets all of these in one lifetime, though—the entire circuit takes 248 years!) For some of us, such change isn't so difficult, because some people are naturally more accepting of change. For those of us who are fearful of change, however, the process of a Pluto transit can be very challenging indeed. It can be difficult, and you may not feel like the same person you were a few years ago once the transit is done, but hey, that's transformation! You'll feel like you're seeing the world—and yourself—through new eyes. You'll be amazed at what you can accomplish in self-awareness during a Pluto transit, and perhaps you won't recognize family members when they're experiencing theirs, but be supportive, and help them grow into the persons they were meant to be. And awareness of this planetary event can be helpful—maybe your brother feels completely unlike himself, as well. Before he gets divorced and buys a red convertible, help him channel that desire for change into some soul searching, for productive change in his life.

That being said, because Pluto ♇ is a generational planet, your own Pluto transit is likely to be right on the heels of your siblings'. (Your parents will likely have a different natal Pluto, with their own midlife crises between ages 35 to 40.) When you experience your own Pluto transit, share the experience with your family, and ask for their help with your exploration of self-awareness. They may have insights into your true self, and memories of a self you no longer wish to be. Use your family resources during this challenging time.

Unlocking Stubborn Problems in Family Relationships

Do you have seemingly insurmountable problems with family members? Difficulty communicating with family members? Or perhaps you sense that the problem is with yourself—maybe you don't easily assert yourself and your own needs in the relationship, or perhaps you find that you don't listen well to the needs of other family members.

We're going to use a key—literally—and your Psychic Intuition to help you unlock some of these family problems. First, you should think about a particular relationship, and try to assess the difficulty and what might be needed to help you better this relationship. Perhaps you need *patience* in your relationship, to slow down and pay attention to the other person. You might find that you need to *listen,* or that you need the *courage* to assert yourself in the relationship.

Tarot's Temperance: Do you need patience in your relationship?

If you can, do this exercise with the other person in the relationship, discuss with this other person what he or she might need to better the relationship, or agree on something you both might need, or do (*listen, love, patience*). Now here's where the keys come in. You should purchase some keys for this exercise, or look around your house for some old keys—some people collect them, and as you'll be looking at this key often, it should be one with an appearance you like.

Tarot's Strength: Is courage what is needed to work on your difficult family relationship?

Now write the word you have chosen on a small card: *patience, love, courage, listen, communicate*. Choose the word that fulfills what your relationship needs. Punch a hole in the card, and attach it to your chosen key with a blue ribbon. (Blue is our choice because it represents peace and thoughtfulness.) If you like, you can perform this process with two keys, and then give one key to the other person in the relationship. If you're not comfortable with that idea, or if the relationship is presently too challenging, keep the key yourself, and use it as an affirmation whenever you think of the relationship or feel confronted by it, or when you find that you have to deal with the relationship on some level (either on your own or with the other person; perhaps you are going through old photographs of your family, or maybe you are expecting your monthly telephone call from your sister). Hold the key and remind yourself that you need to be courageous or patient with the other person.

The key will not unlock this difficult relationship without your help, but it can be used as a tool to make you more thoughtful and intuitive about the relationship, and to give you more control over how you behave within the relationship. Even if you are never able to share a key with the other person in the relationship, this exercise can help you reach a new level of understanding about the relationship, and its joys and difficulties. And changing your own perspective is really most of the battle in any difficult situation. Buddhist monk Thich Nhat Hahn has observed that people are willing to spend many years of effort to achieve an educational or career goal, but grow impatient with difficult relationships and often give up too easily. Unlocking the door to a difficult relationship may take a lot of time and patience, but once the door is open you may find rewards more rich in love and understanding than you'd ever thought possible!

chapter 7

When You Can't Go Home Again

Home is where the heart is ... or may be
Family energy: The asteroids
All in the family
Chiron: The family doctor
(Why) You can't divorce your family
Fortune's wheel
Psychic Intuition: Send it off in a letter

What if your family problems have no obvious or clear solutions, and going home just doesn't seem to be an option? Can your family relationships be salvaged? We introduce you to Astrology's asteroids, and show you how they can help you learn about, deal with, and possibly heal family difficulties. We also take another look at synastry, and use it to help clarify the problems in a difficult relationship. We use the Tarot and Psychic Intuition to help you decide what the next step might be. Use these exercises to bring yourself peace, and to discover new alternatives to your family relationships. Nurture and learn about yourself as you explore the meaning of family and how to create a family—traditional or alternative—that sustains and empowers you.

Home Is Where the Heart Is ... or May Be

Is home where your heart is? Maybe it is, and you still have a difficult family relationship that won't budge, no matter what you try. Most people have (or have had) at least one of these. Perhaps you just don't get along with another family member, or you have been estranged from someone in your family—is there someone you aren't even on speaking terms with? Maybe, in your case, we're not talking about something so drastic. It could be a relationship that seems fine, but that, on a deeper level, is dissatisfying or even hurtful for you.

In this chapter, we consider these relationships, and help you to decide whether you want to continue in the relationship (perhaps altering your expectations of what the relationship will be in the future), or consider your efforts complete, and stop investing your valuable energy and emotions in a relationship that will continue to make you unhappy, angry, or frustrated. Where can you go from here? Let's look at the asteroids—Ceres ⚳, Juno ⚵, Pallas Athene ⚴, Vesta ⚶— and the planetoid Chiron ⚷, and see how they can affect family relationships.

Family Energy: The Asteroids

There are hundreds of thousands of documented asteroids, which are known as minor planets; most of them orbit together on a belt between Mars ♂ and Jupiter ♃. Officially, they are considered material left over from the creation of our solar system. A number of them are named after goddesses. (The asteroids have a very *yin* energy.) Astrologers consider four of them to have noticeable astrological influence. Like the planets, these asteroids also have Tarot card associations.

Asteroid	**Realm**	**Influences**	**Tarot Card Association**
Ceres ⚳	Motherhood	Parenting, nurturing, natural cycles, fertility	The Moon, The Empress
Juno ⚵	Marriage	Partnerships, control	The Empress, Justice
Pallas Athene ⚴	Wisdom	Intelligence, strength, understanding	The Star, Strength
Vesta ⚶	Power	Fulfillment, service, power	The Sun, Judgement

Pushing Your Buttons

Family members most often know how to push your buttons—they know you better (or longer!) than most people, and can hit on a sore spot with the greatest ease. What can you do about it? For starters, it would be useful to find out why your sibling, parent, or child is the way she or he is, and why you are, well, the way *you* are.

Let's look at the Tarot cards associated with each of the four asteroids: the Moon and the Hermit for Ceres ⚳, the Empress and Justice for Juno ⚵, the Star and Strength for Pallas Athene ⚴, and the Sun and

Judgement for Vesta ⚶. Spread these cards out before you and meditate on them for a few minutes, considering each card and its imagery, and then looking at all of the cards together. You can make some notes about your impressions of each card in your Intuitive Arts notebook.

Ceres ⚳

Juno ⚵

Pallas Athene ⚴

Vesta ⚶

Think about a difficult family relationship you're dealing with right now—or one that you aren't dealing with, but that you'd like to work on. This could be *any* family relationship you're dissatisfied with or that you want to improve in some way. What do you feel is the biggest issue you need to deal with or work on in this relationship? Have another look at those Tarot cards, and see if one stands out for how you feel about this family relationship. Choose the card that resonates with you intuitively. Which card did you select? Is the card associated with Ceres and her realm of parenting, Juno's realm of marriage, Pallas Athene's realm of control and intelligence, or Vesta's realm of power over hearth and home? Use the card you selected as a starting point for healing the relationship.

Let's learn a bit about the goddesses for whom each of these four asteroids are named. We also give you a birth chart example from the rock-and-roll Osbourne family for each asteroid. Arlene cast noon birth charts for the Osbournes.

Ceres ⚳: Nurturing Mother

Ceres is the Roman goddess of fertility, and of grain—she is responsible for all things that grow, and was very important in agrarian cultures, as a good (or poor) harvest was in her power. Ceres is associated with fertility, parenting, and nurturing. The obvious choice for this asteroid is Sharon Osbourne.

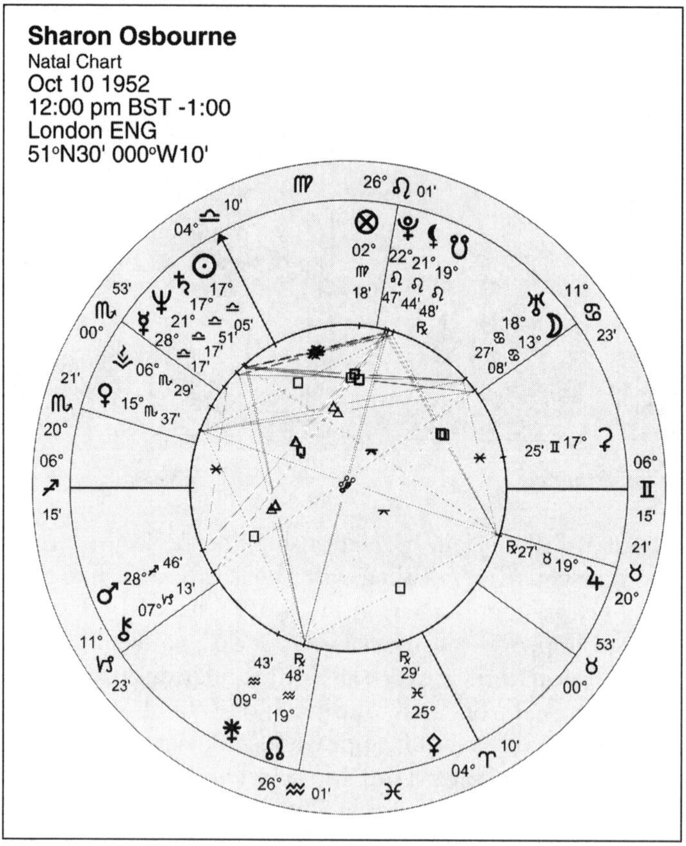

Sharon Osbourne's noon birth chart.

Can you find Ceres ⚳ on Sharon's birth chart? Sharon has Ceres ⚳ in Gemini ♊, in her 7th house of primary relationships. She parents and nurtures in an intellectual way, which doesn't mean that she's not caring, but that she deals with parenting issues in an intellectual, logical way. This obviously works for her family! She focuses her nurturing on her business or marriage partner. Ceres in Gemini means that Sharon nurtures her partner's mind and intelligence, and encourages her partner to speak his mind. Ceres is the asteroid of abundance, the green thumb, and the Earth Mother who plants ideas and gives the mind fertile ground for communication. Sharon nurtures Ozzy's thoughts and ideas and gets him to *feel* what he is thinking. She is also the member of the family who creates intellectual banter about family issues.

Juno ⚵: Partnerships

Juno is the wife of Jupiter, ruler of the heavens and the earth. Juno ruled over marriage, and this asteroid is associated with marriage and partnerships, as well as duty. Ozzy and Sharon Osbourne will be our examples for Juno. Here is Ozzy's birth chart.

Look for Juno in Ozzy's birth chart, and go back to Sharon's chart, and find Juno there, as well. Ozzy has Juno ⚵ in Aries ♈ in his 1st house of identity. Ozzy is impulsive in partnerships, and wants a fiery relationship. Sharon's Juno ⚵ is in Aquarius ♒ in her 2nd house of possessions and self-esteem. She is independent in her partnership with Ozzy, and may feel claustrophobic in a relationship that feels too needy. Juno is the asteroid we look to when we have concern for relationships—she deals with everything from the need for a commitment to the issues of unfair treatment between partners to any injustice that can disturb or deny loyalty. The great thing about Ozzy's Juno and Sharon's Juno is that they are in compatible signs. Aquarius ♒ and Aries ♈ are both independent signs. Sharon would like to be independent with finances and business issues. (She takes care of business for her partner!) Ozzy would like to be independent and creative with his own identity and public image. His marriage partner could elevate him to a secure financial base. Her marriage partner could elevate her public image and bring her personal life to the public's attention.

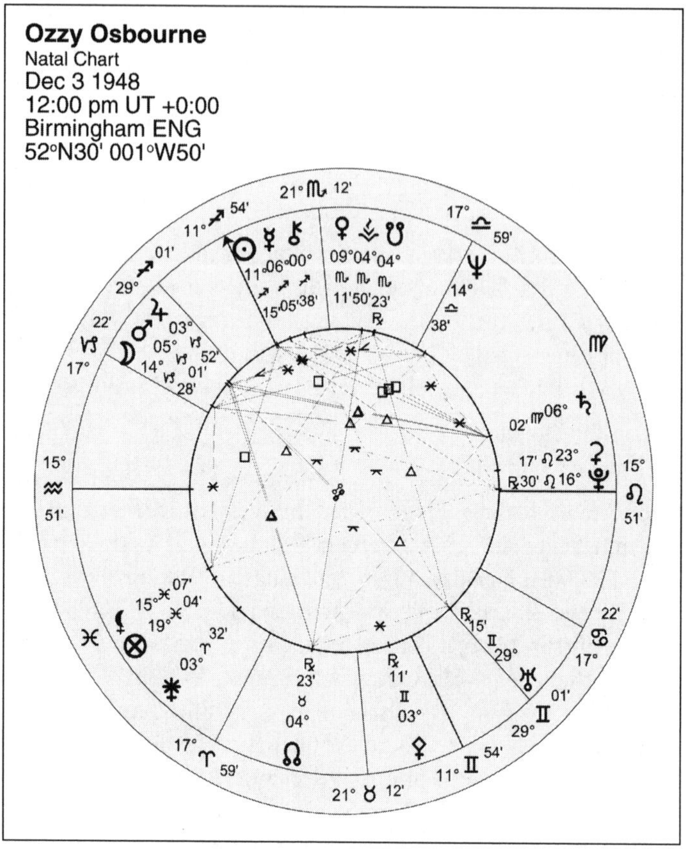

Ozzy Osbourne's noon birth chart.

Pallas Athene ⚴: Strength and Control

Pallas Athene (the Roman goddess Minerva) is the goddess of wisdom and justice. She sprang fully formed from her father's forehead (her dad was Jupiter). Pallas is associated with wisdom and strength, and can be useful in looking at issues of parent/child control, or issues of control and competition in family relationships in general. She can also offer insight into father/daughter relationships. How about if we use Kelly Osbourne's chart, and look for Pallas Athene?

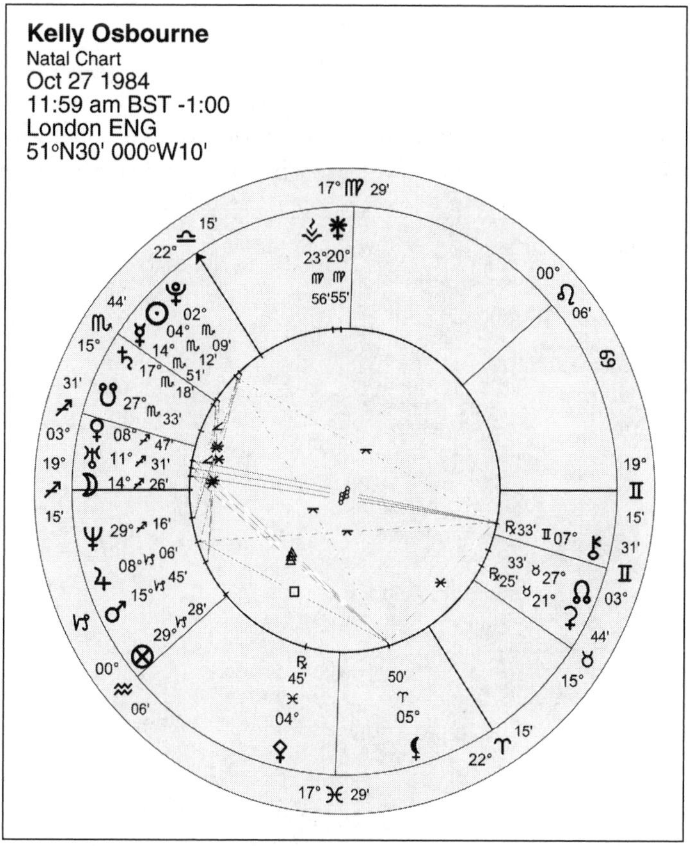

Kelly Osbourne's noon birth chart.

Find Pallas Athene ⚴ on Kelly's birth chart. She's in Kelly's 2nd house of possessions and self-esteem, in the sign of Pisces ♓. This may be a bit surprising, but Kelly finds her strength through her compassion and in how she values life. Her father, Ozzy, has Pallas Athene ⚴ in Gemini ♊ in his 3rd house of knowledge and siblings. He finds his strength through communication—through his voice and in what he learned in early childhood. These two can teach each other to develop their talents, and they can also have intelligent talks about material world issues. Ozzy can teach Kelly how difficult it was to come from a troubled early childhood environment and find success. His trials have made him wiser and he can relate that to his daughter. Kelly can teach Ozzy to be compassionate and true to who he really is.

Vesta ⚶: Powerful, Loyal Family

Vesta is the guardian of the hearth and home, and is responsible for family stability and social order. Vesta is associated with power and focus, as well as commitment and devotion, or loyalty. Let's look for Vesta in Jack Osbourne's chart and see what we can learn.

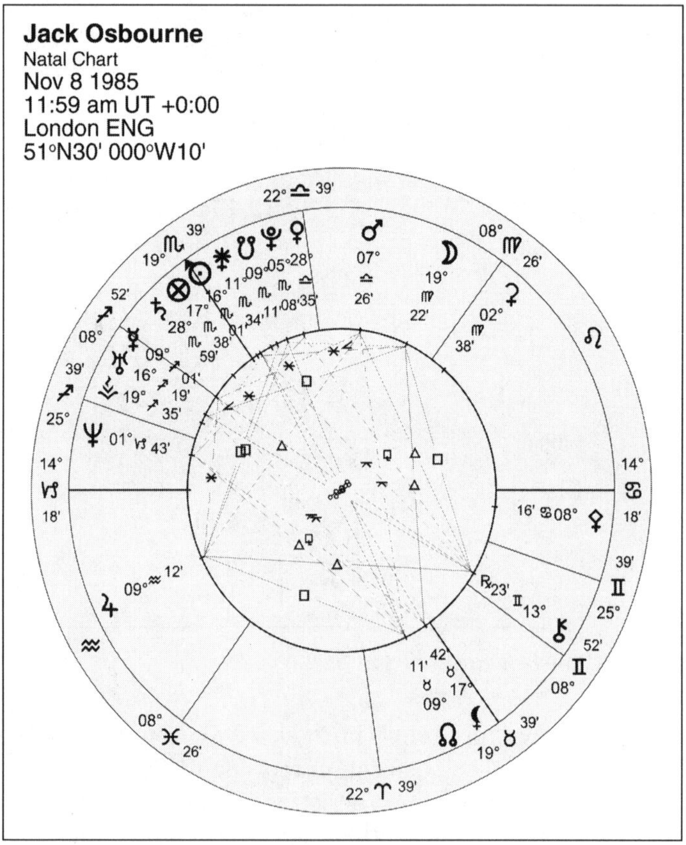

Jack Osbourne's noon birth chart.

Jack has Vesta ⚶ in Sagittarius ♐ in his 11th house of goals and friendship. He is spontaneous with commitment. Vesta in his 11th house means he brings focus to his goals, and commitment to his friendships. He would have a very strong sense of loyalty or commitment to his goals, his friendships, and groups he may belong to. With Vesta in Sagittarius and in a house relating to friends rather than family, Jack creates an extended family for himself. He brings his friends into his hearth and home as if to integrate them into his family. Vesta will help him focus his goals through his friendships rather than through immediate family. Jack's Vesta ⚶ is the same sign as Ozzy's Sun ☉ sign, so the two of them could really clash, because Jack might focus his energy on friends as his leaders rather than his father. Ozzy's Vesta ⚶ is in Scorpio ♏—Jack's Sun ☉ sign—and Ozzy also might have focused a lot of his energy on his friends as leaders. This father and son are alike in this way, and because of this similarity, they will understand each other better as time passes.

All in Your Family

If you look at your birth chart and those of your family members, and find the asteroids we previously discussed, you can learn a lot about yourself and your family, and how your expectations in these areas affect your relationships. These asteroids' signs can reveal how you feel about mothering, partnering, strength, and commitment in your relationships.

The location of Ceres ⚳ in your birth chart will tell you a lot about how you parent and nurture yourself and others, as well as what you expect or need from others in this area of your life. Both the astrological sign and the house are important, but for now we consider the sign. Look at the following table for some keywords for Ceres ⚳ in each sign.

Ceres ⚳ In	**How You Mother**	**The Mothering You Expect**
Aries ♈	Enthusiastically	Demonstrative, assertive
Taurus ♉	Steadfastly	Stable, consistent
Gemini ♊	Intellectually	Lighthearted, thoughtful
Cancer ♋	Empathetically	Nurturing, protective
Leo ♌	Warmly	Generous, sharing
Virgo ♍	Discriminatingly	Self-sacrificing, devoted
Libra ♎	Judiciously	Concerned, loving
Scorpio ♏	Deeply	Powerful, passionate
Sagittarius ♐	Adventurously	Expansive, optimistic
Capricorn ♑	Carefully	Dedicated, loyal
Aquarius ♒	Innovatively	Detached, humanistic
Pisces ♓	Intuitively	Unconditional, compassionate

Juno ⚵ is associated with partnerships of all kinds, though perhaps particularly marriage. What's important to you in a partnership? And how do you enter into a partnership? Again, we've created a table with keywords for Juno ⚵ in each sign.

Juno ⚵ In	**How You Partner**	**The Partnering You Expect**
Aries ♈	Impulsively	Fiery, passionate
Taurus ♉	Committedly	Secure, steadfast
Gemini ♊	Casually	Interesting, stimulating
Cancer ♋	Cautiously	Devoted, nurturing
Leo ♌	Dramatically	Adoring, loyal
Virgo ♍	Practically	Perfect, structured
Libra ♎	Romantically	Balanced, collaborative
Scorpio ♏	Magnetically	Powerful, intense
Sagittarius ♐	Excitedly	Adventurous, enthusiastic
Capricorn ♑	Steadily	Steady, cultivating
Aquarius ♒	Independently	Hands-off, co-partnering
Pisces ♓	Idealistically	Soulful, devoted

Pallas Athene ⚴ is wise and strong. This asteroid can tell you how you (and your family members) find strength, and where you look for wisdom. Pallas Athene's ⚴ keywords for each sign are in the following table.

Pallas Athene ⚴ In	**How You Find Strength**	**The Strength You Expect**
Aries ♈	In leading	Acquiescence
Taurus ♉	In building	Dependability
Gemini ♊	In communicating	Versatility
Cancer ♋	In empathy	Protection
Leo ♌	In creativity	Adoration
Virgo ♍	In sacrifice	Organization
Libra ♎	In harmony	Judiciousness
Scorpio ♏	In power	Magnetism
Sagittarius ♐	In adventure	Enthusiasm
Capricorn ♑	In achievement	Structure
Aquarius ♒	In uniqueness	Freedom
Pisces ♓	In compassion	Connection

Vesta ⚶ is the goddess of the hearth, and she rules the family. She can tell you how you deal with power and commitment in relationships with others, and also what loyalty means to you and how you create focus. Keywords for Vesta ⚶ in each sign are in the following table.

Vesta ⚶ In	How You Commit	The Commitment You Expect
Aries ♈	Thoughtlessly	Unquestioning
Taurus ♉	Generously	Dependable
Gemini ♊	Wittily	Versatile
Cancer ♋	Intuitively	Sensitive
Leo ♌	Warmly	Heart-centered
Virgo ♍	Self-sacrificingly	Sensible
Libra ♎	Sensually	Harmonious
Scorpio ♏	Passionately	Devoted
Sagittarius ♐	Spontaneously	Exciting
Capricorn ♑	Carefully	Practical
Aquarius ♒	Innovatively	Unusual
Pisces ♓	Sensitively	Compassionate

What Can the Goddesses Tell You About You and Your Family?

Let's look at an example, and see how the asteroids come into play in a birth chart. We use Nicole Kidman's birth chart. (Remember, Nicole's is a noon chart, which we first looked at in Chapter 6.)

Nicole has Ceres ⚳ in Leo ♌ in her 11th house of goals and friendship. She's a very warm parent. She nurtures her friends and her goals—and her friends may help nurture her goals. She parents to cultivate her family's and her children's goals.

Juno ⚵ is also in Leo ♌ in Nicole's chart, in her 12th house of subconscious and spirituality. Nicole is dramatically committed in her partnerships, and she needs a rather adoring mate. Nicole needs loyalty in her mate and her family so she can feel free to create.

Pallas Athene ⚴ is in Gemini ♊ in Nicole's 10th house of career. She finds her strength through communicating, and needs others to be versatile. She is highly versatile, and with Pallas in an Air sign, her intellect and her ability to approach her career studiously are evolved.

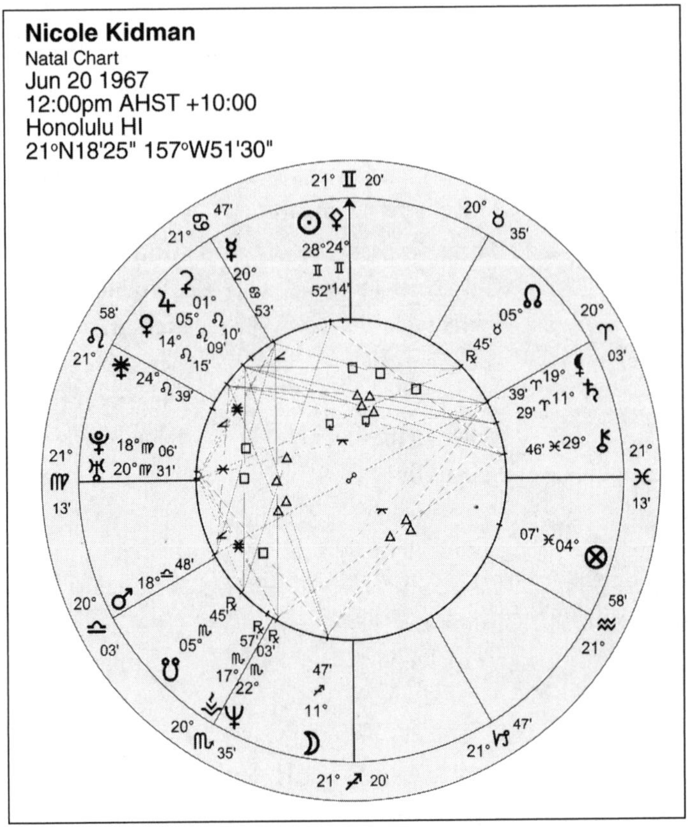

Nicole Kidman's birth chart.

And finally, Nicole has Vesta ⚶ in Scorpio ♏ in her 2nd house of possessions and self-esteem. She is very passionate about her commitments, and expects others to be quite devoted in theirs. She may become self-sufficient financially and will share her resources with her family.

Now try this exercise for yourself by finding these asteroids in your birth chart and using the asteroid keywords in the tables we previously provided. If you can, also do this for a family member, particularly someone with whom you are having difficulty, or with whom you are unable to communicate. Use this form to list the signs and keywords for your (and your family member's) asteroids.

Asteroid	Your Astro Sign	Keywords
Ceres ⚳	________________	________________
Juno ⚵	________________	________________
Pallas Athene ⚴	________________	________________
Vesta ⚶	________________	________________

Asteroid	Your Family Member's Astro Sign	Keywords
Ceres ⚳	________________	________________
Juno ⚵	________________	________________
Pallas Athene ⚴	________________	________________
Vesta ⚶	________________	________________

What are the differences and similarities between you and this family member? Do the asteroids and their influence shed light on this difficult relationship for you? This information isn't meant to be a cure-all, but should give you some insight into how you deal with your family members and what you expect from them, as well as what they expect from you. Knowing that with her Ceres ⚳ in Gemini ♊ your own mother approached motherhood intellectually may not help you with your feelings of neediness, especially if your Ceres ⚳ is in Cancer ♋, but it may help you see that she didn't deprive you of affection intentionally, and that your needs may not be the result of a lack in your relationship with her. You can try to have your desire for affection met in other relationships—look for a family member with Ceres ⚳ in Leo ♌, for example, and use the information you now have to connect with your mother in a different way.

You can add the astrological houses to this equation to get even more information—look back at the keywords for the 12 houses in Chapter 5, and add those to the keywords you recorded earlier.

Chiron ⚷: The Family Doctor

The planetoid Chiron ⚷ was discovered in 1977, which makes it a very recent addition to the world of Astrology. In mythology, Chiron was a centaur—half man, half beast—with great wisdom and healing powers. Immortal, he gave up his immortality to free himself from pain and find peace. In Astrology, Chiron is the wounded healer. The placement of Chiron in your birth chart indicates your psychic wounds—those deep fears and worries you carry with you—which may keep you from fulfilling your potential in life, and can also lead you to self-destructive behavior. Chiron the healer can also show you how to heal your psychic wounds, and once your wounds are healed, you can help to heal others.

We believe that each of us has these psychic wounds, and that we seek others in life who can help us heal them. These might be family members, friends, or lovers. You can look at your birth chart to see where Chiron is, to learn more about this. Let's look again into Sharon and Ozzy Osbourne's birth charts to see how they heal each other's psychic wounds.

Sharon's Chiron ⚷ is in Capricorn ♑ in her 1st house of self. Sharon's wound, or the source of her psychic pain, is fear, which she can heal through courage—no easy feat! Ozzy has Chiron ⚷ in Sagittarius ♐ in his 9th house of philosophy and beliefs. His psychic wound is restlessness, which he can heal by finding inner peace. Chiron's influence is unique in that the healing of the wounds has to be done internally and with constant personal effort. In family and partnerships, the other members of the family will have to accept or realize the wounds in each other first—only then can they help one another heal. Sharon and Ozzy would need to communicate their personal wounds to each other; then they will not only understand but also be able to promote the healing process. In understanding their wounds, Sharon and Ozzy will help each other overcome amazing blockages, improving their relationship and their family dynamics. The family's daily squabbles or confrontations would have a new perspective—the family could acknowledge these blocks and help each other evolve more rapidly, in order to heal!

Now look at your own birth chart and fill in the blanks here.

My Chiron ⚷ is in ______________ *(astro sign)* in my ______________ *(astro house)* house

of ____________________. *(house keyword)*

The house in which Chiron appears will be that area in which you will experience the healing of your psychic wound. (If Chiron is in your 10th house, you will experience and face the wound and its healing through your career and leadership.) The following table indicates what psychic wound Chiron ⚷ symbolizes in each astrological sign, as well as how the wound might be healed.

Chiron ⚷ In	Wound	Heals By
Aries ♈	Impatience	Patience
Taurus ♉	Doubt	Understanding
Gemini ♊	Self-distrust	Wisdom
Cancer ♋	Indifference	Gentleness
Leo ♌	Overenthusiasm	Tolerance
Virgo ♍	Servility	Strength
Libra ♎	Indecision	Steadfastness
Scorpio ♏	Possessiveness	Selfless love
Sagittarius ♐	Restlessness	Inner peace
Capricorn ♑	Fear	Courage
Aquarius ♒	Aloofness	Sharing
Pisces ♓	Paranoia	Self-transcendence

What is your psychic wound, and how might you go about healing it? If you're having difficulty with a family member, ascertain what his or her psychic wound is, as well, and see how this affects that person's relationships, with you and others. Maybe part of your role—or that person's—in this relationship is to help the other person in the healing of his or her psychic wound. Healing is not always a comfortable or pleasant experience. It can be difficult and downright painful, but in the end, you grow. Let Chiron ⚷ help you heal yourself and that difficult family relationship.

(Why) You Can't Divorce Your Family

Why can't you divorce your family, anyway? Sometimes it feels like it would be the very best solution, but even if you're estranged ... your family is still your family. You may in fact decide that the obstacles in a family relationship are so great that all you can do at this point is cut your ties and do your best to move on. But often this is very difficult with family, and breaking off your relationship with one family member can affect your other relationships as well. Not everyone will feel as you do about this family member, and it may be impossible for family members to choose sides, no matter how egregious the situation.

Can you save this relationship? Only you can decide. Before you do, however, use some of the tools we've already presented in this chapter, and then let's consider synastry again.

We first looked at synastry in Chapter 5. (Remember the charts for George Sr. and George W.?) Synastry, you'll recall, is the astrology of relationships. It looks at the aspects between the planets, or their relationship to one another. Aspects can show either the flow of energy between you and your family member (supportive aspects) or a lesson to be learned by one or both of you (challenging aspects). We're going to consider George W. Bush and Jeb Bush, two brothers who, on the surface, at least, would appear to be very competitive. First let's look at their birth charts.

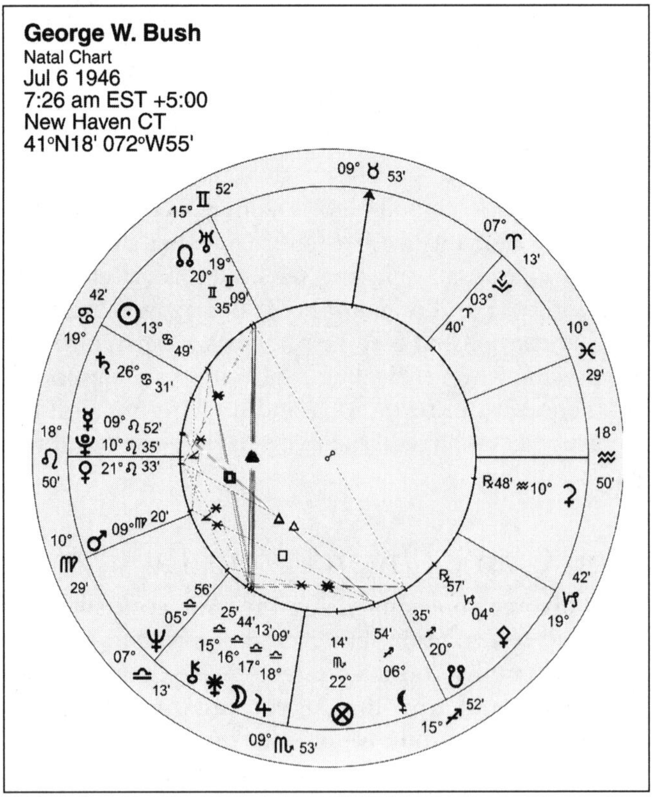

Birth chart for George W. Bush.

What can we see going on here? George has his Sun ☉ in Cancer ♋ in his 11th house of goals and friendship. He's popular and inclined toward leadership, and he may be helped into a position of power by others (!). His Moon ☽ is in Libra ♎ in his 3rd house of knowledge and siblings. George is very social. Family is very important to him. He may be restless, and he feels through others.

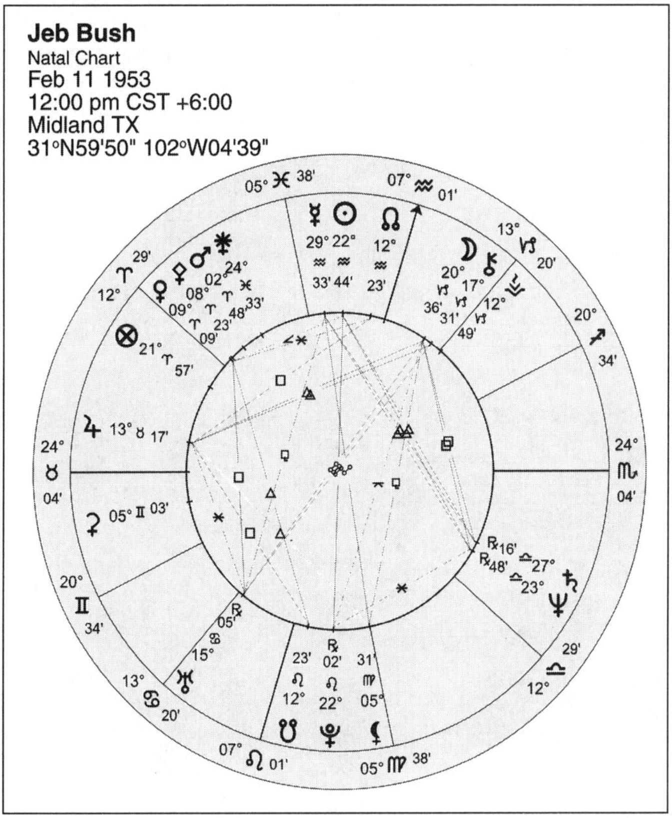

Noon birth chart for Jeb Bush.

Jeb's Sun ☉ is in Aquarius ♒ in his 10th house of career. He has a strong will to succeed, and is very ambitious—this is a good placement for a politician! Jeb's Moon ☽ is in Capricorn ♑ in his 9th house of philosophy and beliefs. He's a natural teacher, and his own beliefs are closely tied to his parents'. He can seem emotionally remote, and is cautious and disciplined with his emotions. He feels through control, and he's likely to be very successful.

Even the best relationships have their challenges, and as we've noted before, the challenging aspects lead to growth, which can make a relationship stronger—and more interesting. That a relationship is fraught with challenging aspects still doesn't make it hopeless; there are so many factors at play! Let's look at the synastry grid for George W. and Jeb Bush, to see where their challenges lie. Turn back to Chapter 5, or look in Appendix A, to review the astrological aspects and their meanings if you need to refresh your understanding before reading this section.

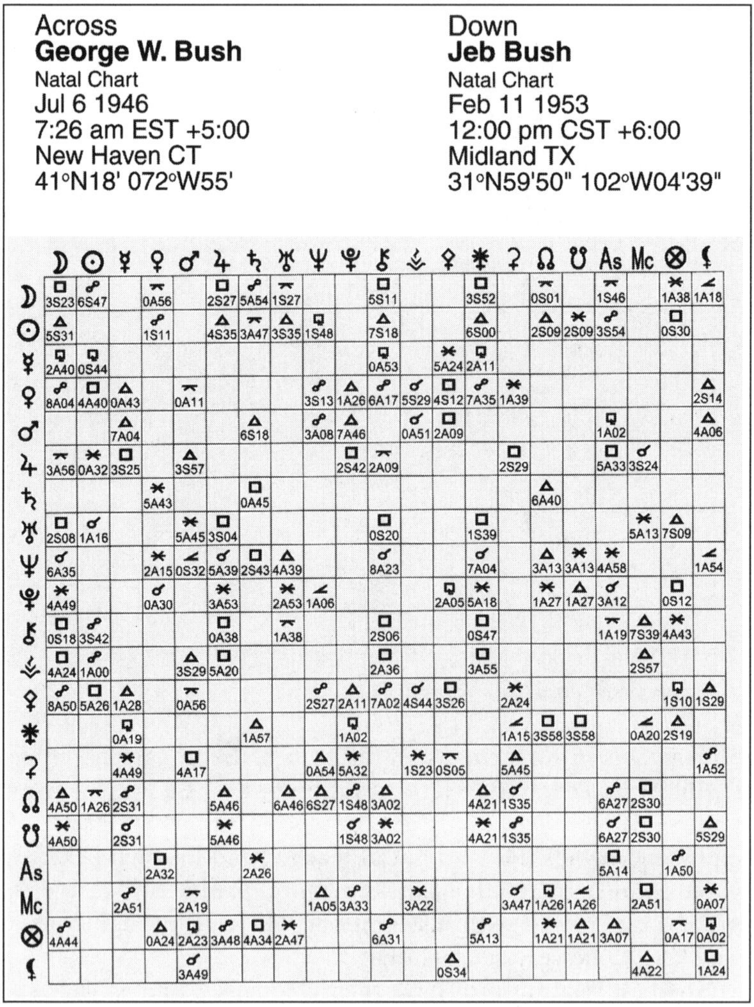

Synastry grid for George W. Bush and Jeb Bush. George: across. Jeb: down.

Aspects between the Sun ☉ and Moon ☽ influence the bonds between people. George and Jeb's Moons are square ☽ □ ☽. This is a challenging aspect, in that they might not understand each other's nurturing or emotional temperament. Their emotional needs could vary so much that they might not feel comfortable relying upon each other for emotional support. But George's Moon trines Jeb's Sun ☽ △ ☉, a favorable aspect supporting the two in talking out their differences and forgiving old wounds.

Mars ♂ represents male energy, power, and competition. Mars forms one challenging aspect between the Bush brothers, with Jeb's Mars in opposition to George's Neptune ♂ ☍ ♆. This has the potential to establish strong competitive energy between these siblings. But several Mars trines help to neutralize and have a balancing effect on this energy as well as on challenging aspects between other planets. Saturn ♄ presents another set of challenges for these brothers, forming numerous aspects between their charts, starting with square each other ♄ □ ♄. However, they have some favorable Saturn aspects as well (Jeb's Saturn trines George's Uranus ♄ △ ♅ and sextiles his Venus ♄ ⚹ ♀) that provide the potential for harmony to develop between them despite their differences.

Their birth charts tell us that George and Jeb might not always see eye to eye when it comes to personal ambitions. Indeed, their personalities, lifestyles, daily habits, and routines are not compatible—we wouldn't want them to share office space! But they can help each other grow in the public eye and help each other's careers to prosper.

Challenging Your Family Relationship Aspects

If you'd like to explore your birth chart and that of a family member for favorable and challenging aspects, you need a synastry grid for the two of you. You may have prepared one of these for Chapter 5, and if you can use that here, do so. If you didn't, or you want to look at a different relationship, you can have an astrologer create one for you, or order one from a number of Internet sites (see Appendix A).

One at a time, go through the following list for your portion of the grid, and then your family member's. Take notes on your findings in your Intuitive Arts notebook. This is fairly complex, and difficult to remember!

1. Look at the aspects between the Sun ☉ and Moon ☽ in your charts. The aspects here are very important to the type of bond you share with this family member.
2. Look for trines △ and sextiles ⚹ in the synastry grid. These are the supportive aspects, which create a harmonious flow between the two charts.

3. Also check the oppositions ☍ and squares □ in the grid. These are the challenging aspects—those that encourage growth—in the relationship.
4. Also look at Saturn ♄ and Nodal ☊ ☋ connections, which indicate relationship longevity and strength. These aspects also relate to karmic lessons.
5. Conjunctions ☌ are perhaps the strongest aspect; conjunct planets focus and emphasize one another. Depending on the planets and the other aspects in the chart, conjunctions can be supportive or challenging.
6. Finally, look for quincunxes ⚻, which indicate a lack of energy and need for adjustment.

Letting Go of a Difficult Relationship

If you've decided that you can't continue in a difficult relationship, what should the next step be? You can choose to end the relationship and cut off your ties with that person, or you can simply decide that the status quo is where the relationship will stay: Perhaps you feel your relationship with your mother is not satisfying, but you don't want to end the relationship; you've just decided to stop trying to change it. This won't be a satisfying conclusion, because you'll still feel those needs your mother hasn't been able to fulfill for you. Where can you go? We suggest looking at your own birth chart again, and seeing what your needs are, as well as your strengths. You can then work on developing relationships that will help you fill those needs and also explore your strengths. You can look for fulfillment from other family members, or from friends—remember, your family is what you make it! If you have a family friend or an aunt with whom you feel a strong bond, work on strengthening that relationship and making this person part of your family, whether that person is related to you by blood or not. It's not just blood, but *bonds* that make a family.

Where do you look in your birth chart for this information? We use Nicole Kidman as our example again.

Supportive aspects (trines △ and sextiles ⚹) between other planets and the Sun ☉ and Moon ☽ can be very helpful in dealing with a loss due to conflict (such as the end of a family relationship). When we look at Nicole's chart, we see that her Moon trines three planets—Venus, Jupiter, and Saturn (☽ △ ♀ ♃ ♄). These supportive energies indicate that Nicole's ability to love is passionate and runs very deep. She has an ability to create her own prosperity and to share it with her family or partner. And she has the self-discipline and ability to withstand adversity. These qualities give Nicole great inner strength and faith in herself. What other supportive aspects do you find when you look at Nicole's birth chart?

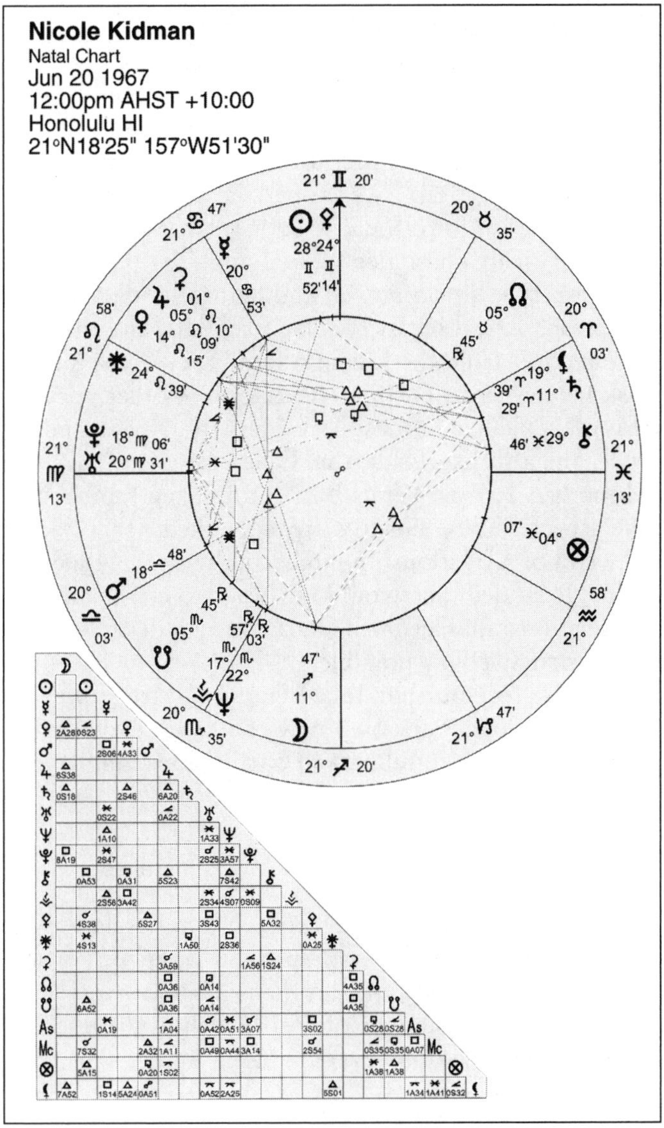

Nicole's birth chart and aspect grid.

Nicole's challenging aspects (squares □ and oppositions ☍) identify where she may have difficulty, but will also experience growth. Again, we look to aspects with the Sun ☉ and Moon ☽ to start—and right away we see that Nicole's Moon squares Pluto (the planet of transformation) and Chiron ☽ □ ♇ ⚷, with her Sun squaring Chiron ☉ □ ⚷. These aspects can represent her need to break down any situation into simpler components to get to the core of the challenge. She would ask, *Is it me? Is my karmic past? Is it something from childhood, is that where this wound comes from?* A caution for her would be do not overanalyze, and do not make a mountain out of a molehill! Most Geminis ♊ have a tendency to think too much! Mercury in Cancer square Mars in Libra ☿ ♋ □ ♂ ♎ shows that mental healing can take place by finding a cause for difficulty, but overworking this intellectual side of things can create continued mental anguish.

Mars ♂, with its focus on power, and Saturn ♄, with its focus on discipline, can each reveal our particular strengths, and this can be helpful as we recover from the loss of a family relationship, as well as begin to look for new relationships (or to look at other relationships in a new way). Nicole has Mars square Mercury ♂ □ ☿, and sextile Venus ♂ ⚹ ♀. She also has Mars trine Pallas Athene ♂ △ ⚴. Saturn is trine her Moon ♄ △ ☽, trine Venus ♄ △ ♀, and trine Jupiter ♄ △ ♃—very positive aspects! These positive aspects indicate that Nicole would approach the end of a relationship intellectually, seeking help from others to keep her grounded. She would not want to create an enemy from the end of a relationship. Her birth chart shows a desire to end things in the most constructive way possible.

Try this exercise for yourself. Take what you learn from your birth chart, and get ready to embark on a new challenge: exploring new relationships to create the fulfilling and harmonious family you are looking for.

Fortune's Wheel

If you're still mired in doubt about a difficult family relationship, and don't know where it's going, why not spin the Wheel of Fortune and see where it takes you? The Wheel of Fortune is a Major Arcana Tarot card that represents the ups and downs of life, as well as the unchanging spiritual reality in the face of an ever-changing world. This card symbolizes fate.

Tarot's Wheel of Fortune: What is fate?

This Tarot reading is meant to give you a sense of perspective and perhaps offer insight into your difficult family relationship. We begin by placing the Wheel of Fortune card in the center of the spread. Then, while shuffling the cards, you should think of the family relationship, and your question about it: *How can I repair this relationship? Can this relationship be salvaged?* Now lay out, *face down*, four cards around the Wheel of Fortune in a clockwise direction. Look at the Wheel of Fortune card: Lay out the first four cards in alignment with the T-A-R-O on this card.

These cards go face down because they represent the factors over which you have no control—they are fate. Next place four cards *face up* on top of the four face-down cards, in the same clockwise order. These cards represent change, and are the factors you can influence in the relationship.

Finally, draw one last card, and place it *face down* over the Wheel of Fortune card in the center of the spread. This one is the wild card—the real element of chance in any spin of the Wheel of Fortune.

Let's take a look at a reading Arlene did for Magda, who was looking for answers regarding her relationship with her brother, Kevin. Their relationship wasn't awful, but it also wasn't good. She and Kevin couldn't seem to communicate, and they had almost nothing in common. They had been close as children, but had grown apart, and Kevin went through a very difficult period during which Magda lost touch with him altogether. They were in contact now, and as she got older, Magda longed for a closer relationship with her brother, though she wasn't sure how to go about achieving this, or if it was even possible.

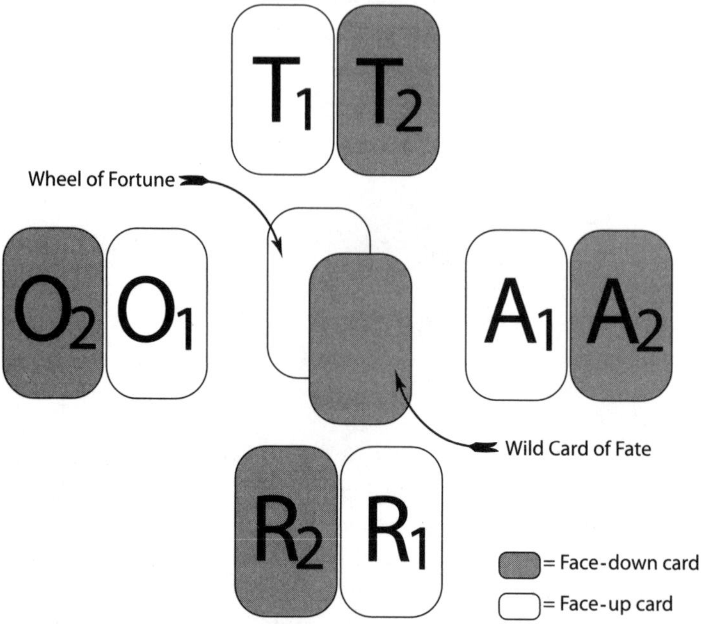

Wheel of Fortune Spread.

Magda's Wheel of Fortune Tarot spread: Will she develop a closer relationship with her brother Kevin, and if so, how long will it take?

The face-up cards indicate those factors Magda can influence, and we look at those first.

Factors Magda can influence are revealed in the face-up cards.

King of Cups. This is a kind and quietly powerful figure. This is what Magda may feel is her past memory of her brother and what their relationship could be: kindness and gentleness. Kevin was close to her and the possibility of that happening again is shown in this card upright—Kevin likely wants the same close relationship as Magda.

The Moon. This card has a lot of psychic energy, and can indicate intense emotions, perhaps even an emotional outburst. They are psychically attuned and have the ability to communicate with each on their own wavelength. A lot of emotions have come between Magda and Kevin, and they need to heal the emotional wounds or the trauma either of them has been through in order to heal their relationship.

Page of Pentacles. This card depicts a studious and generous messenger. It may indicate that Magda should be careful and thoughtful in her decision-making. She needs to be thoughtful and logical in dealing with her brother now. This card may also represent who Magda was as a child, because pages are children or the childhood self! She really wants to communicate with Kevin, as she did when they were children.

King of Swords. This king is logical and reasonable, and again, he would be counseling Magda to be careful, firm, and fair in the decisions she makes about her relationship. This king can also represent their father or a wise counselor, and Magda and Kevin may need to talk about how they were raised by him and what type of influence he had over them. Was it good? Was it frightening? Did he mean well, but perhaps did not express that to them when they were young? We ask Magda these questions and suggest that she relate these ideas to her brother.

The four cards beneath the face-up cards are those factors out of Magda's control, but they might provide her with valuable insights into the relationship and whether she will be able to take it where she wants it to go. Arlene had Magda turn these four cards face up.

10 of Pentacles. This is the card of success, and particularly success and security in family. As the first of the cards Magda cannot control, this card has very positive portent. It is always a wonderful feeling to receive a destiny card that doesn't create worry or stress! Arlene told Magda that the 10 of Pentacles represents the collective family traditions, which will be considered and discussed again, and that Magda will resolve old family issues or separations and return to a solid, secure base.

Magda's face-down cards revealed.

The Hermit. The Hermit is open-minded and wise. He indicates the ability to give (and receive) wise counsel. Just as we saw in the King of Swords, we again have the idea of a counselor. This means that Magda is destined to receive wise advice and counsel from a mentor or spiritual leader—or perhaps from her own inner voice. Magda should go inward and contemplate her inner voice, and ask how to handle her relationship with her brother. She has an answer within herself, because she knows Kevin well.

Page of Swords R. The page of communication has arrived. Reversed, the Page of Swords brings unpredictable change. Upright or reversed, this card brings great communication ability, which is just what Magda and Kevin need. They will write or talk to each other often in the future and will relate the issues of their childhood, finally removing any misconceptions either one of them had.

King of Wands R. This card reversed can indicate a lack of self-esteem and self-confidence, as well as a lack of enthusiasm. This card has the same strength and ability to lead as the Page of Swords upright, but without the belief in that ability, it can be misdirected, and the person may be temperamental or emotionally detached. Arlene believes that this king is one facet of Kevin's personality and he will appear at first to be inward, not necessarily forthcoming to Magda. However, the King of Wands R can also represent what Kevin thought of his father. Magda can only know by taking a kind and gentle approach to Kevin. Kevin might have had crises in his past that Magda doesn't know about, and it would be wise to deal with him gently and respect any negative feelings he has (perhaps of his own self-worth) in her approach to him.

Finally, Arlene had Magda turn over the last card, the "fate" card that is face down over the Wheel of Fortune.

King of Pentacles.

The King of Pentacles. This is Magda's wild card, representing that elusive element of chance that exists in every situation. This card is a generous and prosperous one. The King of Pentacles may represent how the relationship will finally smooth out or resolve. Either someone will negotiate between Kevin and Magda or the king will prove to be Kevin, who will become calm and serene about their childhood past and be able to enjoy a peaceful relationship with his sister in years ahead.

The timetable for the Wheel of Fortune Spread lies in the last four cards of the spread. The first and the last cards of this destiny section are the 10 of Pentacles, which can be the season of winter, and the King of Wands R, which is the season of spring. Between the next winter and spring, there will be action within this relationship to help Madga answer her question.

For Magda, this reading was useful; you might want to try it as well. First, think about your question while shuffling the cards—pull out the Wheel of Fortune card first, and place it in the center of your spread. Now, as Magda did, place four cards face down, in clockwise order, around the Wheel of Fortune in alignment with the T-A-R-O.

Next, face up, and in the same clockwise order, place four more cards around the Wheel of Fortune, atop those face-down cards. Now place that final card face down over the Wheel of Fortune. Follow Magda's earlier reading, and read your cards, in clockwise order, beginning with the four face-up cards in the T-A-R-O positions. Note your thoughts on each card here.

T: ____

A: ____

R: ____

O: ____

Next, turn over the four face-down cards, again in that T-A-R-O order.

T: ____

A: ____

R: ____

O: ____

And finally, turn over your face-down Wheel of Fortune card.

Wild card: ______________________________________

What does the reading say to you? Were you able to gain some insight into your relationship question from the cards?

Send It Off in a Letter

If you've done all of the exercises in this chapter and you're still at a loss about what to do in your difficult family relationship, try this Psychic Intuition exercise. It's meant to bring you some peace and healing about the relationship, even if the relationship doesn't change at all. Chances are that whatever the situation you're dealing with, there are things you'd like to say to this person. Perhaps there are things that you've even said, but don't feel that this person heard or understood. We're going to have you say some of those things, but we don't want this letter to be a way for you to vent your anger toward the person. What we want you to do is write this person a letter from a positive perspective. We want you to think of the things you love or loved about this person, the things you admire. Tell this person your fondest, happiest memories of him or her, write what you hope for his or her future. If this is someone from whom you are estranged, forget why for a moment, and even imagine that the relationship is on solid ground. Meditate on what your relationship could be if you were reconciled, and the love that you would share with this family member.

This can be a difficult exercise, but it's meant to take you out of the conflict of the relationship, to see what you love or loved about this person, which could help you decide if you can or if you wish to repair the relationship.

The final part of this exercise is to send the letter. You don't have to do this, of course—you might not feel it's what you want to do; you might find that you don't want to salvage the relationship, or that you simply aren't comfortable sending the letter; but if you are, *send the letter.* You might have just told this person things they have no idea you ever felt. Wouldn't you love to receive a letter like this—a *loving* letter from someone with whom you feel you have an impossible relationship? If you *do* send the letter, however, *you must do so without expectations.* The letter won't work miracles, and you should prepare yourself to have no response whatsoever. Would you still want to send the letter, even if it brings no change? If so, send it.

If you don't send the letter, keep it, and reread it yourself when you're considering this relationship or dealing with a conflict in the relationship. Try to open yourself up to the possibility of change in the relationship, to manifesting the best in yourself and in the other person, and you could be surprised what happens—if nothing else, you may find *yourself* beginning to transform!

chapter 8

Sharing Life's Journey: Family for Eternity

What is karma?
The Karmic Tarot spread
Karmic lessons in family
North Node, South Node
What's in your 12th house?
The Horseshoe Tarot spread
Tarot's 10s: The house you're building

Whether or not you believe in reincarnation, you probably believe in choice, right? What about karma? What is it, and how does it work within your family? We all choose the people we travel with on life's journey, and they help us learn karmic life lessons. In this chapter, we do a Horseshoe Tarot spread and a Karma Spread to help us figure out what our lessons might be, and how they affect the choices we make and the situations we face every day. We also look at Saturn, Jupiter, and the Nodes to see what insights they can shed on family. And we take a peek into your 12th house of karma and see what your ruling planet in this house says about you. Finally, we complete a Psychic Intuition exercise that looks at the home you're building for your family, and the many homes you've shared with family in your lifetime. We may meet the people we choose to journey with us again and again—sharing, evolving, growing—learning the souls' lessons together on a mutual journey through space and time.

What Is Karma?

You don't have to believe in an afterlife or in multiple lives to believe in karma. Though karma is your past life lessons, you can also look at it as what you have learned already, or those things that come more easily for you. Are you a great listener? A natural cook? A wonderful nurturer? These can all be seen as the lessons you've learned, the things you've already dealt with and mastered. If you believe in past lives, the people you know and are close to in this life are all likely people you knew in earlier lives. Your family has been your family for some lifetimes, and you change roles depending on the lessons you have to learn in this life. The lessons we are learning now, and will learn in the future, are our dharma. Dharma is also our purpose in life, and how we fulfill it relates to our karma.

In Buddhism, karma is like a law of action and reaction: For every action, there will be a new action, and what kind of action it is basically depends on the intent of the action before it. When we speak of karma, we are looking at how those previous actions—our previous life lessons—affect us now. The karma you come into life with is like an energy you carry with you; some speak of karmic debt, which is just a way of saying that you brought some issues with you that you must still work out. Your karmic lessons are those you have to learn before you can move on in life. Sometimes it takes a long time to learn these lessons, particularly if you aren't sure what they are.

The Tarot Karma Spread

Ever wonder why you keep winding up in the same situation? Or why your family keeps coming back to the same place? The Karma Spread is a four-card Tarot spread that explores the karmic lessons you need to learn in this life.

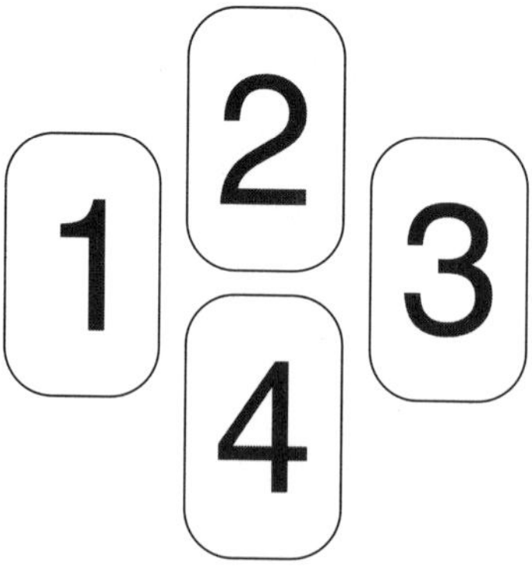

Tarot's Karma Spread: What are my life lessons?